W9-AYN-257

100
BEST
U.S. Wedding Destinations

KATHRYN GABRIEL LOVING

INSIDERS' GUIDE®

GUILFORD, CONNECTICUT
AN IMPRINT OF THE GLOBE PEQUOT PRESS

The prices, rates, and hours listed in this guidebook were confirmed at press time. We recommend, however, that you call establishments to obtain current information before traveling.

To buy books in quantity for corporate use or incentives, call **(800) 962–0973, ext. 4551,** or e-mail **premiums@GlobePequot.com.**

INSIDERS' GUIDE®

Text design by Mary Ballachino
All photos © Kathryn Gabriel Loving

ISSN 1558-5921
ISBN 0-7627-3707-7

Manufactured in the United States of America
First Edition/First Printing

TO ALL THE COUPLES SEEKING
THAT SPECIAL PLACE
TO DECLARE THEIR LOVE AND
SHARE THEIR VOWS — MAY THE BLESSINGS BE!

Help Us Keep This Guide Up to Date

Every effort has been made by the author and editors to make this guide as accurate and useful as possible. However, many things can change after a guide is published—establishments close, phone numbers change, facilities come under new management, and so on.

We would love to hear from you concerning your experiences with this guide and how you feel it could be improved and kept up to date. While we may not be able to respond to all comments and suggestions, we'll take them to heart and we'll also make certain to share them with the author. Please send your comments and suggestions to the following address:

The Globe Pequot Press
Reader Response/Editorial Department
P.O. Box 480
Guilford, CT 06437

Or you may e-mail us at:

editorial@GlobePequot.com

Thanks for your input, and happy travels!

100
BEST
U.S. Wedding
Destinations

a photo essay

Hacienda Doña Andrea
de Santa Fe

Hacienda Doña Andrea
de Santa Fe

Mission at Pecos
National Historical
Park

Casa Rondeña Winery

Inn at Mountaintop,
Santa Fe

The Manor House
Restaurant

Fess Parker's
DoubleTree Resort

Mendenhall Glacier,
Juneau, Alaska

Four Seasons Resort
Santa Barbara

Little Chapel
of the Flowers

Cherokee Ranch
and Castle

The Bishop's Lodge
Resort & Spa

La Playa Hotel

Camarillo Ranch

CONTENTS

Florida

Georgia

Hawaii

Louisiana

Maine

Massachusetts

Minnesota

Nevada

New Jersey

New Mexico

New York

North Carolina

Rhode Island

South Carolina

Texas

Vermont

Washington

Wisconsin

Wyoming

ACKNOWLEDGMENTS

I owe a debt of gratitude to data girl Janet Gabriel for helping to input each site's wedding prices and policies, and for accompanying me to the venues during all forms of weather and flu. I also owe Susan Coté a wheelbarrow of thanks for calling the venues. The following people were gracious in their assistance with local information: Irene Swain, Santa Fe wedding officiant; Ray Jones, travel writer and expert on lighthouses; Patty Gabriel, Denver resident; Phil Knepper, Web master of Online Wedding Planner for the Ventura–Santa Barbara area; Janise Witt, Sedona wedding photographer; and Kellie Sharpe, St. Augustine enthusiast. A battalion of Globe Pequot editors pulled this book together: Erin Turner, Lynn Zelem, Sue Preneta, Leah Gilman, and Laura Jorstad. Margo and Marv Richardson and Jennifer and Dan Kasse deserve gold stars for their patience in waiting for their own wedding albums until after this book was complete. Finally, I would like to thank my husband, David Loving, for living up to his last name.

INTRODUCTION

The face of the American wedding has changed in the past dozen years. The majority of couples are spending more than ever on elaborate weddings, while one in ten are conducting "destination weddings" with up to sixty of their friends and family. For these couples the world is their chapel; their ceremonies are set in nature, in antiquity, and in meaning.

Credit Sandals Resorts International for creating WeddingMoons—the first wedding–honeymoon combination package in the tropics—in 1994. While American couples are coaxed to fly to the Bahamas, Bermuda, the Caribbean, and Mexico with the promise of free weddings with extended stays, Europeans and Japanese are coming to the United States. Not only are they taking advantage of the strength of foreign currency against the dollar, but they are also finding our historic sites, botanical gardens, and national parks glorious settings for reciting vows. The best destination weddings, as it turns out, might be within our own borders. Hawaii and Las Vegas notwithstanding, anywhere in the country where there's a scenic backdrop, there's likely a wedding and a competitive industry to support it.

Why are destination weddings so popular? Geographically dispersed families need a neutral, accessible ground to congregate. Also, many couples these days are paying for weddings themselves, and would rather put their savings toward a car or home. Hometown weddings now average more than $26,000, but when a wedding is moved out of town, the guest list and trappings are proportionately downsized. A three-day destination wedding can cost one-tenth the price of a hometown weekend wedding, including air fare and lodging for the couple. (Guests typically pay their own way for travel and accommodations.)

Destination weddings appeal to a couple's sense of adventure, unique style, and departure from convention. The bride can wear black and the groom can wear sandals—without socks—if they so wish. More often than not, of course, he will don a tuxedo, and she a full-length white gown complete with train and veil—bridal bouquet *not* optional. The juxtaposition of black-and-white formal wear against a reddish Indian ruin, the ocean at sunset, or an evergreen-wreathed ski slope makes for vivid memories and an even more stunning wedding album.

Destination weddings come in all shapes and sizes. Some couples splurge on expensive resorts and catering for their guests; if the guest list is short, the reception can still be a tremendous savings. Not all destination weddings are small, for that matter.

Those who opt for destination weddings are typically in their thirties and beyond, are settled in their careers, and are launching encore marriages. Getting caught up in the flowers, the cake, and the veil becomes less important the second time around. They might even omit bridesmaids and groomsmen. Some couples forgo the nightmare of group travel altogether and perform a ceremony for two—but they *don't* consider it eloping. The wedding itself isn't the destination; their lives together are. Never mind the something old, new, borrowed, or blue—they just want something simple before flying back to work.

The World Wide Bride: Finding the Best Wedding Destination

With the media focus on destination weddings, literally thousands of potential venues are vying for a piece of the $125 billion industry that is spreading across the country. Most wedding venues have Web sites; indeed, most away weddings are planned over the Internet via e-mail. (The groom does just as much of the planning for a long-distance wedding as the bride, if not more.) The Web is one of the first resources couples go to for choosing a destination, but it isn't reliable as a sole resource; search engine results are log-jammed by the savvier Web masters with large advertising budgets, leaving the best venues, as well as the bride and groom, lost in cyberspace.

Research for the one hundred best destinations in this book began with the Web, but it didn't stop there. Once a potential venue was discovered, we either contacted the owner or appropriate personnel, or visited the property. We also cross-checked the sites with local vendors such as photographers and wedding officiants, or with on-line bulletin boards. If the venue was unresponsive to our e-mails or phone calls, or received more than a few scathing reviews, all with the same complaints, the venue got dropped from the list. The entire process took a full year.

Wedding destinations needed to fit the following criteria:

- Picturesque (for the wedding album), romantic, historical, spiritual, or quirky, great ceremony and/or reception sites.

- Oriented toward the wedding market with prices or packages oriented toward less than seventy-five guests.

- A range of lodging and food accommodations on the property or in the area.

- Plenty of wedding vendors in the area.

- A range of pricing options.

- Easily reached as well as wheelchair accessible and accessible to the elderly.

- Easy marriage license requirements.

- Great vacation spot for guests, with plenty of activities other than The Wedding.

- A staff person to help coordinate long-distance wedding planning.

- Reputation for excellent service, with high recommendations from vendors and former nuptial clients.

In selecting the best destinations, we broke some of our own rules. A few of the destinations are not easy to get to; Orcas Island, for instance, is accessible only by seaplane or a long ferry ride—but then that's half the fun. Although the marriage license laws are being amended all the time, Texas still has a three-day waiting period, which can be part of the vacation or honeymoon. An overriding factor is the number of people the venue and its packages can accommodate. Statistically, destination weddings average forty-six to fifty-six guests; some venues in this book require a minimum of seventy-five guests, while others can only accommodate a limited number. A few of the venues are quite expensive, but again the cost is workable and is proportionate to what a couple would spend at home. A wedding on Palm Island, Florida, for six people might come in at less than $5,000, for instance—a once-in-a-lifetime alternative to a large wedding! This book also includes many free sites or permit fee sites, such as national parks in California, for do-it-yourself weddings, but they won't have a wedding planner on staff.

All told the final list of one hundred best destinations is a survey of the American wedding from sea to shining sea. The notable places—the ones with the most established gardens, the prettiest accommodations, the best views—represent a piece of American history. Considering that more than a few historic homes, gardens, and resorts were built in the late nineteenth century, we have renewed respect for the industrialists who built them, along with such visionaries as the Rockefellers who restored these buildings or created new landmark resorts in their place. This book looks at chapels that have been around since Spanish and European colonial times, as well as the more modern "quickie" chapels of Las Vegas and the Mall of America, resorts built by southwestern Indians, and a cosmopolitan rooftop in Seattle. Whether a redwood cathedral in California, a mountaintop alpine garden, or a chapel railcar in Wisconsin—there's an altar for every couple in this book.

Special Considerations

Most historical lodgings are, by definition, old—and that's half their charm. This means that many rooms are in need of restoration or are in the process of being restored and modernized. Thin walls, small bathrooms, and creaky slanted floors are the hallmark of the former, while guests must endure noise and dust with the latter. When making reservations, ask for a newly renovated room, or one that is as far away from the sound of jackhammers as possible.

Some feel that destination weddings mean freedom for the wedding party and guests to be themselves. One woman recounted that her wedding had ended in a food fight with guests jumping into the pool to wash the cake off their clothes. As tempting as this might sound: refrain. Most

of these venues are historic, and because the structures are ancient or the preserved habitat is fragile, permits and contracts will stipulate restrictions on wedding furniture (chairs, tables, arches, etc.), decorations, and what can and cannot be released into the environment (birdseed, doves, butterflies, petals, etc.). Wedding parties also must adhere to noise ordinances and contracts will specify if and when amplified music can occur. Many venues will require couples to use the site's preferred vendors, who are competent, insured, and used to working with the property. Sites without a preferred list often have a list of recommended vendors.

Many locations have developed wedding packages that include flowers, photography, cake, and champagne. They have learned to throw in the honeymoon suite for free, if the couple spends a certain amount on the reception catering. They regain their profit with so-called site fees. At the high end, resorts are used to catering for hundreds of guests, not just fifty or sixty, and they would actually lose money on a small destination wedding. Most catering venues, therefore, earn their profit on the reception and will have food and beverage minimums on their reception rooms, and these are listed in this book. At the low end a bed-and-breakfast might only have ten guest rooms, and because a wedding is disruptive to their nonwedding guests, it may require a so-called buy-out of its rooms for the weekend so that the wedding can have the run of the house. All such pricing issues need to be weighed in the balance. When known, this book lists each venue's price policies.

The facility rental fees and catering prices listed in this book are meant to serve as general guidelines to assist couples in determining affordability. Prices were collected in 2005, however; they are subject to increase (usually no more than 10 percent), and do not include tax, service charges (usually 20 percent), or gratuity. Furthermore, each establishment also requires refundable and nonrefundable deposits, and issues a payment schedule that begins the moment the space is reserved. These deposits are not listed in this book. In some cases a historical venue or museum will require liability insurance; this will be mentioned where applicable, but won't be detailed.

Catering establishments must purchase the correct amount of food supplies in preparation for each reception, and therefore each reception venue also has a schedule for ordering buffets and plated dinners months in advance with final guest numbers confirmed so many days prior to the wedding. These catering policies are not stipulated in this book.

Finally, a number of venues were chosen based on their courteous and attentive staff. Of course, personnel can change.

Planning a Destination Wedding

For places other than Las Vegas and Hawaii, the wedding business is seasonal and usually a weekend affair. Most will offer discounts for a weekday or off-season wedding. Once a date has been decided, consider hiring the photographer first. Photographers often stay at the wedding from beginning to end, and can advise on the best locations, time, and suppliers.

When selecting a destination, consider the cost to guests. If possible, negotiate group rates, reception costs, and a complimentary honeymoon suite. Planning should start six months to a year in advance to book the most coveted spots and to allow guests enough time to reserve flights and schedule vacations. Some cou-

ples travel to the wedding site and meet with vendors personally before the wedding, while others handle arrangements over the phone or by e-mail and then arrive a few days early to apply for their license, tie up loose ends, and get their hair done; it depends on the complexity of the arrangements and the couple's need for control over details. There's plenty of room for spontaneity with ample flexibility—and venues are almost always willing to accommodate.

Most resorts and inns have on-site wedding planners to handle the varying phases of a wedding, and are experienced in working with a couple long-distance. Some will go so far as to help coordinate all of the functions held on their property as well as book activities for the guests. A few venues require couples to hire an independent wedding planner. Such planners, indeed, are often essential for do-it-yourself weddings at places besides a resort or inn; they know where the hidden beaches of Hawaii are, for instance, and they offer all-inclusive packages themselves.

Buy the dress to fit the location. Consider that it has to be flown, shipped, or packed in a suitcase. Also consider that all of these sites were chosen for their natural and historic beauty and do not require much by way of flowers and decoration.

Weatherproof Your Wedding

The phrase *whirlwind wedding* took on a new meaning with the hurricane seasons of 2004 and 2005. Experts say that at least two hurricanes of high magnitude should be expected every year, and, yes, they do strike twice in the same place. Hurricane season runs from late June to mid-November, randomly hitting anywhere along the Caribbean, Gulf of Mexico, and Atlantic coast. Most wedding venues and vendors offer hurricane guarantees, but terms vary widely. In the event of a legitimate hurricane watch or warning, the venues and vendors should offer a full refund or a chance to reschedule upon cancellation. Also, check to see if your destination has recovered from the last hurricane if it has been hit recently.

The best time to book a wedding in the Gulf states is winter and spring. If summer and fall are best for you, then go to California, Hawaii, Colorado, or the Southwest, where the heat is more comfortable. Also consider tornadoes; late-summer monsoon rains in the Southwest; winds and fires in the Southwest and California; and, of course, snow. You don't have to avoid these areas during risky seasons, but keep the weather in mind when making plans.

If you're spending thousands on a getaway wedding, spend another $100 (usually per person) on travel insurance, which not only protects against cancellations, but can also protect in cases of illness and accidents requiring hospitalization. Travel insurance is available from a travel agent or on the Web. Make sure the policy is underwritten by a third party. Insurance to cover mishaps and liability for weddings is also available.

STATE MARRIAGE LICENSE LAWS

Couples must apply for a marriage license in the state where they are getting married. Some states, such as New Mexico, allow couples to obtain a license in one county and marry in another. Marriage laws vary from state to state, and even by county, and are changing all the time, so check with the appropriate county for local rules. Typically applicants must both appear in person far enough in advance and with proof of identification. They usually, but not always, need to bring a picture ID, birth certificate, a Social Security card, military ID, and divorce decree or death certificate of previous spouse. There is often a waiting period between the time a couple applies and the time the license can be picked up, or from the time the license is issued to the time the couple can get married. None of the states in this book requires blood tests (Georgia dropped the requirement in 2003, and Massachusetts in 2005), but all applicants have to be at least eighteen years of age without parental consent. Some states require the officiant to be registered with the state; others do not. The chart below offers some general information pertaining to fees, waiting periods, special conditions, and the length of time a license is valid in the states included in this book.

Couples from other countries should first check with their own marriage laws as well as with their chosen state before marrying in the United States.

State	Fees (may vary within state; most require cash)	Waiting Period	Special Conditions	License Valid
Alaska	$40	3 days	Couple can fax notarized application, and should do so weeks in advance.	90 days
Arizona	$50	None		1 year

State	Fees (may vary within state; most require cash)	Waiting Period	Special Conditions	License Valid
Arkansas	$35–47	None		60 days
California	$45–80	None	Can apply for confidential license to keep off public record; no witnesses required in that case.	90 days
Colorado	$10+	None	One party can apply with notarized absentee application of other party. Couples can solemnize their own marriage if they apply with court.	30 days
Florida	$93.50	3 days	Waiting period is for Florida residents only who have not taken 4-hour course.	60 days
Georgia	$26–30	None		No expiration
Hawaii	$60	None	Download form and file with marriage agent in person.	30 days
Louisiana	$25+	3 days	Waiting period can be waived by judge for residents only.	30 days
Maine	$20+	None		90 days
Massachusetts	$4–15	3 days	Waiting period can be waived by judge.	60 days
Minnesota	$20 or $85	5 days	Lesser fee is for those who have taken premarital course. Waiting period can be waived by judge.	6 months
Nevada	$35–65	None		1 year
New Jersey	$28	3 days		30 days
New Mexico	$25–40	None		No expiration

State	Fees (may vary within state; most require cash)	Waiting Period	Special Conditions	License Valid
New York	$35 in NYC, $40–50 outside NYC	24 hours	Some clerks accept only money orders.	60 days
North Carolina	$50	None	One party can apply with notarized absentee application of other party.	60 days
Rhode Island	$24	None		90 days
South Carolina	$15	24 hours		No expiration
Texas	$31–36	72 hours	Waiting period can be waived for active-duty personnel.	30 days
Vermont	$23+$7 for certificate	None	Only one party need apply, but clerks like to see both.	60 days
Washington	$52	3 days		60 days
Wisconsin	$60	6 days	Waiting period can be waived for nonresidents for $10.	30 days
Wyoming	$25	None	Only one party need apply, but must have a witness present.	No expiration

PEARSON'S POND
BED AND BREAKFAST

Juneau, Alaska

Marrying on solid ground isn't enough for some couples these days; a growing number of hardy souls are helicoptering to the top of a glacier for a ceremony on ice they'll remember forever. The glacier is Mendenhall, just 13 miles from downtown Juneau, so accessible by walkways and viewing platforms that it's the city's main attraction and the most visited of all glaciers in the world. This giant remnant of the distant ice ages is only one of thirty-eight large glaciers that flow from the 5,000-square-mile expanse of rock, snow, and ice known as the Juneau Icefield, North America's fifth largest. Other popular glaciers on this icefield for weddings include Herbert and Taku.

Pearson's Pond Bed and Breakfast is so close to the glacier that a couple can gaze at it from the hot tub deck. The inn is the perfect home base for an Alaskan wedding of any kind. In many ways innkeeper Diane Pearson is as much the destination as the glacier itself. Pearson is, well, many things, most lately innkeeper, tour guide, wedding planner, marriage commissioner—everything a couple needs to get them to Alaska and married. If you want Alaskan salmon (the real thing!) for supper, she's been known to catch it herself. Pearson's Pond started out as a two-bedroom, one-bath cabin, and evolved into its current illusion of being in the Alaska wilderness.

Pearson started out facilitating wedding adventures for friends, and the adventures blossomed into more than thirty ceremonies

a year. She arranges for the couple to be shuttled to the helipad (stopping to pick up the marriage license if needed), and then flown over glacier icefalls and clear blue crevasses to a safe and smooth area on Mendenhall, Taku, or Herbert Glaciers. Time allowing, the couple is given a short "flightseeing" tour over the icefield on the way back to Juneau. Air time is twenty to twenty-five minutes, with thirty-five to forty minutes on the glacier for the ceremony. The helicopter seats four to six, including bride, groom, marriage commissioner, photographer, and, possibly, witnesses. Pearson makes sure the participants are properly outfitted for the glacier with gloves, boots, coats, and crampons. Couples sometimes don wedding attire over the gear, but high heels are not practical. A safety briefing is given before the wedding flight.

If standing on a glacier doesn't sound appealing, Pearson offers an Alaska Wilderness Island Wedding in which couples are shuttled by boat to a vista or cove on a nearby remote island or shoreline in the rain forest along the Inside Passage coast of southeastern Alaska. Pearson's Pond has other options as well, such as a garden gazebo or a pond-side wedding arch on a floating dock, both with glacier views. Open year-round, the Atrium Lounge is perfect for a warm and intimate indoor ceremony and small reception, complete with fireplace, fountain, mezzanine, cathedral ceilings with chandeliers, and windows overlooking the forest.

Pearson's Pond Bed and Breakfast
4541 Sawa Circle
Juneau, AK 99801-8723
(907) 789–3772
www.pearsonspond.com

Location: Pearson's Pond is located in Juneau, Alaska. There are no roads into the town and the only way in is by plane or boat. The bed-and-breakfast is eight minutes from the Juneau International Airport, ninety-seven minutes by air from Seattle, Washington, and seventy-five minutes from Anchorage, Alaska. Couples can be picked up for ceremonies from their cruise ships when they dock in Juneau for the day.

Facility Rental, Amenities, and Policies: Basic weddings start at $600 and include a ceremony by an Alaska marriage commissioner, the site fee for the location at Pearson's Pond, and filing; they go up to $1,850 with the addition of transportation from a cruise ship, pier, or other lodging (if needed), wedding coordination, bouquet and boutonniere, professional photography, cake, toasting beverage, serving ware, setup, and cleanup for two to six people.

The Glacier Wedding, starting at $2,350, includes planning assistance, round-trip transportation, helicopter flightseeing, use of gear, wedding ceremony, professional photographer, flowers, witnesses, and filing of signed paperwork. The Alaska Wilderness Island Wedding, with many of the same amenities as the Glacier Wedding (substituting a boat for the helicopter), is $1,850. For the ultimate wedding Pearson's Pond offers an overnight glacier wedding, trek, glacier camping, and flightseeing package for $4,350.

All of the above packages can be booked on Pearson's Web site, and discounts are given if the couple books directly with Pearson's Pond.

Catering: Small receptions such as a mini reception for $150 for two to six people (including a small tiered cake and toasting beverage) are package options.

Extras: Glacier treks, kayak tours, dog mushing, or helicopter tours chartered through Pearson's Pond.

Accommodations: 5 suites in total, all with romantic canopy bed, fireplace, CD player, kitchenette, private entrance, deck, and a wonderful view. Honeymoon suites have a two-person private whirlpool, living area with loft, skylight for watching the northern lights, and a view of the water and mountains.

The nightly room rate for two adults ranges from $179 (Super Saver Season) or $279 (Spectacular Summer Season) for the Deluxe Fireplace Efficiency Studio; to $229 (Super Saver) or $329 (Spectacular Summer) for the Premium Jacuzzi Fireplace Suite.

Keep in Mind: Glacier weddings are available at the top of the glacier between May and early September, when temperatures average sixty to seventy-five degrees. This means the bride can wear a strappy dress on the glacier in summer, especially from noon to midafternoon. Weddings are welcome year-round at Pearson's Pond.

CASA SEDONA

Sedona, Arizona

Casa Sedona's most spectacular feature is the red rock formations that surround it. In the early 1990s Mani Subra designed the inn—with its teal-trimmed red stucco—to match its environment, in accordance with the philosophy of mentor and architect Frank Lloyd Wright. Although a neighborhood is beginning to grow up around Casa Sedona, every room, deck, and terrace still has a view of the red rocks in all directions; folks travel from around the world to enjoy its serene setting. What sets this inn apart from the dozens in the Sedona area, however, are owners Bob and Donna Marriott, especially when it comes to weddings.

Many weddings that take place on the property are for previous guests of the inn. "We host thirty some–odd weddings a year and we get thirty hugs when they leave," declared Bob Marriott. That's the goal—the hugs. Yes, it is true that the Marriotts (particularly Bob) coordinate the entire wedding down to the finest detail, whether it's an elopement or a wedding-plus-reception for sixty (the maximum). In fact, they insist on it. Every vendor who works on the wedding, including the florist, photographer, and caterer, is hand chosen by the Marriotts. The bride and groom choose the photographer whose style they prefer from the inn's short list, but don't actually meet with the photographer until the inn has negotiated the contract. The couple pays one fee, from which the inn pays the vendors. Most vendors "don't always do what they say they're going to do," Bob Marriott explained. He attributes his attention to detail to his background as a chemist in research and development.

Casa Sedona is actually two southwestern-style stucco homes bridged by a small courtyard. The inn's sixteen guest quarters are individually configured with fireplaces, refrigerators, and baths with spa tubs. The decor throughout is eclectic, from cowboy chic to tea-cozy country French to Mediterranean tranquility.

Couples marry in the Victorian wedding gazebo, on the Sunset Garden Patio, or on the Juniper Terrace. The gazebo is in view of Thunder Mountain. The nearby garden patio, with its bubbling fountains and manicured gardens, is newly tiled and can host a reception for fifty guests with formal beverage service, as well as soft acoustical music such as harp or guitar. A reception for forty can take place on the east-facing, second-floor terrace, which overlooks a panorama of red rock formations and centuries-old juniper trees, and can be covered during a chance rainstorm. Indoor receptions can be held for up to twenty guests.

Casa Sedona
55 Hozoni Drive
Sedona, AZ 86336
(800) 525–3756 or (928) 282–2938
www.casasedona.com

Location: Hozoni Drive is north of Arizona Highway 89A, west of the Y intersection of AZ 89A and Arizona Highway 179. Many travelers take AZ 179 from Interstate 17 between Phoenix and Flagstaff into Sedona, but it is scheduled to undergo major construction through 2007 and is best avoided.

Facility Rental, Amenities, and Policies: Casa Sedona offers an elopement ceremony starting at $829. This Diamond Wedding package is completely planned by the Marriotts and includes exclusive use of the Victorian wedding gazebo, a customized floral bouquet for the bride and boutonniere for the groom, a wedding cake with a fresh flower topper, champagne, witness, officiant, and photography. After the wedding the newlyweds dine at Savannah's, a restaurant in Sedona. The package offers a 10 percent discount on room rates, which comes with a full two-course breakfast and afternoon appetizer buffet. This offer is not valid over holidays or in conjunction with any other package or discount. It must be requested at the time of reservation. The nonguest price for the Diamond Wedding package is an extra $100.

An event fee starting at $750 is required for larger weddings and receptions for up to sixty guests; the average event fee is $1,000. The fee includes site rental and coordination of the wedding ceremony and reception, catering, flowers, officiant, photography, music, wedding-night dinner for two, wedding cake and beverage, in-room massages, and hair and makeup scheduling. Final ceremony and reception prices depend upon the needs and style decisions of the bride and groom in consultation with the Casa Sedona.

Catering: Casa Sedona can arrange catering for up to sixty guests, whether a cocktail reception or dinner, a formal or casual affair. The staff design and prepare a menu fitting any budget and style, from a barbecue buffet to a multicourse gourmet seated dinner. Catering typically ranges from $35 to $75 per dinner (excluding beverages and rental fees). The staff will set up and take down the ceremony and reception tables, chairs, and so on, but these items must be rented elsewhere.

Extras: The inn can arrange for gift baskets and special requests.

Accommodations: Lodging at Casa Sedona is required for wedding services. The number of nights required as a minimum stay depends upon individual packages. Guest rooms are provided for the wedding party to prepare for the ceremony if available, although this does not include overnight accommodations. The 16 guest rooms are $185 to $290.

LA TLAQUEPAQUE ARTS AND CRAFTS VILLAGE

Sedona, Arizona

Called "the Art and Soul of Sedona," La Tlaquepaque Arts and Crafts Village provides several venues for wedding ceremonies, receptions, and rehearsal dinners, including four restaurants, two patios, a ballroom, and the flagstone *calle* itself. One of Tlaquepaque's most remarkable features is its beautiful chapel, perfect for intimate weddings. The antiqued, whitewashed stucco walls, and adjacent courtyards, fountains, landscaping, and shop-lined lanes, transport the imagination to Old World Mexico. The interior is marked by stained-glass windows and hand-carved wood-and-leather pews. Overlooking the altar is a mural commissioned by local artist Eileen Conn, featuring a number of saints. Although distinctly Catholic in flavor, reflecting Mexico's predominant culture, the chapel is nondenominational.

Tlaquepaque (locally pronounced *ta-la-ka-pa-kee*) was inspired by a Guadalajara, Mexico, suburb of the same name. Abe Miller was the driving force behind the construction, which took seven years to complete in the 1970s. He designed the village as a whole, with the chapel and some forty shops fitting into a unifying architectural theme that looks as if it's been there for centuries. And that was the point. Buildings were constructed around existing trees. Where possible, construction methods mirrored those of Mexican artisans and builders; tiles, statuary, lanterns, pots, doors, wrought iron, and even the fountains were largely imported piecemeal from Mexico. To say that it is picturesque is an understatement, and that's good for wedding pictures. In fact, it's a photographer's dream with all its archways and different points of perspective.

Seating capacity in the chapel is for a total of fifty people: thirty-five in the wooden pews and the remainder in extra chairs set up in the back area. Each reservation is for a ninety-minute period, which allows one hour for the ceremony and an additional thirty minutes for setup and guest arrival. A custodian attends the gated doorway and ensures privacy during the allotted time. Once the ceremony concludes, the custodian rings in this joyous occasion with a wedding peal in the bell tower.

Add to the chapel ceremony a reception in one of several venues: Patio de las Campanas, Patio del Norte and Terrace, Calle Independencia, Plaza de la Fuente, or the Tlaquepaque banquet room, known as La Sala de los Milagros (Room of Miracles). **Patio de las Campanas** is the smallest patio, accommodating up to sixty people. This attractive area features a bell tower with a cobblestone courtyard surrounded by arched balconies and stucco walls, a large flowing fountain, flowers, and aged sycamore trees. **Patio del Norte and Terrace,** the larger and more popular of the two patios, accommodates sixty guests. In the center is a majestic fountain surrounded by large, flowing flower gardens and sycamore trees. The patio has its own public restrooms and is sheltered from passing shoppers. An overhang along two walls creates an ideal space for caterers and musicians. **Plaza de la Fuente,** a spacious cobblestone courtyard with fountain, is popular for dances for one hundred.

Larger weddings with up to one hundred guests might want to set up in **Calle Independencia.** Calle Independencia starts at a circular drive that flows around a large Venus sculpture and flower garden at one end, and ends at a fountain at the other. A street party here would look and feel like a *Cinco de Mayo* fiesta. **La Sala de los Milagros** overlooks Patio del Norte and holds up to a hundred guests. The banquet room is 1,500 square feet and provides a timeless setting for all occasions.

Chapel at La Tlaquepaque Arts and Crafts Village
336 Highway 179
P.O. Box 1868
Sedona, AZ 86339
(928) 282–4838
www.tlaq.com

Location: Tlaquepaque is on the right heading south from the Y intersection of Arizona Highways 89A and 179. Note: AZ 179 will be undergoing construction through 2007. Enter Sedona from AZ 89A and allow extra time to negotiate traffic.

Facility Rental, Amenities, and Policies: Reservations for use of the chapel need to be made in advance. Weddings scheduled between 9:00 A.M. and 4:00 P.M. are $300, and weddings after 4:00 P.M. are $400.

Additional time can be reserved for $50 per half hour, and a one-hour rehearsal can be booked for $100. Tlaquepaque offers a changing room with all the amenities a bride and her party will need for an additional $50 per hour.

A straightforward reservation application that doubles as an agreement is available on Tlaquepaque's Web site.

Patio de las Campanas can be rented as a reception venue for $850. The larger Patio del Norte and Plaza de la Fuente each cost $1,000. Tenting and disc jockey systems are not allowed on either patio. Renting the spacious Calle Indepencia costs $1,000. Amplified entertainment is permitted, and tenting is optional for an additional fee beginning around $700. Rental of La Sala de los Milagros is $500 for two and a half hours between 9:00 A.M. and 4:00 P.M., or $850 for four and a half hours between 5:00 and 11:00 P.M. Each additional hour runs $100.

Catering: Tlaquepaque only provides the venue; all coordinators, catering, decorations, flowers, rental equipment, and the like must be secured from outside vendors.

The village does not have a liquor license, so the wedding group must also provide liquor.

Extras: Tlaquepaque presents special wedding packages put together by outside wedding planners. These include such items as chapel rental, officiant, witnesses if needed, flowers for the altar and the bridal party, professional photography or videography, musicians, keepsake marriage certificates, a unity candle, a night's stay in a local lodge or bed-and-breakfast, and even a neck massage. The packages range from $1,300 to $3,000; day of the week determines prices.

Accommodations: Tlaquepaque is centrally located and convenient to a number of lodging facilities, but one possibility is Los Abrigados Resort starting at just above $100 per night (www.ilxresorts.com; 928–282–1777). The resort is completely separate from the arts-and-crafts village, but bordering the south side of the property. Tree-shaded areas along Oak Creek on the property would also make for a beautiful ceremony backdrop, while receptions can be held in a number of function rooms.

RED ROCK COUNTRY
PUBLIC SITES AND CHAPELS
Sedona, Arizona

Several years ago *USA Today* declared the red rock spires and canyons of Sedona to be *the* most beautiful place in the country. The eighty-million-year-old formations are like mammoth (albeit special-shaped) wedding cakes with layered deposits of sandstone, limestone, and siltstone; the red color palette comes from iron oxide, or hematite, that

actually rusted when the area was a wetland. These are reds of every hue, from the palest peach to the deepest vermilion, contrasted by evergreens and an intensely blue sky.

The town itself, founded in 1902, branches off from two main arteries—Arizona Highways 89A and 179—that meet at an upside-down-Y-shaped intersection.

CHAPEL OF THE HOLY CROSS

Catholics would definitely want to consider the Chapel of the Holy Cross near Sedona, designed by a student of Frank Lloyd Wright and identifiable by a giant cross that seems to support the structure as it juts out from the red rock.

Some four million people pour through this intersection every year for various reasons: recreation, sightseeing, or shopping and dining in the tiny town itself. All, however, have red rock fever in common. The University of Northern Arizona found that 64 percent of those who travel to Sedona seek a spiritual experience from the inspirational and regenerative essence the red rocks seem to emanate. Little wonder this is a popular place for those who want to get married near a so-called vortex, or just want to be photographed in their wedding garb against Cathedral Rock in the background.

Local photographers mention such areas as Boynton Canyon, Courthouse Butte, Bell Rock, and Merry-Go-Round as popular and picturesque places for weddings. Many of the favorite ceremony sites, however, are in federally designated wilderness areas, and weddings are not, by law, "appropriate use of a wilderness," which makes up 60 percent of the area around Sedona.

Despite this hurdle, there are several sanctioned places for a ceremony. Most brides don't necessarily want to hike too far and are happy to pull into a scenic overlook and exchange vows with a formation in the background. Any wedding officiant, photographer, or planner would be able to guide couples to the best spots, but please keep the environmental impact of your wedding in mind. The wedding party is asked to help preserve the very aspects that attract them to the space. Although the red rocks are millions of years old and are not prone to wind or water erosion, the top veneer of the soil is full of living organisms and is paradoxically fragile beneath trampling feet.

Red Rock Crossing and Crescent Moon Ramada

One of the more popular and picturesque wedding places is Red Rock Crossing, just 7 miles west of Sedona. Symbolizing the American West, it has been featured in dozens of feature films and documentaries. Many a ceremony has taken place on the flat sandstone area next to Oak Creek, with Cathedral Rock standing witness and reflecting in the water. The Crescent Moon Ramada, a covered picnic area at Red Rock Crossing, can be reserved for a wedding. People come here to fish, swim, and wade in the creek, as well as to picnic and photograph the scenery, so it can become quite crowded. Early mornings or weekdays, however, it's possible to have the beauty of Red Rock Crossing nearly all to yourself.

Red Rock State Park

Red Rock State Park allows ceremonies under its Wedding Tree, a short hike across the Oak Creek bridge in a grassy meadow. This majestic cottonwood is actually two trees joined at a 4-foot base, said to represent the union of the bride and groom. The park's acreage and trail network are well maintained, and it offers reception and changing rooms.

Sedona Creative Life Center

Renting chapel space in the Sedona area is another simple wedding alternative. The Sedona Creative Life Center is just five minutes from Sedona's tourist section, yet it sits quietly in the middle of a fifteen-acre setting of hills and trees. Once you know where to look, the center's signature 40-foot blue-tinted glass steeple is visible from many places in the village. The chapel's altar is formed by a right-angled corner of the steeple that is open to the top, bringing the views and light inward; even the restrooms at the base of the steeple have a glorious view through the tinted glass. The observation deck above the chapel also has panoramic views. The Great Room, seating 200 theater style, and the Peace Garden can host ceremonies as well. The Universal Room and a picnic terrace are perfect for receptions. The chapel and facility are nondenominational with a decidedly exploratory spiritual bias. But as the quite friendly and helpful directors we spoke with said, the center is "not New Age, or old age, but rather it is ageless."

Red Rock Ranger District, Coconino National Forest
P.O. Box 300
Sedona, AZ 86336
(928) 282–4119

Crescent Moon Ramada
(877) 444–6777
TDD: (877) 833–6777
www.fs.fed.us/r3/coconino/recreation/red
_rock/crescentmoon-picnic.shtml
www.reserveusa.com

Location: From Sedona, drive west on AZ 89A and turn left onto Upper Red Rock Loop Road. At the bottom of the hill, turn left onto Chavez Ranch Road to the Crescent Moon Recreation Area, which ends in the Red Rock Crossing area.

Facility Rental, Amenities, and Policies:
The formations around Sedona fall into the Red Rocks Ranger District of the Coconino National Forest. According to *general* USDA Forest Service policy, noncommercial groups of fewer than seventy-five people,

such as weddings, do not need a permit. As soon as a couple hires an officiant, photographer, or musician, the wedding becomes a commercial event.

All marrying couples and wedding professionals who are planning weddings in the Sedona–Oak Creek forest areas are asked to contact the Red Rocks Ranger District to either obtain a confirmation number for the wedding or to apply for a permit. At the writing of this book, the ranger district permit administrator was in the process of developing a permit system that was to replace the temporary registration system. Until the time that a permit system is in full operation, the wedding party will also need a Red Rocks Pass of $5.00 per day per car. The passes can be purchased from self-serve machines near trailheads, most gas stations and retail stores, and all of the ranger stations.

While the Crescent Moon Ramada picnic area is in the Red Rocks Ranger District, reservations are made through a national center. Day use of the facility accommodates up to fifty people for $75 per day, plus a $10 service fee. The ramada has a grill, drinking water, and restrooms.

Red Rock State Park
4050 Red Rock Loop Road
Sedona, AZ 86336
(928) 282–6907
www.pr.state.az.us/Parks/parkhtml/redrock
.html

Location: From Sedona, drive west on AZ 89A and turn left onto Upper Red Rock Loop Road. At the bottom of the hill, bear right on Upper Red Rock Loop Road, which goes to the state park visitor center and Wedding Tree.

Facility Rental, Amenities, and Policies:
Red Rock State Park's wedding package options include a ceremony under the Wedding Tree ($50), use of the Black Room

for dressing ($50 for 25 to 30 people), and the Twin Cypress Ramada for a reception ($20 for 75 people, $35 for more), totaling a four-hour block. Guests must also pay the park entrance fee of $6.00 per vehicle for up to four adults per vehicle and $1.00 for each additional passenger over the age of thirteen. The ramada has electricity, picnic tables, grills, and restroom facilities. No chairs are provided by the park at the wedding site or Black Hawk Room without prior agreement, and decorations are restricted. The park is open 8:00 A.M. to 5:00 P.M. October through March; 8:00 A.M. to 6:00 P.M. April and September; and 8:00 A.M. to 8:00 P.M. May through August.

Sedona Creative Life Center
333 Schnebly Hill Road
Sedona, AZ 86336
(929) 282–9300
www.sedonacreativelife.com

Location: The Sedona Creative Life Center is on Schnebly Hill Road, off AZ 179, a quarter mile south of the Y intersection of AZ 179 and AZ 89A. Allow enough time for construction and traffic construction on AZ 179.

Facility Rental, Amenities, and Policies: The site fee is $300 per two-hour period. The Sedona Creative Life Center might just be the answer for a nondenominational wedding involving fewer than fifty people. Weddings are held at the center any day of the week year-round, but tend to taper off in July and August because of the heat. The center is flexible about booking requirements as long as space is available, but call three to six months in advance to book.

Catering: Receptions can be held at the Sedona Life Center, or any of the fine restaurants in the area.

Accommodations: Lodging is available in Sedona and Oak Creek Canyon.

SANCTUARY GOLF COURSE AT WESTWORLD
Scottsdale, Arizona

Golf courses make for stunning ceremony and wedding sites, with their unobstructed views of the scenery from the best perspectives, impeccably kept greens and bordering gardens, and relatively private, expansive space. By their very nature golf courses are natural habitats for all kinds of wildlife. Sanctuary Golf Course at Westworld proves that it's possible for all to exist together in harmony. This Scottsdale, Arizona, golf course was designed to provide an exceptional experience for golfers while preserving and maintaining a healthy, thriving natural environment. Given that the site is also a wedding venue, *sanctuary* might carry a deeper meaning—whether you're a golf enthusiast or not.

Built on the western slope of Scottsdale's McDowell Mountains and adjacent to the nationally recognized Westworld equestrian center, Sanctuary is more than a stunning eighteen-hole, daily-fee golf course. Acclaimed golf course architect Randy Heckenkemper transformed the Bureau of Reclamation's storm-water retention area into a 6,624-yard, par-71 layout that provides a haven for native plants and wildlife.

Sanctuary at Westworld is the first golf course in Arizona and the seventeenth course in the world to attain the coveted Audubon International Institute's Signature Status by incorporating Audubon requirements into the earliest design phases of course development to manage issues such as wildlife habitat enhancement, water-quality management and conservation, waste reduction, and pest control. The golf course has incorporated a feature beneficial to the entire area: onsite recharge wells that repurify runoff water from the golf course and return it to the ground, replenishing the area's natural water. The Sonoran Desert's native quails, roadrunners, and jackrabbits watch quietly as golfers play on the rolling terrain featuring seventy-one acres of turf and sixty-five sand bunkers. Hole eight incorporates one large water feature complete with two multitiered waterfalls.

With such attention paid to the cohabitation of golfers and wildlife, the Sanctuary Golf Course is an amazing venue for weddings. Watch from the patio as the sun makes its majestic descent beyond Camelback Mountain, coloring the McDowell Mountains to the east and the valley in pinks and purples. Sanctuary's outdoor pavilion offers a picture-perfect setting for weddings and receptions. The Sanctuary Golf Course's 10,000-square-foot stone-and-stucco clubhouse is an inviting retreat that features a host of amenities, including a comfortably elegant dining room for up to 44 guests, the West Patio for 50, and a multiuse, covered outdoor pavilion that can accommodate up to 150 guests. The Ceremony Lawn is, as the name implies, ideal for a ceremony and can be tented for an additional fee for 150 to 170 people.

Westworld, comprising approximately 120 acres, is a premier, nationally recognized, user-friendly equestrian center and special-events facility. Scottsdale itself, with sunny days and warm temperatures, is a golfer's paradise of more than 200 golf courses. Ample spas, wellness resorts, shopping, art galleries, and cultural attractions make pleasure and relaxation in Scottsdale par for the course.

Sanctuary Golf Course at Westworld
10690 East Sheena Drive
Scottsdale, AZ 85255
Wedding and Reception Information: (480) 502–8642
www.sanctuarygolf.com

Location: Sanctuary Golf Course is in the Westworld gated community in Scottsdale, off McDowell Mountain Ranch Road and 105th Street.

Facility Rental, Amenities, and Policies: Facility rental in 2005 was $250, with a ceremony site fee of $10 per guest. This fee includes setup of white wood chairs and a wedding arch. A one-hour ceremony rehearsal the day prior to the ceremony is also included. White table linens and napkins are provided for every event.

Catering: Catering must be provided by Sanctuary unless otherwise approved. Buffets are $23 to $37 per person. Entrees include Monterey chicken with avocado, chicken piccata, Southwestern chicken pomodoro, roast pork loin with pineapple salsa, and others.

Extras: Dance floor rental is also available starting at $250.

Accommodations: Lodging is available in Scottsdale and the Greater Phoenix area.

SHERATON WILD HORSE PASS RESORT AND SPA

Chandler, Arizona

The bride and groom will walk in beauty at the new Sheraton Wild Horse Pass Resort and Spa just south of Phoenix, Arizona. Named for the feral mustangs that still roam the area, this expanse of rugged Arizona landscape affords views of the Sierra Estrella and South Mountain Ranges, the Gila River, and two championship golf courses. The resort's design is meant to represent the architecture, art, and basket-weaving and pottery-making lifeways of the two Sonoran Desert peoples who built the resort—the Pima and the Maricopa.

The 500-room AAA Four Diamond resort is located on the 600-square-mile Gila River Indian Community shared by the Pima (Akimel O'otham) and Maricopa (Pee Posh). Since ancestral times of Hohokam (or Huhugam), the land has remained relatively pristine. Casino revenues have enabled several southwestern tribes in this millennium to break the centuries-old cycle of dependence, disease, and inhumane treatment by building luxurious theme-park resorts that bridge high-end hospitality with cultural education.

Part of the $175 million Indian-park design includes a replica of the Gila River, cascading waterfalls, and a 111-foot water slide modeling the ancient Casa Grande Ruins of the Hohokam. The grand entrance faces east to the rising sun; giant boulders pile high in an atrium crowned with wrap-around murals of Indian life. Pima and Maricopa traditions inspired guest room and function room decor with artwork that specifically represents each of the two tribes.

The Wild Horse Pass resort includes two eighteen-hole Troon-managed golf courses, a 17,500-square-foot spa, and the Koli Equestrian Center for riding lessons, trail rides, and outdoor events; it's also equipped with tennis courts and jogging trails. Guests are shuttled to the Whirlwind Golf Club and nearby Wild Horse Pass Casino in surrey-covered boats along a 2.5-mile waterway that wraps around the resort.

The resort offers an array of both indoor and extensive outdoor venues and can transform a room with such themes as Old West and Native Spirit. The desert setting allows for year-round outdoor events on riverside lawns, the poolside terrace, or the Koli Equestrian Center, topped off with sunset views and heart-shaped fireworks. Sixteen indoor reception rooms, named for Sonoran Desert animals and featuring earth tones and cultural designs, offer a variety of seating options. The Main Ballroom murals display ancient figures representing music and dancing, while baskets and pottery designs adorn the Junior Ballroom.

Besides golf and the spa, wedding guests will be able to enjoy the Koli Equestrian Center, which organizes horseback rides, hayrides, and even cattle drives and rodeos.

Sheraton Wild Horse Pass Resort and Spa
5594 West Wild Horse Pass Boulevard
Chandler, AZ 85226
(602) 225–0100
www.wildhorsepassresort.com

Location: Sheraton Wild Horse Pass Resort and Spa is 11 miles from the airport and 15 miles from downtown Phoenix, off Interstate 10, exit 162.

Facility Rental, Amenities, and Policies:
The Deluxe Ceremony package is offered in conjunction with on-site receptions or dinners, and is priced for up to 150 guests; additional guests are $3.00 each. The package includes the use of a ceremony site for three hours, a wrought-iron arch, padded white wooden chairs, and a wedding specialist on site for the ceremony. Ceremonial sites are reserved for three-hour periods to accommodate setup and after-ceremony photography. They include the Akimel Lawn (fountains, flagstone, and grass surrounded by the Gila River), $1,500; Beehive Patio (lawn area bordered by the Gila River and a decorative fireplace), $1,500; Estrella Sunset Point (cascading river site with mountain and golf course views), $1,800; and Whirlwind Golf Course (near clubhouse, which includes parking and shuttle service), $3,500.

Catering: With fifty or more guests, reception packages include wedding-night accommodations for the bride and groom with chilled champagne and a special surprise in the room; reduced room rates for out-of-town guests (based on availability); personalized wedding cakes; a champagne or sparkling cider toast; white linen and napkins; votive candles for a centerpiece; dance floor and entertainment staging; and elegant decor on buffets and the cake table.

Plated lunches average $47 per guest, and dinners average $92 per guest, October through April; there are discounts May through September. A dinner might include tower of buffalo mozzarella and beefsteak tomatoes with eggplant caviar, micro greens, and saffron tangelo and sun-dried tomato oils, followed by sliced beef tenderloin and mushroom dusted Atlantic salmon dripping in champagne butter and pan juices, Yukon potato mash, and broccoli rabe. Buffets are designed for a minimum of fifty guests (with an extra charge for fewer guests) and per person prices range from $47.50 to $54.00 for lunch and $75.00 to $80.00 for dinner. Add $100 per station for carving and chef fees. The resort also offers a casual reception of displays, passed hors d'oeuvres, baked potato bar, and pasta, griddle, and carving stations—plus champagne toast and wedding cake—for $85 to $90 per person plus a chef's fee of $100 per station.

Extras: In-house floral experts can create fresh-cut flower bouquets and twinkle lights to enhance the wedding arch and reception site. The in-house audiovisual specialists provide lighting packages to uplight the foliage in a variety of hues, or highlight the walls in heart-shaped or customized gobo designs.

Accommodations: The 500 guest rooms offer a choice of river, golf course, pool, and mountain views. High-season rates start at $289 for a double room. In autumn regular room rates go down to $269; from late May to early September, the regular room rate is $139.

WESTWARD LOOK RESORT

Tucson, Arizona

A desert oasis wedding is a subtle journey of the senses. Westward Look Resort begins that journey with bath tea included in every information packet mailed to the bride. The combination of rose petals, citrus peel, lavender, rosemary, chamomile, sage, and fireweed immediately opens the imagination to the promise of being pampered. Read on to find that Westward Look Resort sits on an eighty-acre refuge in the heart of the Sonoran Desert. Guests relax with sensuous spa treatments using an array of natural elements such as jojoba or desert mud. Feast on Four Diamond cuisine accented with chiles, herbs, and other regional produce from the chef's garden.

The suite-size accommodations all have a private patio or balcony, and there's golfing, mountain biking, horseback riding, and birding along nature trails. You might spot a bobcat strolling on the horse trail in the early morning, a great horned owl sitting in a palm tree, roadrunners darting beneath a pomegranate tree. After dinner you might stargaze through the resort's Celestron 2000 telescope. As the nineteenth-century English poet Arthur Hugh Clough wrote, "But westward, look . . . the land is bright."

Tucson grew along two rivers, and the valley is surrounded by mountains known as Sky Islands to the Native peoples. Westward Look Resort began as a homestead purchase shortly after the territory of Arizona became the forty-eighth state admitted to the Union. At the time the 172-acre plot was considered the most desolate, unreachable part of the emerging city of Tucson. The original homesteaders hired a local architect to build their dream home in the popular adobe style. So convincing was the adobe appearance of the facade that it was not discovered until the 1940s that the home was actually cleverly disguised concrete and steel.

In the 1920s tourism became an important part of the Tucson economy, during which time the ranch's owners added fifteen cottages to the original homesite and invited guests to enjoy the ranch experience. The ranch became a resort in the 1940s and took its name from the Clough poem. Ownership changed hands several times over the decades as the resort expanded—but with an aim toward staying in balance with the cultural and biological environment.

In 1996 lobby and guest rooms were refurbished to reflect the property's multicultural influences, while the historic Vigas Room was restored to its original hacienda decor. At that time the resort added its desert-inspired spa featuring ayurvedic treatments and organic facials in an "East meets Westward Look" fashion. In 1998 the resort launched efforts to create greater awareness of the unique Sonoran Desert ecosystem. By the following year it was nationally recognized as Tucson's most authentic southwestern resort experience, attracting nature lovers, bird-watchers, and outdoor enthusiasts from every region. A multimillion-dollar renovation added a new ballroom (with rooftop terrace), Stargazer Spa Rooms, and executive suites.

The serenity of this desert oasis and the Santa Catalina foothills at sunset offers a romantic setting for any ceremony. The banquet rooms can host receptions for as few as 10 or as many as 300 guests. The largest venues are the Sonoran Ballroom, with its rooftop terrace for panoramic views, and the Catalina Ballroom featuring 14-foot windows for city views. For something smaller and more intimate, the Palm Room is perfect for receptions up to eighty guests and offers an easy indoor/outdoor flow with French doors opening onto a brick terrace overlooking the city. The Mesa and Canyon Rooms open onto terraces with lush desert and mountain views. The white-canopied terrace pavilion combines the outdoors with the comforts of an indoor venue. Outdoor locations are also available.

Westward Look Resort
245 East Ina Road
Tucson, AZ 85704
(800) 722–2500
www.westwardlook.com

Location: Westward Look Resort is near the Ina Road exit off Interstate 10 west.

Facility Rental, Amenities, and Policies: The site fee ranges from $250 to $1,000. Package specials are likely offered in the summer months, and incentives periodically throughout the year. In the past one package for a minimum of 150 people included the choice of three of the following: a 10 percent discount on a Sunday-through-Friday wedding, a 10 percent discount on bridal spa packages, a fifty-minute massage for bride and groom, a groom's cake, an upgrade for the wedding night in the Stargazer Room with private outdoor hot tub, a horse carriage ride from the reception to the room, or dinner for two in the Gold Room restaurant.

Catering: Reception catering at Westward Look includes floral table centerpieces with mirror tiles and votive candles, cake service (when the cake is purchased from the resort), a champagne toast for the head table, complimentary overnight accommodations for the bride and groom, and a wedding consultant and coordinator. For

10 to 250 guests, brunch starts at $50 to $75 per person, plated lunch at $30 to $37, buffet lunch at $33 to $57, plated dinner at $44 to $75, and dinner buffet at $50 to $95. Banquet chairs are rented for $3.00 apiece.

Extras: Westward Look offers a number of tempting spa packages for wedding groups. For instance, the bride receives a free fifty-minute massage upon purchasing spa treatments for nine or more members of the wedding party.

Accommodations: Westward Look Resort offers 244 spacious guest accommodations, 16 meeting and banquet rooms, a highly rated tennis facility, a world-renowned gourmet restaurant, a bar and Sonoran grill with first-rate entertainment, and a breathtaking view of Tucson. Note that the property is hilly and spread out, making it tiring to move about for some. You can arrange to be taken anywhere on the property, or can request a room closer to the main building where the restaurant and bar are located. Rooms higher on the hillside are quiet and have great views, and are also close to the main building. Depending on the season, rates start at $89 June through September, and $179 January through April. Guest room rates for out-of-town guests are discounted.

Keep in Mind: The peak season for weddings at Westward Look is January through April, before the summer heat begins. Spring temperatures climb from sixty degrees in March to ninety degrees in May, averaging ninety-five degrees throughout the summer—although low humidity lessens the discomfort. Fall is a bit cooler than spring, and winter temperatures average fifty-eight degrees from December through February. Monsoons in late summer are one of the great attractions for visitors to the Arizona desert.

THORNCROWN C

Eureka Springs, Arkansa

Hearts stir at first glimpse of the wood-and-glass Thorncrown Chapel soaring 48 feet amid a cluster of giant oak, hickory, magnolia, and maple trees. Made of cross-braced native Arkansas pine and 6,000 square feet of glass atop one hundred tons of native stone, the chapel has been ranked (by the American Institute of Architects) as the nation's fourth greatest building of the twentieth century. With 425 windows, the chapel of light was designed by prominent architect E. Fay Jones, an Arkansas native and disciple of Frank Lloyd Wright. Jones used Wright's principle of melding architecture with its environment. Exchanging vows inside will feel like a marriage made in heaven.

Thorncrown was the dream of Jim Reed, a native of Pine Bluff, Arkansas. He had brought his wife to Eureka Springs on a honeymoon before he went off to World War II. In 1971 Reed purchased land for his retirement home, but when he realized how often people stopped on his property to gain a better view of the beautiful Ozark hills, it occurred to him to build a glass chapel in the woods to give wayfarers a place for inspired relaxation. Shortly thereafter he enlisted architect Jones, a professor at the University of Arkansas. With starts and stops, the chapel finally opened on July 10, 1980. Since then four million people have visited this little chapel on the hillside—600 of them joining in matrimony there every year.

Thorncrown Chapel is not the only attraction in the area. The springs in this region of the Ozark Mountains have long been known for their restorative qualities, first noted and revered by Native Americans. The miraculous waters eventually gave rise to the founding and naming of the city of Eu... the road... covered"... out that... of thousands to set... rapidly grew into one of the top reso... the Victorian era. Called America's Little Switzerland, the gingerbread-laden houses and boutique-lined streets of Eureka Springs recapture the small-town charm of a bygone era. Visitors enjoy a leisurely stroll along winding avenues in one of the most walkable cities in America. The entire downtown, with its well-preserved Victorian architecture, is listed on the National Register of Historic Places. Eureka Springs has also long been a mecca for honeymoon and romantic getaways. It is increasingly a popular destination for weddings.

Thorncrown Chapel
12968 Highway 62 West, Eureka Springs, AR 72632
(479) 253–7401
www.thorncrown.com

Eureka! Springs Visitors Bureau
35 North Main Street
P.O. Box 522
Eureka Springs, AR 72632
(866) WISH–EUREKA or (479) 253–7333
www.eurekasprings.org

Location: 3 miles west of Eureka Springs on U.S. Highway 62. The chapel is 250 feet down a pathway from the parking lot large enough for buses and RVs. Thorncrown Chapel is open daily from 9:00 A.M. to 5:00 P.M.

ety-minute reservation of
eating 100 guests) or Worship
ting 300) is $395. For large
s involving musicians and extra
dants, couples may rent either facility
a one-hour rehearsal with the chapel
minister or host for an additional $200.
Reservations must be made for the
rehearsal as well as the wedding.

A full-time minister is available to conduct the service for no additional charge, although a donation is appreciated. Couples who decide to use the chapel minister are required to listen to a Christian marriage counseling tape provided free of charge. The Thorncrown Chapel music minister is also available to play or sing at the wedding for an additional charge. Guest ministers licensed with the state of Arkansas must submit a copy of their wedding ceremony to the chapel a month prior to the wedding. Since Thorncrown Chapel is a Christian organization, all ceremonies must be Christ-centered and scriptural.

Thorncrown Chapel provides only the facilities and a minister for the wedding; it does not provide dressing rooms, organ, or drive-up access. A piano, sound system, cassette and CD players, recorded wedding music, small restrooms, and an office with a full-length mirror are offered for the couple's convenience at no extra charge.

The wedding party should arrive more than thirty minutes prior to the scheduled time. No smoking, food, or drinks are allowed on the chapel or Worship Center grounds.

Catering: Thorncrown does not provide a reception area. Reception and rehearsal dinners are all available locally in Eureka Springs.

Extras: Photographer, flowers, candelabra, musicians, and ministers (if the staff minister is not used) are available locally.

Accommodations: Lodging is available in Eureka Springs. Thorncrown recommends that the wedding party dress in their rooms before coming to the chapel.

Keep in Mind: Early reservation is helpful, especially during the summer months. Ceremonies held in the chapel during the busiest months of April through October may only be scheduled at 8:00 A.M., 4:30 P.M., and 6:30 P.M., although the Worship Center is available almost anytime day or evening. Chapel ceremonies November through March may be scheduled anytime. Weddings involving just the bride and groom are sometimes charged only $295.

ASILOMAR CONFERENCE GROUNDS
Pacific Grove, California

Monterey pines and cypresses shade the forty redwood-and-granite buildings that make up the 107-acre Asilomar Conference Grounds. An S-curved boardwalk takes visitors down to the sand dunes where vegetation grows wild and whitecapped waves create a constant roar. Deer graze in meadows, monarch butterflies cluster thickly in the pines, and seals swim in the protected coves. This is nature in the raw; critics call it summer camp, but many others call this rustic retreat enchanting.

More than seventy marrying couples find Asilomar the perfect place to hold ceremonies every year. Since Asilomar is located at one end of the famous 17-mile Drive, guests can easily trek to the local golf courses, boutique shops, restaurants, wharfs, and museums of Pebble Beach, Carmel, Pacific Grove, and Monterey.

Asilomar is roughly a Spanish composite word meaning "refuge by the sea." The complex of buildings was originally created as a YWCA conference center. It was designed by Julia Morgan, who was the first woman architect licensed in California and known for designing Hearst Castle. All but one of her thirteen buildings were created in the Arts and Crafts style. Redwood beams and round stones supported by massive trusses create spacious interiors dominated by stone hearths. Exterior dormer windows and weathered shingles blend in with the environment. Thirty years later John Carl Warnecke (best known for John F. Kennedy's grave site memorial) created seven more complexes.

The Grace H. Dodge Chapel, seating 350, is one of several locations offered for ceremonies. A panoramic window behind the stage looks west through the pines to the spectacular Asilomar dunes, and the slanting floor creates the illusion of sitting among them. Natural light pours through surrounding windows at all times of the day.

A venue for exceptionally large weddings is Merrill Hall, Morgan's final structure. Flagstone replaces rubblestone on the building's western effacement, a departure from her style. It is a well-lit building with French doors, wood floors, and a fireplace with a fossil imprinted on its center keystone. The interior also features arch trusses and an upper clerestory with pointed-arch style windows. Asilomar also offers a number of smaller, cozier venues for more intimate weddings.

A favorite ceremony site is the meadow facing the sea; the sculpted Monterey cypress forms a broad canopy over the meadow in a cathedral-like manner. Beach weddings are also popular and encouraged, with the boardwalk providing a dramatic processional.

Asilomar Conference Grounds
800 Asilomar Boulevard
Pacific Grove, CA 93950
Room Reservations: (831) 372–8016
Guest Phone: (831) 372–8016
Group Sales Office: (831) 642–4222
www.visitasilomar.com

Location: Asilomar is 105 miles from San Francisco International Airport and 310 from LAX between Monterey and Pebble Beach.

Facility Rental, Amenities, and Policies: Booking a wedding at Asilomar is a year-long process, although it is possible to book weddings within a shorter time frame. Asilomar usually books two weddings per weekend and sometimes as many as three per weekend in the summer. Flexibility is the key to finding an opening, and one can almost always be found. A staff coordinator is assigned to every wedding and assists in all stages of planning the menu and event.

Asilomar schedules weddings and receptions between 11:00 A.M. and 4:00 P.M., and between 5:00 and 10:00 P.M. Ceremonies in the chapel are $660, and those in the meadow or on the beach are $3.20 per chair (up a dime from 2004). Be sure to confirm time of high tide when booking a ceremony on the beach!

Room rental fees for receptions increase only slightly from year to year, and range from $450 for the Surf and Sand (accommodating 45) to $1,400 for Merrill Hall (accommodating 600). Rooms are booked for four hours for the actual reception, plus two hours for setup and decoration. Overtime or excessive cleanup may incur additional charges. Full-service banquet amenities such as tables, chairs, standard linens, china, silver, glassware, setup, and cleanup are included in all wedding packages.

The grounds have a natural beauty; a simple arch with flowers is all the decor that is necessary.

Catering: Catering starts at $20 per person. Reception favorites include Asilomar Chicken with lemons, cashews, and capers, as well as themed dinners such as a Hawaiian luau and signature Boardwalk Barbecue. No outside food and beverage may be brought onto the gorunds, with the exception of the wedding cake.

Accommodations: Guest accommodations, if available, can be booked for less than $100 per room. Based on availability, a block of rooms may be reserved for wedding guests, and conference rates and rules

apply. Otherwise guests may call the "leisure reservations" department ninety days prior to the event, although weekend accommodations tend to sell out to conferences years in advance. Plenty of hotels exist in the four-city area of Pacific Grove, Carmel, Salinas, and Monterey.

Keep in Mind: Annual temperatures at Asilomar average sixty to sixty-five degrees, but coastal weather does vary throughout the day. Fall is the warmest season, while winter is the rainiest. Dressing in layers and carrying an umbrella is always a good policy. All outdoor events are booked at Asilomar at the client's own risk. However, should the weather become inclement on the day of a wedding, the ceremony might be transferred to the banquet room where the reception is being held, or to an appropriate function room, if available. Guests should plan to arrive early enough to park in designated areas, and to wear comfortable shoes to walk to the event.

CAMARILLO RANCH
Camarillo, California

Camarillo Ranch is a historic, popular refuge in the heart of a manufacturing and agricultural region. Located within sight of the Ventura Highway, the suitability of Camarillo Ranch as a wedding and reception venue might not be apparent at first arrival. But a tour of the house and grounds reveals its perfection as a special-events location. Such noncommercial, noncrowded sites are rare in Southern California. Yet the Pacific Ocean is just fifteen minutes away, and Santa Barbara or Los Angeles, just forty-five minutes away.

That Camarillo Ranch is located in fertile farmland is not to understate its romance. The house itself is preserved in the decor of the Victorian age. Hints of the horse ranching that went on here are found in the red barn, the carriage lane, and the rein ties at the side porch. With the site's seventy-degree temperatures, weddings can be conducted here at any time of the year. The same coastal plain climate that allows for agriculture also nourishes the ranch's prolific flower gardens and towering trees. Three of these trees, planted before 1900, are on the

California Historic Tree Registry. Although as many as 2,000 guests can sit concert style on the lawn between the bunya-bunya and the Norfolk pine, a simple ceremony for two is often conducted beneath the grand boughs of the Morton Bay fig. The gardens feature mature trees, water fountains, and extensive planting for butterflies, which means something is always in bloom as the perfect backdrop for photography.

Camarillo Ranch now sits on what was once a Mexican land grant given to Jose Pedro Ruiz by Governor Alvarado in 1847, and purchased by Portuguese explorer Juan Camarillo in 1875. Following his death five years later, his oldest son, Adolfo Camarillo, took over ranch operations at the age of sixteen. He and his wife, Isabella Menchaca, moved into an adobe structure on the ranch in 1888 that was soon destroyed by fire. The family moved into the Camarillo Mansion, a three-story, fourteen-room Queen Anne, complete with spindles and gingerbread towers, upon its completion four years later.

Adolfo Camarillo is often called "the Last Spanish Don," partly because of his prominence as a community leader. He died on December 10, 1958, the father of seven children. The city of Camarillo's seal bears his resemblance riding a white horse.

In 1997 Centex Corporation acquired four and a half acres of the ranch, including the mansion, and turned it over to the city of Camarillo. Since then both the city and the Camarillo Ranch Foundation have completed extensive renovations inside and out. Facilities now include a Victorian-style bride's dressing and powder room, along with a more masculine bathroom where the groom can prepare. Guests will enjoy cocktails in the front parlor featuring a tower bay window. The Adolfo Camarillo Mansion interior can accommodate 60 for ceremony seating, 80 for reception seating, and 125 for a standing reception and cocktails. The main lawn with its canopy of trees can accommodate 2,000 for concert seating, 600 for ceremony seating, and 500 for a seated reception. The red barn (undergoing renovation as of this writing) will hold a maximum of 299 for ceremony and reception seating. The West Garden seats 75 for a ceremony and 50 for a reception, and the East Garden seats 250 for both the ceremony and reception.

Wedding guests should find plenty to do in the area, which has more than 30 miles of bicycle routes, plus sixteen public and private golf courses within a 20-mile radius. Channel Islands National Park, the Santa Monica Mountains Recreational Area, and the Los Padres National Forest are all within easy driving distance. Camarillo Premium Outlets features more than 125 stores, including some upscale names not often found in outlet malls. Camarillo also has a number of smaller, specialized shops and an old-fashioned farmers' market that takes place every Saturday morning on Ventura Boulevard in Old Town.

Camarillo Ranch
201 Camarillo Ranch Road
Camarillo, CA 93012
(805) 389–8182
www.camarilloranch.org

Location: North of the Ventura Highway (US 101), near the intersection of Mission Oaks Boulevard and Camarillo Ranch Road. Camarillo Ranch Road is a relatively new street; specific directions are found on Camarillo Ranch's Web site.

Facility Rental, Amenities, and Policies: All of the wedding and reception packages include the choice of five main event venues. All site rental packages include use of grounds and mansion for wedding photography, use of the bridal room, a white wooden wedding arch, and 200 bistro chairs.

Ceremonies without an on-site reception are only allowed before 1:00 P.M. Every effort is made to schedule events when no public tours are being offered. The Garden Ceremony Only package is $950 for three hours of site use, including two hours to set up and break down, and a one-hour event. The Mansion Ceremony package is $1,400 for the same three hours (maximum sixty seated).

The Garden Reception package is $3,000 for five event hours. The Garden Reception package with Cocktail/Appetizer Hour in the mansion is $3,225 for six event hours. The Mansion Reception is $3,600 for five event hours (maximum eighty to one hundred people seated) inside the mansion, and use of the kitchen for catering, sink, and staging tables.

Catering: Camarillo Ranch is strictly a site rental facility and offers no other services. Although cooking is not permitted in the kitchen, couples may bring in their own food or hire caterers.

Extras: Camarillo Ranch can provide a list of area vendors.

Accommodations: Lodging is available in Camarillo, Ventura, Los Angeles, and Santa Barbara.

DESCANSO GARDENS
La Cañada Flintridge, California

One of the more celebrated places in Southern California for weddings is Descanso Gardens, twenty minutes from downtown Los Angeles. Unique among comparable botanical gardens for its forest of camellias—more than 700 varieties (some 20 feet tall)—it has as many as 34,000 plants blooming under a canopy of California oak trees. These evergreen flowering shrubs from China and Japan were the passion of *Los Angeles Times* publisher E. Manchester Boddy, who began planting them here in 1941. This urban oasis encompasses 160 acres of native chaparral-covered slopes, with paths and streams that wind through the towering forest and pass by a lake, a bird sanctuary, the Japanese Garden and Tea House, and the Boddy House Gallery. Descanso also features the nine-acre International Rosarium, which holds 1,700 varieties of antique and modern roses; daffodils, azaleas, tulips, and lilacs in the spring; and chrysanthemums in the fall.

Descanso Gardens can usually accommodate up to three weddings at a time: one at Boddy House and one each on the East Side and West Side of the gardens. The scheduling of three weddings at a time is possible because all ceremonies and their accompanying receptions must be held in the same zone.

Boddy House, where Boddy and his family lived, is a twenty-two-room Regency–style mansion sited above lush oak woodland. The lawn and terrace of Boddy House have a maximum capacity of seventy-five guests, while up to fifty guests can be invited into the living room, dining room, or solarium and foyer. All ceremonies and receptions must be held together at the house venue.

The Japanese Garden on the East Side lends itself to stylish outdoor events in a serene setting of Asian elegance for fifty. Tranquil and colorful, the Japanese Garden is graced by a blue-tiled Tea House, a raked rock garden, and a koi-filled pond surrounded by giant pink azaleas. The Minka, on the edge of the Japanese Garden and reached by a red Shinto bridge over a softly flowing stream, is ideal for an intimate gathering of up to twenty people.

Other outdoor ceremony sites in the East Side include: Feather Falls (80), Sundial Lawn (150), Magnolia Lawn (200), and the Main Lawn (up to 400 guests). The Under the Oaks Theater on the Main Lawn can seat up to 250 guests on open-air natural redwood benches.

All ceremonies held at the East Side locations have their receptions in the Van de Kamp Hall. Van de Kamp is a Craftsman-style building that seats 180 and is part of a complex of buildings near the visitor center. It also has an outdoor courtyard suitable for after-hours receptions.

The popular Rose Garden on the West Side provides a historical overview of the rose, with examples from the Middle Ages, the Renaissance, Victorian England, and the early American colonies planted in a circular arrangement. Rose Garden ceremony venues include the Rose Garden Gazebo (200), Rose Pavilion (140), and "other" Rose Garden Nooks (up to 100). Other outdoor ceremony sites on the West Side include the Oak Forest (300) and the Promenade (150). Ceremonies on the West Side of the gardens have their receptions in the Rose Pavilion.

No Southern California venue is complete without an amusement ride. For the young (and the young-at-heart), the Descanso Gardens Enchanted Railroad offers the chance to climb aboard a tiny replica of a diesel train and travel around a small section of the gardens. The train runs every weekend and tickets are $2.00.

Descanso Gardens
1418 Descanso Drive
La Cañada Flintridge, CA 91011
(818) 949–4200
Weddings: (818) 949–4203; Catering: (818) 790–7932
www.descansogardens.org

Location: Descanso Gardens is easily accessible from Interstates 2 or 210, and is just twenty minutes from downtown Los Angeles and the Burbank airport.

Facility Rental, Amenities, and Policies: Site fees for Boddy House locations range from $3,200 for an exterior ceremony (no reception) to $5,200 for both ceremony and reception, indoor and out. East Garden ceremonies range from $2,500 for Feather Falls to $3,000 for the Main Lawn, or $4,500 to $5,000 at the same sites with an accompanying reception at Van de Kamp Hall. A reception at Van de Kamp without a ceremony is $3,500. West Garden location fees are around $3,200 for the Oak Forest and Rose Garden for a ceremony only, or $5,200 with a reception at the Rose Garden. A reception at the Pavilion without a ceremony is $3,800. Discounts are given for winter ceremonies and receptions, November through February, although a $300 surcharge is added to Saturday weddings. To rent the entire East or West Side for both a ceremony and reception is $8,000. All rental fees include staff coordinator, security guard, parking, and unlimited admission to Descanso Gardens prior to the event for planning, photography, and rehearsal, as well as for visits within three months after the event.

Although each venue has its own set of time restrictions, ceremonies are generally scheduled from 8:00 to 10:00 A.M. or 5:00 to 7:00 P.M., and ceremonies with receptions are from 8:00 A.M. to 1:00 P.M. or 5:00 to 10:00 P.M.

Catering: Patina Catering at Descanso Gardens is the exclusive caterer. The banquet menu features a wide selection of traditional and creative fare. Four-hour receptions for a minimum of one hundred people include champagne toast, house wine and imported beer selections, passed hors d'oeuvres, and essential tables, linens, place settings, and serving dishes. Plated dinners start at $65.00 to $76.50 per person, and buffets are $68.50 to $78.50.

Accommodations: Numerous hotels and motels exist within 10 miles of Descanso Gardens.

Keep in Mind: Reservation books for all events at Descanso Gardens open on the first of June for the following year. At that time all wedding information for the current year is removed from the Descanso Gardens Web site and it can take a couple months for new pricing information to be posted for the following year.

FESS PARKER'S DOUBLETREE RESORT

Santa Barbara, California

The Fess Parker DoubleTree stands on what was once the site for two consecutive locomotive roundhouses constructed by the Southern Pacific Railroad. The first was severely damaged by the 1925 earthquake. The planning committee of the community arts association convinced the railroad to design the replacement building in the Spanish style for which Santa Barbara was becoming famous, and the resulting construction resembled—of all things—the bullring in Seville, Spain. In September 1982 the roundhouse was demolished to make way for Fess Parker's resort, which opened four years later. The old roundhouse served to inspire the architectural design of the new resort, which was further meant to capture the mission and Spanish colonial history of Santa Barbara.

Echoes of the old roundhouse remain in the roofless Plaza del Sol, which recalls the bullring and coliseum motif, with gigantic arched-window views of East Beach and an unobstructed view of the sky. It serves as a unique venue for grand weddings and receptions in the round, particularly when adorned with one of the resort's signature lighting packages. Guests have cocktails on the open Rotunda above the Plaza del Sol as wait staff clear the wedding chairs to set the reception.

Actor Fess Parker of Santa Barbara, California, has been called by some an American icon. In 1954 Walt Disney signed Parker to play the title role in *Davy Crockett, King of the Wild Frontier*. In 1964 he began starring in the network television series *Daniel Boone*. Parker continued to star in numerous box office hits while laying the foundation for his second career as a real estate developer.

Blending his Texas hospitality and eye for land development, the DoubleTree was Parker's first resort hotel, built on twenty-three and a half oceanfront acres. Parker purchased a 714-acre ranch in the Santa Ynez Valley 35 miles north of Santa Barbara in 1987, where he promptly established Fess Parker's Winery & Vineyard, made famous by the 2004 movie *Sideways*.

In 1998 Parker purchased the Grand Hotel in Los Olivos near his winery. This charming twenty-one-room Victorian-style inn is now called Fess Parker's Wine Country Inn & Spa and also hosts weddings. Visiting guests may have the opportunity to see the legend himself, as he frequently dines in the restaurant.

Fess Parker's DoubleTree Resort
633 East Cabrillo Boulevard
Santa Barbara, CA, 93103
(805) 564–4333
www.fpdtr.com

Location: Cabrillo Boulevard is the beachfront harbor drive.

Facility Rental, Amenities, and Policies: Plaza del Sol and the Grand Ballroom can accommodate receptions for 1,000 people, but much smaller weddings can be booked there as well. The Plaza and the President Ronald Reagan Room, which has a capacity of 160 to 200 (and has been used by the Reagans for fund-raising), have catering minimums of $10,000 to $13,800. The ballrooms and the Fiesta (capacity 80 to 110) and Solstice (70 to 90) on the Rotunda do not require minimums.

In addition to the catering prices, the resort charges a setup fee for receptions, ranging from $450 for the smallest banquet rooms to $1,900 for Plaza del Sol. Ceremonies in Plaza del Sol are $1,000, while those in the Rose Garden or Anacapa Patio (capacity 200 to 400) are less than $600. The resort requires a wedding planner for weddings with a hundred or more guests; the bride and groom may hire a professional coordinator or use the services of a staff professional for $1,500.

Catering: Reception packages include champagne toast for guests during the event, mixed nuts, an assortment of hors d'oeuvres, a three-course dinner or buffet, wine service, a wedding cake provided by the resort's specialty bakery with ceremonial cutting, freshly brewed coffee, iced tea, and function room set to specifications.

Wedding menu prices for 2006, up slightly from 2005, start at $52 to $57 per person for lunch and $69 to $77 for dinner. Luncheon buffets start at $64, and dinner buffets at $77. The signature Celebration of Stations—entertainment with food prepared or cooked on site by uniformed chefs—starts at $82 per person with a minimum of four stations; for additional stations, add $15 per person. Children can choose from their own menu.

Extras: Couples will want to purchase lighting packages to enhance their venues, especially in the Plaza del Sol. Technicians can paint the area with a colored wash, create a sunset effect with colored uplights on the columns and dance floor gobo (projected patterns such as stars), or an aurora effect with uplights on the trees. Packages are priced per number of people, and are also available for the ballroom.

Accommodations: With a minimum of sixty guests at Fess Parker's DoubleTree Resort, the bride and groom receive a deluxe ocean-view room for the evening of the wedding and breakfast for two.

The resort was scheduled to have 360 newly redesigned rooms by the summer of 2005. Group discounts are available for blocks of 10 rooms or more. The resort offers free shuttle service to and from the Santa Barbara airport and Amtrak station, easy access to the Santa Barbara trolley and the downtown waterfront shuttle, a full spa and salon, a steak house, and two cafes. Ocean-view rooms are available upon request. Rooms are $199 to $399; suites are $359 to $899.

FOUR SEASONS RESORT SANTA BARBARA

Santa Barbara, California

The Four Seasons Resort is the gem of California's Côte d'Azur, combining Old World standards of service with beauty, indulgence, and exclusivity—without the brusqueness. Surprising to most newcomers, however, is the feeling of privacy. Yes, all of this luxuriousness comes at a price that is prohibitive to most, but the grounds are situated geographically—with cemetery, freeway, and sprawling Montecito mansions as barriers—so that the resort turns a shoulder to the more public East Beach just around the bend. The result is the feeling of being one of the privileged few to experience the quiet stretch of Butterfly Beach and panoramic ocean views.

The hotel (formerly the Biltmore) was constructed in the 1920s in Santa Barbara's now classic Spanish revival red tile and white stucco. It was Robert Odell who brought the hotel (then the Biltmore) into its prime during his forty-year reign, building the resort's exclusive Coral Casino, with an enormous pool and glamorous ballrooms. His legendary style included a strict dress code and a private poker room accessible by a staircase hidden in the coat closet. The usual Hollywood glitterati, from Lana Turner to Rock Hudson, played croquet on the lawns.

Beanie Baby baron Ty Warner purchased the property in 2000 and brought it to a new level with a $26 million pool, spa, and state-of-the art fitness center. Today guests can swim in the abalone shell-lined pool or undergo chromotherapy while soaking in a Jacuzzi lit in the chakra-tuned colors of their choice.

Although the resort is undergoing a $60 million guest room restoration, its glorious past is still reflected in its architecture and service.

This is twenty acres of tropical paradise: Open arches frame gardens where gardenias and jasmine perfume the air, while bougainvilleas cascade from iron balconies. What an intoxicating place for a ceremony. Vows can be exchanged in the Palmera Garden, a flagstone courtyard bordered with flowers and palm trees (accommodating 50 to 150 guests). Wedding chairs can be set in the Escala Garden, oriented toward the resort's signature tower with its spiraling staircase (50 to 150). The Monte Vista's expansive croquet lawn and putting green offers a breathtaking view of the Santa Ynez Mountains (up to 400). The Mariposa Garden provides a view of the ocean (50 to 100). La Pacifica opens to a large lawn (200 to 300) overlooking the Channel Islands and the crashing surf; wedding guests might spot some of the 20,000 whales that migrate through here between late February and May.

Reception sites are glamorous. The Loggia Ballroom, accommodating receptions for up to 350 guests, features an 18-foot ceiling, crystal chandeliers, a fireplace, and three French doors opening onto an outdoor patio. For receptions with as many as 150 guests, El Mar has high wood-beamed ceilings, fireplace, windows, and a red-tiled terrace overlooking the Pacific Ocean. La Pacifica Ballroom has a wall of windows opening onto the Pacific Ocean for a reception of 500. The resort has a number of smaller rooms for smaller events.

Four Seasons Resort Santa Barbara
1260 Channel Drive
Santa Barbara, CA 93108
(805) 969–2261
Weddings: (805) 565–8323
www.fourseasons.com/santabarbara

Location: At the end of Olive Mill Road from the Ventura Highway (US 101).

Facility Rental, Amenities, and Policies: The fee for wedding ceremonies in the Mariposa, Palmera, Escala, La Pacifica, and Monte Vista Gardens is $2,500. Outdoor events are scheduled no earlier than 9:00 A.M. and no later than 9:00 P.M. to ensure the comfort of other hotel guests. The resort requires a coordinator for all ceremonies held on the property. Complimentary services provided by the hotel are in-house centerpieces, umbrellas, dance floor, heaters, and staging. Four Seasons offers superior linens, cutlery, china, and glassware for all banquet tables. Special colors, patterns, or designs may be obtained for a nominal rental fee. A Four Seasons on-site expert will work with the couple or wedding consultant to reserve dates, plan the schedule of events, and coordinate all food and beverage details, from menu design to linens.

Catering: For the three larger ballrooms, the resort requires minimum food and beverage orders from $8,000 for lunch in El Mar to $35,000 for dinner in La Pacifica. Wrap your taste buds around these sample wedding menu items: lobster medallion caramelized fennel puff pastry, roast Chilean sea bass with a crab and potato crust, and grilled tenderloin of beef topped with sweet corn brioche and Cabernet reduction.

A minimum of fifty guests is required for a buffet; a small labor fee is charged for all buffets with fewer than fifty guests, and all functions with less than twenty. The hotel provides one server for every twenty guests for breakfast and lunch, and one for every fifteen at dinner. An extra fee may be required for additional servers.

Extras: The wedding couple will want to set aside two and a half hours for a his-and-her spa package to melt away wedding day nerves.

Accommodations: There are 217 guest rooms, suites, and cottages on twenty acres of lush gardens overlooking the Pacific Ocean, starting at $450 to $500 per night. Rates are higher in summer when rooms in Santa Barbara book solidly. Recreational facilities include a swimming pool, health club with spa services, three lighted tennis courts, putting green, croquet, and complimentary bicycles.

A complimentary night for the bride and groom is offered with a catered event of seventy-five people or more. An additional 5 rooms are offered at a preferred rate for wedding guests (subject to availability). Special-rate room blocks will be released four weeks prior to the event. A two-night minimum stay is required when staying over a Saturday night.

GOLDEN GATE
NATIONAL RECREATION AREA
San Francisco, California

For scenic outdoor weddings Golden Gate National Recreation Area (GGNRA) in the San Francisco area has it all: cathedrals of redwood, rugged beaches, a working lighthouse, and prominent views of the Golden Gate Bridge. Under the National Park Service (NPS), GGNRA has designated twenty areas for outdoor weddings, fourteen of which can accommodate 100 to 200 people, with restrictions and caveats. The logistics of a large wedding might be problematic, but for a smaller group any of these locations would be well worth the effort.

Golden Gate National Recreation Area, one of the largest national urban parks in the world, sprawls across more than 74,000 acres of the San Francisco Bay and ocean shoreline, Marin Headlands, the Presidio, Point Reyes National Seashore, and John Muir National Monument. GGNRA protects more than 1,250 historic structures, twenty-seven rare and endangered species, and many small "islands" of threatened habitat.

When selecting a ceremony site, consider the mood you want to strike—enclosed and intimate, or expansive and inspired. The coziest site would be **Muir Woods,** located in a small valley where it is foggy, cool, and damp all year long. Creating an atmosphere of quiet reverence, the majestic virgin redwood trees tower as high as 252 feet; some are nearly 800 years old. Pathways cross streams, but are wheelchair accessible. The most popular site for ceremonies (and tourists) is the circular Cathedral Grove half a mile from the entrance. Thirty people can close in around the couple, but only ten can attend

a ceremony in the Walk-In Tree. Muir Woods also allows ceremonies in seven other sites for five to thirty people. Ceremonies must be held before 10:00 A.M. or after 4:30 P.M., and no receptions, chairs, singing, or music allowed. The park is a mere 12 miles north of the Golden Gate Bridge, but with traffic it can take an hour to drive there on the steep, winding road (long vehicles prohibited).

If beaches are more your thing, GGNRA has six of them in various shapes and sizes. **Muir Beach** (one hundred people), near the town by the same name one hour north of San Francisco, is a small, sandy shoal studded with boulders and surrounded by high bluffs. **Rodeo Beach** (200) is a large, picturesque strand located at the westernmost edge of the Marin Headlands. **Ocean Beach** (200), on the western edge of San Francisco, is a wide expanse of sandy shoreline extending from the Cliff House south to Fort Funston. Ocean Beach tends to be chilly, though September and October have optimal weather conditions. **Stinson Beach** (200), one hour north of San Francisco, is an immense stretch of white sand tucked below the steeply rising slopes of Mount Tamalpais State Park. (*Tip:* Hire a monitoring ranger to reserve the south parking lot.) **Baker Beach** (200) is San Francisco's most popular, located west of the Golden Gate Bridge on the western edge of the Presidio. Nearby, Battery Chamberlin—named for a Union hero of the Civil War—is the site of a historic seacoast fortification completed in 1904. **China Beach** (fifty) is a tiny cove located between Baker

Beach and Lands End in San Francisco, named for the Chinese fishermen who anchored their junks in the cove.

Always fancied a lighthouse wedding? Ceremonies involving up to sixty-five people are permitted just outside the **Point Bonita Lighthouse** (which is within the GGNRA purview) on Saturday, Sunday, and Monday before 11:00 A.M. or after 4:30 P.M. Situated on the extreme southwestern tip of the Marin Headlands, and accessible by a steep half-mile walk, the point has exceptional views of the Golden Gate Bridge and the Pacific Ocean. Constructed in 1855 and moved to its current location in 1877, the lighthouse is still active and maintained by the U.S. Coast Guard. Two rangers must be hired to monitor the event at $65 per hour for a minimum of four hours.

The **Muir Beach Overlook,** half a mile north of Muir Beach, has a large lawn area, breathtaking views of the coastal cliffs of the Pacific Ocean, and potential sighting of migrating gray whales in June and November. Ceremonies may not take place on the promontory, but photography there will be considered. Resist parking in the neighborhood around the overlook. **Sutro Park** (200), on the western edge of San Francisco across from the Cliff House, has quiet lawn and garden areas, a parapet with spectacular ocean views, and a cute, miniature pavilion structure quite popular for ceremonies.

Military buffs will enjoy the World War I and II gun emplacements of **Battery Mendell** (50), **Black Point Battery** (100), and **Battery Rathbone/McIndoe** (100), but others shouldn't discount them. By definition they all have the best vantage points and unobstructed views of the ocean, San Francisco, the Golden Gate Bridge, or the Marin Headlands. Spanish soldiers first fortified the Fort Mason area in 1797; it became a U.S. Army military reservation in 1850. Some of the buildings date back to the Gold Rush and were occupied by the army during the Civil War.

Other Area Options

Park Partners. "Park Partners" in the San Francisco–area NPS system also offer space and catering for weddings and wedding receptions. The Presidio of San Francisco, for example, was a military post that served the Spaniards (1776), the Mexican army (1821), and the U.S. Army after the Mexican-American War of 1846. Transferred to NPS, the Presidio has a number rental facilities: the Golden Gate Club, Golf Course, Officers' Club, Chapel of Our Lady, Main Post Chapel, Glass Palace & Log Cabin, San Francisco Film Centre, and Presidio of San Francisco. Other NPS Park Partners include the Fort Mason Chapel and Officers' Club, San Francisco Maritime National Historic Park Museum & Historic Ships, Marin Headlands Facility (handled by the Golden Gate Club), Golden Gate Youth Hostel, Headlands Center for the Arts, and Headlands Institute. See the GGNRA Web site for more information on these sites.

Cliff House. One of the more interesting places for a reception, and even a ceremony, is the Cliff House on a rocky point called Point Lobos, the westernmost point of the San Franciscan peninsula. Considered an NPS Park Partner, Cliff House's latest renovation turned it into a modernistic complex while maintaining a nod to its 140 years of dining history. The first Cliff House was built in 1863; it was rebuilt in 1896 and 1909 after the first was destroyed by fire, the second by earthquake. The NPS took charge of it in 1977.

Cliff House today encompasses a mechanical museum and Camera Obscura, a gift shop, a playland at the beach, and four dining areas. For receptions the Terrace offers breathtaking views of the Pacific Ocean. The adjoining room is reserved for four hours, accommodates from 35 to 145 guests in gracious surroundings, and opens to an outdoor terrace for cocktails or the wedding ceremony itself. The $400 ceremony package includes two large floral arrangements, two white trellises, an aisle runner, chair setup and cleanup, and an additional half hour. Banquet menus are $40 to $75 per plate, and buffets are $55 to $65 per person. There is a $100 setup fee and a $350 dance floor.

Cliff House is located at 1090 Point Lobos, San Francisco, CA 94121 (415–386–3330; Fax: 415–387–7837; www.cliffhouse.com).

Golden Gate National Recreation Area
Office of Special Park Uses
Building 201, Fort Mason
San Francisco, CA 94123
(415) 561–4300
www.nps.gov/goga/spug/weddings/outside/

Location: In and around San Francisco.

Facility Rental, Amenities, and Policies:
The permit fee for most of the GGNRA beaches, overlooks, lighthouse, and John Muir sites is just $400 for three hours, which must be paid by credit card or money order. Twenty million people visit these areas each year. This means parking is always extremely limited; carpooling or shuttling is recommended. Six sites have public restrooms, six sites have portable restrooms, four have none, and for the rest, restrooms are as much as half a mile away. Wedding permits at some sites are suspended on weekends and holidays from mid-March to mid-October during peak visitor times, but a number are open year-round. Most of the sites pose difficulties for guests with disabilities, and in some cases would be a hike in wedding heels. Please carefully read the limitations and conditions for each site on the GGNRA Web site.

Catering: Receptions, catered by either a professional company or the wedding party, will be considered for the Fort Barry Parade Ground (200), the Fort Mason Parade Grounds (200-plus), West Fort Miley (125), the Fort Mason Great Meadow, and the restored Crissy Field Airfield and Amphitheater (200 to 500). See Park Partners for more reception options.

Accommodations: Lodging is available in the Greater San Francisco area.

Keep in Mind: The Golden Gate National Recreation Area is not to be confused with the 1,000-acre urban Golden Gate Park, which also rents outdoor and indoor space for just $250 to $500 for two hours, accommodating groups from 50 to 250. Contact the Permits and Reservations Division of the San Francisco Recreation and Park Department at (415) 831–5500, or search "weddings" on www.sfgov.org.

HIGHLANDS INN, PARK HYATT CARMEL

Carmel, California

There are views, and then there are *views.* Terraced across a twelve-acre bluff overlooking the ocean, the Highlands Inn furnishes each guest room with binoculars—and for good reason. Point Lobos, a state reserve with jagged rock outcroppings, driftwood-strewn beaches, and ornamental wind-twisted cypress trees, is viewable from the inn's mezzanine of decks and floor-to-ceiling glass windows. Everywhere are panoramic ocean views, waves crashing and spewing on the rocks, arrays of Monterey pine and juniper branches—even a migrating whale or two passing by the shore. It is no wonder the inn has been a favorite wedding site since it opened in 1917.

The inn declares itself a "rustic refuge," but after an $8 million renovation, there's *rustic* and then there's an artistic shaping of wood, glass, and stone in the hands of a master. The main lodge features a large fireplace, open wooden arches in the ceiling, and more plate-glass windows for ocean viewing.

Those who first visit Highlands rarely want to leave their balconies or the inn's four fine restaurants. When they do venture out, they head south to the beach and redwoods of Big Sur, or head north for shopping, dining, and sightseeing in Carmel or Monterey to the north. Point Lobos, just across the highway from the Highlands Inn and known as the "crown jewel of the state park system," is an irresistible call.

This overwhelming beauty has always attracted newlyweds. Highlands Inn considers each wedding celebrated on its grounds to be part of *its* history. When they stopped counting in 1966, Highlands had already honored 25,000 wedding couples.

Highlands Inn's event rooms can accommodate everything from small gatherings to lavish weddings. For small weddings of just the two of you or fewer than ten guests, the inn suggests an intimate ceremony on the couple's suite balcony, or on the beach just five minutes away. Larger weddings are usually conducted beneath the wedding gazebo, a metal sculpture of connecting squares mirroring the architectural lines of the inn. The gazebo's garden-enclosed redwood deck is perched above the rocky ocean and offers an idyllic setting. A changing room with a full-length mirror is available nearby. In the event of inclement weather, the ceremony is usually moved to the Fireside Room, which is only used as an alternate function space. The Fireside Room has two gigantic stone fireplaces, lit during the wedding, wooden floors, and ocean views.

Following the ceremony, guests are escorted to one of the inn's glass-walled banquet rooms, where fine dining and nature dramatically intertwine. The Monarch Room offers garden and partial ocean views with balcony access, encompassing an oak table for twelve. The Surf Room can seat 50 to 125 people for a meal, and also offers terrace access where guests may enjoy the sights and sounds of the natural surroundings. Dancing can be arranged in the Surf Room (95), and the mystical Yankee Point Room (50) offers a stone fireplace and full ocean views highlighted by the crashing waves at Yankee Point 200 feet below. The two rooms can work together for parties of 95 to 125 people.

Highlands Inn, Park Hyatt Carmel
120 Highlands Drive
Carmel, CA 93923
www.highlandsinn.hyatt.com
(831) 620–1234
Weddings: (831) 622–5441

Location: 4 miles south of Carmel on U.S. Highway 101.

Facility Rental, Amenities, and Policies: A wedding on a suite balcony is $150 plus the charge of the room for up to six people. Couples can hold a ceremony (no reception) at the gazebo for less than $1,000, but only during the off-season of November through March, Monday through Thursday; this is limited to twenty-five people. Rental fees for gazebo ceremonies plus reception room range from $1,000 to $4,000. All site rental fees include setup, breakdown, event chairs, and tables with basic ivory or white linens.

Most wedding dates are secured six months to a year and a half out, depending on the time of year. Highlands Inn offers full coordination services for all events; catering, music, and flowers must be arranged through the coordinator. Off-site vendors, such as the florist, photographer, and entertainment, must be hired from the hotel's preferred vendor list because of the unusual property. (Vendors not on the list must show proof of insurance and are subject to a fee.)

Extras: The dance floor is an additional fee.

Catering: A minimum of four courses is required for a seated meal at lunch or dinner. Lunches begin at $65 per person; dinners, $95. Cakes are prepared based on the number of guests—three tiers for thirty-five guests or more, and four tiers for more than a hundred people—beginning at $12 per person (or may count as one of the courses), plus a $4.50 cutting fee per slice. Minimum beverage and bar costs also apply. Site rental fees and menu prices tend to increase significantly from year to year.

Accommodations: Weddings with room fees of $3,200 or more include a complimentary one-night stay for the bride and groom, depending upon availability. Wedding-guest discounts for rooms are based on availability in blocks of 10. This one- and two-story inn has 142 guest rooms (all nonsmoking). Rates start at $205 for a double; $260 to $695 for a spa suite; and $485 to $1,025 for a two-bedroom, full ocean-view spa suite.

Keep in Mind: The coast is consistently mild, with an average temperature near sixty-five degrees year-round. Early autumn is the coast's sunniest time of year.

HORNBLOWER
CRUISES AND EVENTS

Berkeley, San Francisco, Marina del Rey, Newport Beach, and San Diego, California

Envision a nautical wedding in view of California's barrier islands and shimmering city skylines. Cut your cake beneath the cloud-enshrined Golden Gate Bridge, the festive lights outlining the Bay Bridge at night, or the arching Coronado Bridge with the USS *Reagan* or *Midway* standing witness. Dine in the company of sailboats and regattas as they escort you through the harbor and out into the panoramic Pacific Ocean.

Such elegant weddings—and reasonably priced, we might add—are available on twenty-four private yachts out of Berkeley, San Francisco, Newport Beach, Marina del Rey, and San Diego through one single company. Hornblower Cruises and Events is a twenty-three-year-old corporation that grew from a two-ship operation to a $30 million market leader sailing from six ports. (Long Beach makes the sixth port, but does not offer wedding packages.) Hornblower's fleet includes a mix of vintage and state-of-the-art yachts to fit all moods and themes. Hornblower is so popular that in 2002, it facilitated some 900 weddings. Consider catered cruises for rehearsal dinners, engagement parties, bridal showers, wedding brunches, and bachelor and bachelorette parties.

San Francisco sails ten unique yachts, and shares six of them with the Berkeley port. Take the *San Francisco Belle,* acquired in 2001 from Kentucky. This stern-wheeler, featuring three enclosed decks, a spacious sundeck, and complete wraparound decks, is a grand expression of Art Nouveau. Also stationed at San Francisco is Hornblower's flagship, the majestic *California,* featuring three spacious salons, full-service bars, hardwood dance floors, large window, a captain's lounge, and brass, teak, and mahogany appointments.

Newport Beach and Marina del Rey have eleven yachts between them. The most famous is *Wild Goose* (Newport), which first saw action as a minesweeper in the Canadian navy during World War II. John Wayne purchased the ship in 1965, dubbed her the *Wild Goose,* and converted her into a luxury yacht for celebrity events, family vacations, and infamous poker sessions with such buddies as Dean Martin, Sammy Davis Jr., and Bob Hope. Measuring 136 feet long with a 25-foot beam, the vessel still sports the

solid brass plates installed by the navy to protect her prow while hunting for mines.

The handsome *High Spirits,* one of seven Hornblower wedding yachts out of San Diego, was originally constructed as a sister ship to *Sequoia,* President Franklin D. Roosevelt's presidential yacht, and is now considered one of the finest antique yachts available for entertaining on the West Coast. After a dramatic remodel this sleek, 85-foot Skipper-Liner now features a push-button convertible sunroof, which treats guests to fresh sea air and sunshine and dancing under the stars on a 460-square-foot parquet floor.

In addition to the yachts, Hornblower also hosts events in its 1910 Abbey located on the perimeter of Balboa Park in San Diego (capacity 475).

Hornblower Cruises and Events
(888) HORNBLOWER (888–467–6256)
Wedding Planners: Berkeley/San Francisco,
(415) 788–8866; Marina del Rey/Newport
Beach, (310) 301–6000, ext. 6601, or
(949) 574–4313; San Diego, (619)
725–8819
www.hornblowerweddings.com

Location: San Francisco, Pier 3, Pier 33, Pier 38, Pier 40; Berkeley Marina; Marina del Rey, Fisherman's Village; Newport Beach, 2431 West Pacific Coast Highway, #101; San Diego, 1066 Harbor Drive.

Facility Rental, Amenities, and Policies: Packages vary from port to port, as well as among yachts and are even based on time of day. Each port has a wedding planner who creates packages specific to that port and market, customizing them to the desires of the couple. Each yacht has both minimum and maximum guest numbers. To plan a wedding, couples should begin by matching the size of their wedding to the minimum requirements of each yacht, taking into consideration their budget, preferences for menu and wedding extras, climate, and accommodations in the host city.

In the **San Francisco and Berkeley Ports,** complete and elegant packages are offered for yachts with minimums of 30 to 900. The Select package (departing before 1:00 P.M.) begins at $69 to $99 per guest and includes a half-hour dockside ceremony by a uniformed captain at home ports only (otherwise under way), a two-and-a-half-hour cruise, choice of buffet or plated meal, house champagne toast or free-flowing house champagne, and wedding cake. Wedding dinner packages priced from $149 to $219 per person include four-hour cruises, menu and liquor upgrades, and colored linens. Prices include applicable taxes, service charges, and port fees, and may be higher during holidays, special events, and weekends in December. Further upgraded services include a red-carpeted gangway and champagne for boarding guests, white-glove service and maître d' in formal attire, and steward-passed chocolates. Additionally, couples can purchase entertainment, photography, and videography packages.

From **Marina del Rey and Newport Ports,** packages for yacht minimums of 20 to 250 begin at $55 per person for a three-hour cruise departing by 1:00 P.M. and include captain-performed ceremonies, choice of seated lunch or buffet, boarding glass of champagne, hosted soda and juice bar (no host bar), and custom wedding cake. Add $10 per guest for choice of entertainment (DJ or solo entertainer), photography package, flowers, and personalized ring buoy. Four-hour dinner cruise packages are similar and start at $75 to $85 per person. The deluxe package, starting at $120 per guest, includes an upgraded menu and free-flowing champagne. (Prices do not include service charge or taxes, and are subject to change.) Wedding planners can arrange

many enhancements, including invitations and limo service.

From **San Diego Port,** packages for minimums of 30 to 250 start at $68 to $79 per person for brunch cruises (departing by noon), $75 to $93 for lunch cruises (departing by noon), and $89 to $142 for six buffet and seated dinner cruises, plus applicable taxes and service charges. All wedding cruises include four hours of yacht time, a wedding ceremony by the uniformed captain, free-flowing champagne, wedding cake, hosted soda and juice bars, and background music. Price increases reflect menu upgrades, addition of hosted beer and wine bars, and entertainment. The wedding planners for this port can also arrange cruises for other wedding celebrations as well as enhancements—photography, flowers, and so on.

Extras: For groups with fewer than twenty people, Hornblower offers wedding packages on weekend champagne brunch cruises and nightly sunset dinner cruises from any port. (The San Diego ports tend to do the most public weddings of this kind.) The basic package in San Diego starts at $350 to $450 for twenty to thirty guests, and includes a forty-five-minute ceremony performed by a captain, champagne toast and bottle of house champagne at the table, plus a personal wedding attendant. The package increases up to $1,000 with the addition of bridal bouquet, boutonniere, photography, wedding cake, and other enhancements. Add to this either the price of the two-hour wedding brunch cruise at $40 per person, or the three-hour dinner cruise at $60 per cruise.

Catering: All of the yachts have galleys where the staff can prepare fresh food and fully cater every event. Table service, in the Hornblower tradition, includes white linens, fine china and glassware, and service by a well-trained and nautically attired crew.

Accommodations: Ample choices available in the port cities. Check with wedding planners for recommendations.

Keep in Mind: Hornblower is busiest during the summer months for all ports, while September and October are busy in San Francisco, where the weather is so beautiful that time of year. Couples tend to book from six to nine months ahead.

HOTEL DEL CORONADO
Coronado, California

The Travel Channel in 2002 named Hotel del Coronado the best place to get married in the United States and the second best in the world, but this island resort has been a romantic rendezvous for more than a century. The first to marry on the property were the son and daughter of two site engineers, in 1887. Island legend recounts the meeting of Prince Edward and Coronado resident Wallis Simpson (then Mrs. Spencer)—for whom he would later abdicate the throne—during a banquet hosted by the hotel in 1920. Hollywood began flirting with the hotel almost from the beginning, filming a number of features here along with simply finding it a secluded respite. Add to this legacy the hotel's beaches and ocean views, elaborate architecture, and world-class cuisine (for which we can personally vouch), and it's easy to see why the large, red octagonal turret dominating the resort has equally dominated wedding albums for generations.

"The Del" is the last of California's grand old seaside hotels, an 1888 monument to Victorian grandeur spread out over thirty-one acres. This Queen Anne Revival was conceptualized by two midwestern businessmen, who paid $110,000 for 4,100 acres to build a resort that would be "the talk of the Western World." The largest wooden structure in the United States, its materials all had to be imported. Sugar pine was brought in for the enormous Crown Room ceiling, held in place without a single nail. A mahogany bar was built in Pennsylvania and shipped fully assembled around the horn of South America. In 2001 the hotel completed an extensive renovation, returning the grande dame to its turn-of-the-twentieth-century splendor. Dramatic enhancements include oceanfront dining venues, restoration of the intricate wood-beamed lobby, and shops built along paneled hallways. The Prince of Wales fine dining emporium, so named in honor of Edward's 1920 visit, was remodeled from a dark, clubby room to an airy, elegant, ocean-facing salon.

The resort's variety of premier wedding sites combined with forty-two beautifully decorated public rooms provide unlimited options for a wedding of any size. The Crown Room, richly decorated with paneled ceiling, wall coverings, and crown chandeliers, seats up to 450 guests. Crystal chandeliers, tapestry draperies, and a sweeping ocean view make the Ballroom an impressive reception setting for up to 800. The Garden Patio, in the heart of the hotel, can seat up to 350. The Windsor Lawn seats up to 500 and is adjacent to the Windsor Cottage, an elegantly restored bungalow that offers a Southern California oceanfront setting.

The island on which the hotel is located is actually a 5.3-square-mile peninsula that forms the western boundary of San Diego Bay. Today the peninsula is connected to San Diego by a 2.3-mile bridge, or is reachable by the Coronado Ferry, Coronado Shuttle, Old Town Trolley, and San Diego Water Taxi (harrowing, but fun). There's lots to do in Coronado and neighboring San Diego, from shopping to theater, amusement parks, and a world-class zoo. Many hotel guests opt to stay put and enjoy the 18 miles of white sand beaches, two pools, biking, tennis, and dozens of other activities.

Hotel del Coronado
1500 Orange Avenue
Coronado, CA 92118
(800) 468–3533 or (619) 435–6611
Catering Sales: (619) 522–8070
www.hoteldel.com

Location: Coronado Island is accessible by water taxi and commercial ferries at the San Diego Bay front along North Harbor Drive, as well as the Coronado Bridge.

Facility Rental, Amenities, and Policies: Hotel del Coronado offers a variety of ceremony and reception sites for all budgets and wedding sizes. Ceremony site fees are $1,800 to $5,000 for the outdoor venues such as the beach, the Vista Walk, and Windsor Lawn, and each ceremony venue pairs with specific indoor reception rooms. Liability insurance is required.

The hotel maintains an inventory of complimentary white, black, and colored tablecloths. Staff can assist with the rental of specialty linens, china, silver, or stemware, but emphasize that the couple should hire a professional wedding coordinator to assist with wedding planning, ceremony, rehearsal, and reception.

Catering: Meals and buffets are $110 to $140 per person for a daytime event, and $130 to $180 per person for evening events. Some rooms carry food and beverage spending minimums.

Extras: The resort offers myriad romantic amenities and services, including his-and-hers massages, breakfast in bed, fresh flowers, and chocolate-covered strawberries.

Accommodations: Rooms run the gamut from compact to extravagant and are packed with antique charm. For ultimate honeymoon seclusion, consider the 9 private cottages lining the beach's edge or the beachfront junior suites with large windows and balconies. Nearly half the hotel's rooms are in the seven-story contemporary tower; some offer more living space, but none of the historical ambience (although the floors don't slant). Nightly rates range from $300 for rooms to $750 for suites.

Keep in Mind: The hotel is located at the westernmost edge of Coronado Island, where public parking is sparse. The hotel offers special-event rates for self-parking and valet parking, which the couple may decide to have applied to their account.

IL FORNAIO CARMEL CUCINA
ITALIANA AT THE PINE INN

Carmel-by-the-Sea, California

Il Fornaio in Carmel-by-the-Sea is a chain restaurant, one of twenty-three, but what it has going for it as a wedding destination, besides authentic Italian food, is location. The restaurant is attached to the historic Pine Inn, which lies in the cultural heart of Carmel. Couples can marry for free on the restaurant's piazza, with its ocean and street shop views. If preferable, they can marry at the Carmel Mission, the charming Church of the Wayfarer just around the corner, or at the beach a few blocks away, and then celebrate at Il Fornaio. The wedding itself would be almost beside the point when it comes to the trattoria's Old World atmosphere and consistently exceptional cuisine.

Marrying in Carmel-by-the-Sea would be like marrying in Brigadoon. Tucked away in a hidden cul-de-sac off U.S. Highway 1, the town is a blend of English seaside and forest hamlet. Hansel-and-Gretel shops and Arts and Crafts houses line the hilly grid of Monterey pines. Despite the throngs of tourists jamming the streets on summer weekends and the multimillion-dollar price tags on real estate, the tempo and look here belong to former centuries.

The three-story historic Pine Inn connected to Il Fornaio claims to be the oldest hotel in Carmel (c. 1889), and it looks it with its deep red and mahogany lobby and library. Over the years owners have added shops, rooftop dining, and ornate embellishments still visible in the restaurant's architecture. Il Fornaio (pronounced *eel for-nigh-oh,* meaning "the baker") fits into the eclectic Carmel and Pine Inn scheme like an Italian leather glove. The main dining room is dimly lit Italian marble and vintage dark wood, while the side room is open and oriented toward the windows to promote a sense of interaction with the neighborhood in the tradition of most Il Fornaios.

The idea of a "chain restaurant" has to be adjusted when it comes to Il Fornaio, first conceptualized in Milan, Italy, in 1975 as a franchised neighborhood bakery; it is now a multimillion-dollar transatlantic partnership. The chef-partners are nearly all first-generation Italians wearing Italian uniforms. Every year a group of Il Fornaio chefs reschool in Italy to purge them of American habits. The chefs bring back a new palette of dishes; a different region is featured every month in addition to the core menu.

Other Area Options

Church of the Wayfarer. The Methodist Church of the Wayfarer, founded in 1905, is only a block from Il Fornaio. The church can seat as many as 200 guests in the ornate wood and stained-glass sanctuary and 50 in the densely planted garden. The $650 fee includes bride's dressing suite, altar candles, fresh floral arrangements, and two reserved parking spaces in front of the church. The services of a pastor, wedding coordinator (required for large weddings), organ or piano music, and aisle candelabra with candles are extra, but quite reasonable. The Church of the Wayfarer is located at Seventh Avenue and Lincoln Street, Carmel-by-the-Sea, CA 93921 (Voice Mail: 831–624–3550; Fax: 831–624–2530; www.churchofthe wayfarer.com).

Carmel River State Beach. Carmel River State Beach is popular for weddings; its impeccably white sand is a stark contrast to the deep blue water of the river flowing into the bay. That's former mayor Clint Eastwood's renovated dairy farm, called Mission Ranch, across the wetlands. Wedding planners and officiants can suggest other nearby ceremony locations, such as Carmel Beach, Monastery Beach, Lover's Point Park Pacific Grove (one of Monterey's most spectacular views), Berwick Park (a bayside park), Jewel Park in Pacific Grove (with Gazebo and Little House), and Rocky Shores Gazebo. The city of Pacific Grove will reserve an hour (or two) for weddings at Berwick Park or Lover's Point. There is a permit charge to be married in some of these city parks, but state parks are free. Call (831) 649–7118 or visit www.parks.ca.gov for more information.

San Carlos Borroméo de Carmelo Mission. Catholics may well want to marry at Carmel Mission, which sits behind adobe walls in a quiet area of Carmel and is considered one of the most beautiful missions in the chain of nine that stretched along California's Central Coast. Founded in 1770 in Monterey by Padre Junipero Serra and moved to its present location in 1774, it was the seat of power for all the California missions for thirty years. The building, which fell into ruins in the nineteenth century and has since been completely restored, exhibits classic Mission-style, fortresslike architecture, with thick, bougainvillea-covered adobe walls and a central courtyard. A Moorish-style bell tower contains nine bells and is open to the public. A wedding in the basilica, seating 450, is $1,500; the chapel ($900) seats seventy. A permission slip is needed from the couple's home parish. San Carlos Borroméo de Carmelo Mission (Carmel Mission) is located at 3080 Rio Road,

Carmel, CA 93923 (831– 624–1271; Fax: 831–624–8050; www.carmelmission.org).

Il Fornaio Carmel Cucina Italiana at the Pine Inn
Ocean Avenue at Monte Verde
P.O. Box 5655
Carmel-by-the-Sea, CA 93921
(831) 622–5100
www.ilfornaio.com

Location: Buildings in Carmel do not have physical addresses. Il Fornaio is at the corner of Monte Verde and Ocean Avenue, the town's main street.

Facility Rental, Amenities, and Policies: The main dining room can seat groups of thirty, but larger affairs can take advantage of the private and sunny Ocean Avenue room that accommodates sixty seated, one hundred standing for a reception. Twenty to eighty people can be entertained on the adjoining outdoor piazza, weather permitting. Even the Rotunda, housing the bakery, retail goods, and espresso machine, would be interesting for a reception of around forty to fifty people (after 5:00 P.M.). This unique round dining area hosts a large round oak table in the center with intimate seating around the perimeter. Larger groups can be accommodated through the use of multiple rooms, or a buy-out of the restaurant (about $18,000 for 150 meals in 2004), with a month's notice. While room charges are not imposed, there are minimums, which can easily be absorbed by the meals. There are, however, charges for bar setup and staffing, and cake-cutting service.

Catering: Large groups typically order from one of six preset catering menus, ranging from $37 to $56 per person (in 2004). The meals include salad, one of four entrees, and dessert. There is also a children's menu at $10 per plate.

Accommodations: At the Pine Inn (www.pine -inn.com; 800–228–3851) next to Il Fornaio, reviewers say the most affordable rooms (doubles) are small; pay a bit more to secure a larger room with a half canopy. Prices are $135 to $260 for double occupancy.

LA PLAYA HOTEL
Carmel, California

True to all great romances, La Playa Hotel and Carmel-by-the-Sea have stayed together through thick and thin. The bond began in 1904, when Norwegian landscape painter Christopher Jorgensen built a Mediterranean-style villa for his bride, the daughter of the Ghirardelli chocolate dynasty of San Francisco. Known for his paintings of missions and Yosemite landscapes, his mansion of stone and heavy beams was inspired by the nearby Carmel Mission. His hospitality, along with the villa's commanding view of the ocean just a couple of blocks away, drew many intellectuals like himself, thus contributing to Carmel's budding reputation as an artists' village.

By 1916 Agnes "Alice" Signor, a charismatic hotelier and earthquake survivor from San Francisco, had acquired the wedding villa and turned it into a full-service resort. Fire swept through the building in the 1920s, leaving just enough of its footprint to be reconstructed. Signor's nephews were now managing the place and cultivating a new breed of tourist. Nephew Fred Godwin became a pioneer in California's fledgling hospitality industry, organizing excursions and picnics along the nearby 17-Mile Drive. As housing sprang up around the property and the streets became paved, the Godwins expanded the hotel to a luxurious eighty-room destination with a grand dining room overlooking the bay.

The hotel changed hands two more times, bringing in world-class management and European clientele, but by the time the Cope family purchased it in 1983, it had become run down. Owners of the prestigious Huntington Hotel in San Francisco, the Cope family began renovating La Playa back to its original beauty.

Owner John Cope knew that people still loved La Playa no matter what shape it was in, but he respected the hotel's legacy to Carmel, and felt duty bound to restore the property to its past grandeur. The hotel was really two buildings: the original mansion plus the guest room building first built in the 1920s. Guest rooms were repainted and refurbished to complement the stunning views of the ocean, garden, patio, and residential Carmel using pieces from the Cope family's collection of European antiques, artwork, and California memorabilia.

The Cope family installed a two-level brick patio, replaced the wrought-iron gazebo with a larger one, and upgraded and expanded the surrounding gardens to the award-winning status they enjoy today. The English cottage gardens, with their Mediterranean influences, greet weddings with colorful flowers year-round: delphiniums, foxgloves, pansies, Peruvian lilies, and daisies of all kinds, against a background of sweet pea, roses, Spanish lavender,

Mexican sage, and, of course, bougainvil-lea. Colorful bowls accent walkways and seating areas amid cypress trees, man-zanita, Pacific Coast iris, and other indige-nous plants. The effect might well look like a Jorgensen painting.

Knowing a little of Carmel's love affair with La Playa Hotel, it is easy to see why many of the locals marry at its ornate, wrought-iron gazebo. Receptions take place in several period rooms, including the Patio Room, with French windows that open onto the garden (reception and dining capacity of 10); the Fireside Room (18 to 20); the Carmel Room (54 to 70); the Garden Room, with high ceilings and view of the gardens through arched windows (36); and the Poseidon Room, with views of ocean on two sides (110 to 150).

La Playa Hotel & Cottages-by-the-Sea
Camino Real at Eighth
Carmel, CA 93921
(800) 582–8900 or (831) 624–6476
www.laplayahotel.com

Location: Carmel does not have street addresses. La Playa Hotel is on the corner of Eighth and Camino Real, 3 blocks from the beach.

Facility Rental, Amenities, and Policies: The site fees for a ceremony in the gazebo area are $500 for one hundred guests, for one hour. The hotel does not rent the gazebo without a reception also being booked at the hotel. Rental fees for recep-tion rooms for a four-hour period range from $275 for the Fireside Room for 16, to $1,750 for the Poseidon Room for 112 with dance floor. Only the Poseidon Room is suitable for live or amplified music, and only between noon and 10:00 P.M.

Catering: All catering is provided by the hotel's acclaimed Terrace Grill Restaurant. Reviewers praise the Terrace, saying the food holds up next to the scenery, and the service is so good that servers will cover plates if diners step away from the table. This is not a tourist trap, yet all are wel-come, whether they show up in beach garb or black tie. Catering prices for events are reasonable. For example, a Benedict Buf-fet runs $21 per person (with a minimum of twelve people). With a minimum of forty people, dinner buffets range from $38 to $48 per person, and plated dinners top out at $46 per person. The Jorgensen Buf-fet at $48 per person, for example, includes carved tenderloin of beef, roast chicken with Marsala and mushrooms, hot planked salmon, seasonal fresh vegeta-bles, gratin potatoes, three cheese tortellini, traditional Caesar salad, mari-nated mushrooms with sherry and shal-lots, and chilled pasta primavera with artichoke and basil salad. Cakes are baked by the hotel pastry chefs for around $4.00 per person with a $75.00 minimum, and the couple can choose from a menu of eight.

Accommodations: Weekend accommoda-tions routinely sell out months in advance, but the hotel will block up to 10 guest rooms upon confirmation—though this is not automatic. 5 guest cottages have been recently added to the hotel's accommodations, all with large fireplace, two bedrooms, complete kitchen, storage alcove, and private patio. Residential-view rooms start at $175 to $195, gar-den- or ocean-view rooms at $235, suites at $375, and cottages at $350. Review-ers suggest splurging for the view rooms or cottages.

THE LODGE AT RANCHO MIRAGE

Rancho Mirage, California

Seventeen million viewers watched "the wedding of the decade" in December 2003, when Trista Rehn married Ryan Sutter, the suitor she selected on ABC TV's *The Bachelorette*. The setting for this $4 million extravaganza: The Lodge at Rancho Mirage's croquet lawn overlooking Palm Springs, transformed by a blizzard of pink Ecuadorian roses and rows of hot-pink-covered chairs. Trista descended the cascading garden staircase in diamond-frosted stilettos and floated toward her groom standing at the wedding gazebo. Food flown in from fourteen countries was served to 300 guests beneath a Waterford crystal chandelier in the grand ballroom.

Long before the wedding took place, the hotel was known for its friendly staff. Built in 1987, it is a RockResort owned by Vail Resorts. The 240-room hotel is perched atop a 650-foot panoramic plateau surrounded by the Santa Rosa and San Jacinto Mountains, home to some 500 endangered bighorn sheep. The Lodge is approximately twenty minutes from Palm Springs, the golf capital of the world with 120 courses. Guests enjoy a spa, tennis, swimming, and access to nearby golf courses.

The Lodge at Rancho Mirage recently completed an extensive renovation of its public areas and meeting spaces, as well as a number of its guest rooms. The remaining guest rooms are expected to be completed by fall 2006. Complementing its desert location, the color palettes make use of pale blue and Dijon accents in the furniture. Large windows have been added to the lounge area to bring in more light, and lighting and fixtures have also been changed to create a brighter, more inviting

atmosphere. Custom-designed floorings appear throughout the hotel, including the meeting space with its new carpeting. The Lodge has also expanded and updated its art collection, adding original limited-edition lithographs by international modern masters such as Matisse, Hodgkins, and Albers to the Gallery, which connects the lobby to the lounge.

The Lodge at Rancho Mirage
68-900 Frank Sinatra Drive
Rancho Mirage, CA 92270
(877) 770–ROCK or (760) 321–8282
http://ranchomirage.rockresorts.com

Location: Between Cathedral City and Rancho Mirage off California Highway 111, twenty minutes from the Palm Springs airport.

Facility Rental, Amenities, and Policies: Event fees for a gazebo lawn ceremony with ballroom reception and dinner run $3,000; ballroom reception and dinner only, or gazebo lawn ceremony only, is $2,000. Evening use of the gazebo lawn with the ballroom requires a food and beverage minimum of $10,000 to $15,000 from October 15 through June 1, when nighttime temperatures are seventy degrees, and $8,000 to $10,000 for June 2 through October 14, when daytime temperatures regularly break one hundred degrees.

For smaller weddings (and budgets), the Lodge now offers an Intimate Wedding package costing $1,500 for thirty-five guests or less. The package includes a gazebo ceremony with white lawn chairs, a bridal bouquet and boutonniere of white roses and stephanotis, one-night deluxe guest-room accommodations and one-hour spa treatments for the bride and groom, and champagne with chocolate-dipped strawberries. Restrictions may apply.

In response to many inquiries, the Lodge now offers "Trista and Ryan" packages—the ultimate themed destination wedding. The Above It All fantasy package, priced per person at $2,500 with a minimum of 200 guests, celebrates in the style of the television couple's wedding *sans* news helicopters and television cameras. The package includes a replica of their wedding altar, the five-course wedding dinner, signature wines and champagnes, personalized champagne glasses bearing Trista and Ryan's wedding logo embossed with the bride's and groom's names, their wedding logo illuminating the mountainside, and exquisite decor and florals. For guests the packages include bridal-party gifts, one dozen roses in the bridal color for each guest, in-room Avanyu spa treatments for bridesmaids, rounds of golf for groomsmen, guest suites for the parents, and limousine transfers. The bride and groom will stay in the Trista and Ryan Suite, previously named for President Gerald Ford, which has a premier view of the Coachella Valley, a baby grand piano, a formal dining room, and an expanded master bathroom with a Jacuzzi bathtub. Finally, a poolside rehearsal dinner and Sunday brunch for the family and bridal party are also built into the package.

Wedding bookings with catering sales costs of more than $15,000 are eligible for a complimentary five-day/four-night stay at any RockResort. This offer is nontransferable and based on Sunday or Monday arrival. Travel must occur within three months of the wedding event.

Extras: The Luxury Escape ($2,450) includes two nights in the Trista and Ryan Suite,

where they spent their wedding night, and use of a Jaguar or Mercedes, with pickup and drop-off service from any location in Southern California (including airports). Caviar and Dom Pérignon are presented upon arrival with engraved Trista and Ryan champagne flutes, a private dinner for two in the gazebo where the couple was married, the VIP valet parking spot in front of the hotel where their limousine was parked, private breakfast or brunch prepared in the suite by the chef who prepared the same for the couple, rose-petal turndown on the night of the arrival, and an engraved Trista and Ryan photo album. If this isn't enough, memorabilia of the couple is also on sale.

Catering: In case a half-million-dollar wedding is not within your budget, the Lodge also suggests three reasonably priced packages for a minimum of seventy-five guests: Casual Elegance (starting at $50 per person) for a luncheon or dinner buffet, with California red and white wines and imported and domestic beers; Wine and Roses (starting at $80 per person) for butler-passed hors d'oeuvres with the choice of a four-course plated luncheon or dinner, wine and beer, or buffet stations; and the California Classic (starting at $120 per), featuring cuisine specialties from all regions of California, a five-course plated luncheon or dinner, California champagne and wines, imported and domestic beers, specialty linens, chair covers, pinspotting at each table, and customized menus.

Discounts are granted on reception, if the couple's guests stay in the hotel.

Accommodations: There are 240 guest rooms, including 20 suites and 31 Lodge Club rooms and suites, each with a private patio or balcony and a view of the mountains, the valley, or the pool. Rates start at $189, with discounts for weekday and off-season months.

THE NAPA INN & SPA

Napa, California

The Napa Inn is literally steps away from both Napa's historic district and the wine country of Napa Valley. How can it be in two places at once? The complimentary Napa Trolley picks up guests on Napa Inn's corner every twenty to thirty minutes and takes them to the American Center for Wine, Food & the Arts (COPIA), the Wine Train, the town center, and factory outlets.

Napa, the busy urban hub of the Napa Valley wine country, was established in 1848. The city has been undergoing a cultural rebirth since the opening of COPIA in 2001 and the grand reopening of the 1880 Napa Valley Opera House in 2003. Many new restaurants have opened in the refurbished downtown area. Visitors are making Napa their base camp as they explore the 280 wineries and quaint towns in the rich agricultural area surrounding the city. Summer is the peak season, but the late-winter, early-spring season has become increasingly popular.

Then there's the Napa Inn itself, which actually comprises two houses painted in complementary shades of blue. The main house, where guests check in and go for breakfast, was built in 1899 as a wedding gift. This beautiful Queen Anne Victorian, complete with turret tower and gables, is furnished in antiques reminiscent of a bygone era. The Italianate Buford House, built in 1877, is on the National Register of Historic Places and located next door. The properties face different streets but share the back parking lot and gardens.

All fourteen guest rooms and suites are individually decorated, each with its own private bath and fireplace. All have air-conditioning, cable television, and wireless Internet service (for instantly broadcasting your ceremony); many have a two-person whirlpool tub. All are sweetly decorated in that fussy yet welcoming decor of the nineteenth century. Miss Tessa's Room, for instance, is a large second-floor room with high windows, a fireplace, and a carved mahogany, queen bed. The bathroom features a skylight and tiled tub and shower. Simeon's Quarters, in formal creams, golds, and green, convey the feeling of sleeping in a French chateau. Relax in a two-person whirlpool tub amid handmade tiles and gilded furnishings.

William's Hideaway, featured on the Learning Channel's *Trading Spaces,* has a private entrance on a balcony, high beamed ceilings, and tall windows. A unique room divider creates a cozy two-room feeling. There's also a fireplace, queen bed, and bathroom with tub/shower and skylight.

Although they have lived in Northern California most of their lives, innkeepers Jim and Brooke Boyer had always dreamed of owning a special place away from the hectic pace of the big city. They love the rolling hills, the green grass and yellow mustard in spring, and the oranges and yellows of the vineyards in fall. They know all the back roads, the best restaurants, and the best wineries. They have put their artistic talents to work detailing the inn, including wall murals and faux paintings in guest rooms.

All of these ingredients go into the perfect wedding ceremony at Napa Inn.

Other Area Options

Napa Valley Wine Train. Celebrate your nuptials on the Napa Valley Wine Train through vineyards and woodlands. The dinner train departs from Napa at 5:00 P.M., and rates for the five-course gourmet meal start at $85 per person. See the Web site for other excursions, including the Moonlight Escapade Dinner. The Napa Station is located at 1275 McKinstry Street, Napa, CA 94559 (800–427–4124 or 707–253–2111; www.winetrain.com).

The Napa Inn & Spa
1137 Warren Street
Napa, CA 94559
(800) 435–1144 or (707) 257–1444
www.napainn.com

Location: 1 block north of First Street off California Highway 29 in Napa, California.

Facility Rental, Amenities, and Policies: Napa Inn's Intimate Wedding package for just over $2,000 for up to fifty guests includes lodging in one of inn's luxury suites for two nights, use of the parlor or gardens for the ceremony, the minister's fee (a list of available officiants is provided), a professional photographer (a list is provided), bridal bouquet and boutonniere, a small wedding cake, and a bottle of champagne or sparkling cider. The inn provides assistance with music and special requests. Depending on the size of the ceremony, the inn may request that couples book the entire inn.

The Elopement and Vow Renewal package for $800 for up to six guests includes lodging in one of the inn's luxury suites for two nights, use of the parlor or gardens for the ceremony, assistance in contacting an officiant, a small wedding cake, and a bottle of champagne or sparkling cider. An additional fee applies for arranging further requests.

Catering: The inn will help make reservations for a celebratory dinner at a nearby restaurant.

Accommodations: Rates for standard guest rooms and suites start at $120 to $220 in winter. Wake up the next day to a full gourmet candlelight breakfast served in the dining room or on the garden patio. The inn also offers afternoon refreshments of fresh-baked cookies and wine or specially blended coffee. Dessert and liqueurs are offered throughout the evening.

POST RANCH INN
Big Sur, California

Yearning for a quiet ceremony at the edge of the world, a place to simply breathe and "be"? The Post Ranch is just such a place. Dug into the cliffs a thousand feet or so above the Pacific are thirty camouflaged units on a hundred acres of pure tranquility. The inn's wedding package invites a cere-mony for eight, but couples might not want to share it with anyone.

Architect and local resident G. K. "Mickey" Muennig designed the resort using the "organic style" that's won him tribute. "Building with the land instead of on it," as the inn's press release states, Muennig shaped wood and glass to follow the contours of the terrain, raising some units to avoid tree roots, cutting some into the earth, exploiting ocean and mountain views at every turn. The Tree Houses truly give the illusion of being in the trees; the Earth House roofs are covered in grass and wildflowers, attracting the occasional deer. The result is what might have happened had Frank Lloyd Wright lived in a Hobbit village in Middle-earth.

Visitors can relax in the basking pool set against a spectacular view of the ocean or in the heated lap pool that gives a panoramic view of the surrounding mountains. Even views from the glass-enveloped Sierra Mar, the Post Ranch Inn's award-winning restaurant, leave diners in awe of the turbulent ocean. Little wonder *Los Angeles Magazine* called the Post Ranch Inn the "world's most powerful aphrodisiac."

One of the inn's massage therapists can come to the couple's unit for a side-by-side massage on the private deck. They might head for the Mongolian-style yurt for morning yoga, or pick up one of the walking sticks provided in all guest rooms and attend a stargazing lesson or nature walk through a lagoon, wildflower meadow, redwood forest, and fern grotto. Billy Post, great grandson of the original homesteader and now in his eighties, guides all who are game on two-hour nature walks through his ninety-eight-acre property.

The inn has a resident wedding officiant who helps couples plan a personalized ceremony. "This isn't the classic wedding site by any means," says Soaring Starkey, the current wedding planner, and if she senses that the site isn't the appropriate venue she will suggest other places in the area that might better suit the couple. One of her primary goals is to provide a celebration with the least amount of stress and pressure. "The intent is to honor the uniqueness of each relationship, create a sense of sanctuary, and help the bride and groom feel present during the ceremony."

The dramatic meeting of land and sea are the Big Sur area's greatest single attraction to the public. A dozen or so state parks and campgrounds in the area attract hikers and backpackers, particularly the redwood groves of Pfeiffer Big Sur State Park and the 80-foot waterfall of Julia Pfeiffer Burns State Park. An equal number of gift shops and art galleries, including the Post Ranch Mercantile, fill an afternoon of milling about.

Post Ranch Inn
Highway 1, P.O. Box 219
Big Sur, CA 93920
(800) 527–2200 or (831) 667–2200
www.postranchinn.com

Location: 30 miles south of Carmel on California Highway 1, the Pacific Coast Highway. *Caution:* CA 1 might be closed in places north of Los Angeles because of mudslides. Signage on the west side of the highway for the Post Ranch Inn is subtle.

Facility Rental, Amenities, and Policies: Post Ranch Inn's Elopement Experience wedding package, at around $2,000, is a supplement to the room rate, and is designed to simplify arrangements for those who want a small and graceful wedding on the terrace of their guest room. The package includes a keepsake script of the ceremony, with a bottle of champagne and a keepsake pair of crystal champagne flutes as well as complimentary flowers and photography and licensing services. The wedding party is limited to eight people, which is about the largest wedding that they do (primarily because of the number of guest rooms available). A couple might want to consider renting one of the houses on the property that accommodate up to six people. The package can be adapted for vow renewals and unions.

Catering: Post Ranch weddings are ceremonies only. A celebration can be arranged
at the inn's restaurant, Sierra Mar. For larger
weddings consider a reception at Nepenthe,
just south of Post Ranch Inn. This family
owned restaurant, once an infamous hippie
hangout, is one of California's most picturesque dining spots overlooking forty miles of
coastline. Nepenthe does weddings for a
$3,000 event fee for up to eighty guests.

Extras: The Post Ranch Inn also offers
Sweetheart Getaway—a honeymoon or
romantic escape package that includes a
three-night stay in a Tree House for $3,130.
This package begins with a delivery of champagne and farm-raised osetra caviar, perhaps
shared in the room's spa tub scented with
Sensual Blend bath salts. Over the next couple of days, the couple receives spa services
and a private class in yoga or meditation.

Accommodations: Overnight guests have a
choice of rooms in four styles, including 5
Ocean Houses recessed into the side of the
ridge; 7 Tree Houses suspended on stilts 9
feet above the ground; 10 Coast Houses,
including 2 cylindrical Mountain Houses;
and 6 rooms located in the three-level Butterfly House.

Room rates are quite diverse and depend
on ocean or mountain views. Prices range
from $495, $550, and $595 for the Butter-
fly Rooms; to $745 for the Tree Houses; to
$715 and $745 for the lower and upper
Mountain House (which includes a buffet
breakfast at the Sierra Mar). Service is laid-
back yet attentive; for those who come to
decompress, this down-to-earth attitude is
refreshing.

Keep in Mind: For weather and clothing
tips, see the Highlands Inn.

SANTA BARBARA COURTHOUSE, GARDENS, BEACHES, AND PARKS

Santa Barbara, California

If there is an American wedding capital in
this day of countrywide destination shopping, it would be Santa Barbara. On a given
weekend in July, it wouldn't be unusual to
drive past half a dozen ceremonies being
performed in oceanfront parks and open-air
facilities. The more glamorous hotel and
mansion reception sites can rent for
$2,000 to $5,000, plus catering, but pru-
dent Californians take advantage of the sur-
prisingly free or nearly free venues.

Wedding parties are drawn to the same
Mediterranean ambience, the ocean's posi-
tive ions, the grape-growing climate, the red-
tiled buildings, and the Hollywood cachet

that prompted the Convention and Visitors
Bureau to trademark Santa Barbara's epi-
thet, the American Riviera. The Santa Barbara region, a cluster of towns tucked
between the Pacific Ocean and the Santa
Ynez Mountains, is epitomized in its Spanish
Revival architecture. This style was inspired
by a combination of influences ranging from
the Moors to southwestern Pueblos, unified
by the arches, courtyards, form-as-mass philosophy, plain wall surfaces, and tile roofs
derived from the Mediterranean world. The
1925 earthquake presented an opportunity
for visionaries and financiers to rebuild the
city in the unique, consistently eclectic style

now seen in nearly every building, including the humblest home.

One such masterpiece is the Santa Barbara Courthouse, called the most beautiful government building in America, and likely the most famous wedding site in Southern California. Designed by William Mooser III, the 1929 Spanish-Moorish-style building occupies a square block in downtown Santa Barbara. Hundreds of weddings are held on the attractively landscaped Sunken Garden every year on a first-come, first-served basis—and it is absolutely free! A couple can apply for a marriage license at the county clerk recorder's office and have a minister meet them on the grounds. Larger weddings even set up chairs and an arch, with the caveat that there are no site reservations or wedding coordinators, and therefore weddings might abut one another. Few realize that the mural room upstairs seats seventy-five people and can be used as an alternate location on one of those rare rainy days.

Santa Barbara is famous for its beautiful beaches, which lie along a unique south-facing stretch of coastline that affords beachgoers sun all day long and greater shelter from winds and surf than many other coastal beaches. (This south-facing anomaly can be confusing—and it doesn't help that there is an East Beach and a West Beach.) The white sand is thick and the cliffs are steep, leaving some wedding vendors in the area to charge by the foot if they must walk or climb any farther than their packages stipulate.

Shoreline Park can be reserved through Parks and Recreation. Situated high on the bluffs, the lawn has a spectacular view of the ocean and the Channel Islands. With a capacity of 125, it has parking and a playground. Intimate weddings are often held beneath a large tree that has a makeshift wooden arbor. Follow the narrow wooden stairs to the beach below and discover a local secret, a beach and tidal pool area (when the tide is low) that is both private and beautiful.

Alice Keck Memorial Park, also reserved through Parks and Rec, is in the heart of downtown Santa Barbara on the corner of Arrellaga and Garden Streets. One step beyond the outer gates transports a couple into Eden. Surrounded by winding, secluded pathways and Japanese-inspired footbridges, this lush garden overflows with exotic and native botanical treasures, including a koi pond dotted with pink water lilies. The park's grass area by the arbor is designated for wedding ceremonies. Although the park will not close for the wedding, park officials will post signs to reserve the area.

Another popular spot is the **Mission Rose Garden** on the corner of Los Olivos and Laguna Streets just across from the Santa Barbara Mission. The garden features 1,500 rose plants that begin blooming about mid-April. Weddings for fifty are held in the large grassy area just outside the garden on its mission side. The Rose Garden itself may not be used for your event.

Other Area Options

East Beach–Cabrillo West and Cabrillo Pavilion Arts Center. Have your ceremony right on East Beach–Cabrillo West, then walk to your reception at the nearby Carbillo Pavillion Arts Center, both reserved through Parks and Rec. The reservation area on the beach is just west of the pavilion's parking lot and has a capacity of 200. A monitor fee is added to all reservations. Parking is a commodity in this area, and the bathhouse beneath the pavilion is public and leaves a lot to be desired, especially if dressed in wedding attire.

The pavilion center is about as close to the beach as possible without being directly on the sand. Although the interior of this space has dated decor and plain interior architecture, it is one of the most popular reception sites in Santa Barbara and rents months, if not years, in advance; the views of the ocean from the large balcony that overhangs East Beach are spectacular. The room itself is open and airy, and a talented designer could easily transform this space to suit any taste as long as decoration policies are followed. The center's capacity is 180 theater-style, 200 for a seated dinner, 250 for cocktails and hors d'oeuvres. There is an eight-hour rental minimum on weekends and holidays, beginning at $1,557 (on Thursday the facility is rented by the hour). Check the Parks and Recreation Web site for further information on policies and fees. Couples will have to hire their own catering company, available in abundance in the Santa Barbara area.

El Presidio Chapel. El Presidio Chapel, part of El Presidio de Santa Barbara State Historic Park, is a faithful reconstruction of Santa Barbara's first church of the eighteenth century, built with the authentic materials and techniques of early California's Spanish Colonial architecture. Interior walls and the altar rail are painted to represent marble or tapestry, and the chapel is furnished with period artifacts, down to the statuary in the niches and the paintings and candle sconces on the walls. The altar is dressed with a reredos (altarpiece). The chapel is available for morning, afternoon, or evening wedding celebrations for 2 to 200. A reception site is available outdoors under the orchard trees. The rental fee is $600. As many as 140 chairs can be provided for $100, although you may also choose to rent chairs. Chapel attendants will light the candles along the walls and on the altar. Wedding couples provide their own minister, musicians and instruments,

flowers, unity candle, and aisle runner. A parking lot is available in the lot next door. El Presidio Chapel is located at 129 East Canon Perdido Street, Santa Barbara, CA 93101. Call (805) 965–0093 or visit www.sbthp.org/rentals.htm for more information.

Santa Barbara Courthouse
1100 Anacapa Street
Santa Barbara, CA 93101
(805) 962–6464
www.sbcourts.org/general_info/cthouse_info
.htm

The City of Santa Barbara Parks and Recreation
620 Laguna Street
Santa Barbara, CA 93101
(805) 564–5418
www.sbparksandrecreation.com

Location: Santa Barbara is 92 miles north of Los Angeles off U.S. Highway 101, and these wedding locations are either within the city limits or along the ocean.

Facility Rental, Amenities, and Policies: A dozen or so parks are available for wedding ceremonies and receptions through the City of Santa Barbara Parks and Recreation Department, some near the ocean or on the beach, others hidden in the foothills. Fees normally run between $120 and $650, and are based on the number of people attending and what furniture will be brought in for the ceremony; there is an extra charge for nonresidents. A reservation guarantees that you get the site over anyone else who decides to "drop in," and events are limited to a four-hour span (two hours to set up, one hour for the ceremony, and one hour for breakdown). The Parks and Recreation Web site gives a description of each park and provides an online calendar of dates that have already been reserved. Call or e-mail for a facility information sheet that details prices and policies. Reservations are usually two weeks to a year in advance, but apply as early in the year as possible.

Catering: In most cases receptions catered by the wedding party or professional vendors are allowed in the parks and beaches. Check the Parks Department's Web site.

Accommodations: Although the parks and beaches might be available, hotels in the Santa Barbara area for the summer sell out by spring. The closer to the ocean, the higher the rates. The lowest-priced accommodations are along State Street in Goleta, as well as in Carpenteria.

TOWN AND COUNTRY RESORT AND CONVENTION CENTER
San Diego, California

If the objective of your wedding is to introduce families to each other in a beautiful, relaxing atmosphere with plenty of nearby attractions for all tastes, the Town and Country is your place. And it is aptly named. This forty-acre resort, buffered by a lush landscape, feels as secluded as a country motor inn, yet because of its location in San Diego's Mission Valley, it is accessible to everything a sprawling coastal city has to offer.

The T and C was originally built in 1956, in the California bungalow style so popular in its day. The accommodations are a mix of charming cottage-style single-story units, two-story garden units, and two multilevel towers, with all-white facades and fences. Walking along the lanes between facilities amid arching palm trees and scented tropical plants is pleasant. The gardens are the pride and joy of the owner's wife, Mrs. T. Terry (Charlene) Brown, who is often found in her grubbies pruning, weeding, or planting.

Everything about the Town and Country numbers in the thousands: 2,500 palm trees, 7,000 rosebushes, more than

165,000 square feet of meeting space for as many as 5,000 conferees, 1,000 sleeping rooms, and nearly 1,000 employees. This might seem too huge for one little wedding, but with forty acres of gardens and grounds, five restaurants and lounges, four pools, a golf course, a spa, and a health club, there is plenty of room for conventions *and* weddings to coexist. Because of this resort's layout, the guest room area is relatively quiet, even while conventions and balls are crowding the (humongous) ballrooms. City noise is negligible.

The Brown family has owned the hotel since the 1950s—and a family-operated hotel translates into personable service. Staff are accommodating; a few have worked for the resort for more than forty-five years. The hotel has recently started bringing back turn-down service free of charge. What a treat to come back to the room after an active day to find chocolates on pillows against neatly refolded bedding, with fresh towels in the bathroom to boot.

Some rooms are decorated in the deep blue florals of Williamsburg Colonial, while others are being refurbished in California pinks. The T and C is not the Ritz and the rooms are not spacious, but they are clean and comfortable. Besides, with so much to do, who wastes their time in their rooms?

The Town and Country can host a convention for 3,000, but can it do a wedding for, say, 30? Yes, and happily. A rose garden gazebo, as well as a number of other garden settings and private salons, stand at the ready. Popular reception rooms include the Windsor Rose (125 capacity), Le Chanteclair (100), and Sunset (200), plus a variety of rooms for cozier groups. Rumor has it that the rose garden, with its adjoining pool, will be paved over for a beautiful outdoor venue for 1,500.

Family members involved in the wedding will have so much to do, it might be difficult to rein them in for the actual event. A footbridge connects the hotel to the Fashion Valley Mall. The trolley adjacent to the hotel leads to Old Town, the Gas Lamp Quarter, and Tijuana, Mexico. Beaches, SeaWorld, the San Diego Zoo, Seaport Village, and Balboa Park and Museums are all within a ten-minute drive.

Town and Country Resort and Convention Center
500 Hotel Circle North
San Diego, CA 92108
(619) 291–7131
www.towncountry.com

Location: From Interstate 8, exit Hotel Circle. The hotel is located on the north side at Fashion Valley Road.

Facility Rental, Amenities, and Policies: The fee for a ceremony in the Rose Garden Gazebo or a private wedding salon is $5.00 per chair and includes a wedding arbor decorated with silk flowers. Additional services include ice sculptures, specialty linen and decor rentals, baby grand piano rentals, and

fresh flower arrangements or centerpieces. The T and C provides a complimentary bridal consultant to each couple, and all of the events and necessary guest accommodations can be arranged through one contact, at one convenient location.

Catering: The banquet and catering staff at the Town and Country Resort Hotel have offered competitive, customized wedding services to new brides for more than forty years. With fifty or more guests, the hotel offers a generous, reasonably priced package that averages $50 per person for catering. The packages include one of four seated dinner menus, one glass of champagne per person for toasting, a wedding cake made in the hotel's European bakery with complimentary cake-cutting service, white-glove and silver service, silk floral centerpieces with mirrored rounds and votives, and complimentary room setup with dance floor and staging.

Elegance, one of the four meal selections, features a petite filet of beef in brandy-Dijon sauce. Unforgettable, a wedding buffet, is available for a minimum of seventy-five guests and centers on breast of chicken with Pommery cream sauce, roast of top sirloin, and "chef's sweet presentation." A hosted beverage hour is available for $16 per person.

Accommodations: A complimentary bridal room is included in a wedding with more than 100 guests, which is upgraded to a bridal suite with a minimum of 300 guests. Room rates peak at $150 per night, but are generally much less and are specially reduced for room blocks of wedding guests.

Keep in Mind: The hotel can often sell out during the week for conventions. However, conventions typically follow the school year, and therefore, weddings are best booked when school is out.

VIANSA WINERY &
ITALIAN MARKETPLACE

Sonoma, California

No list of the best wedding destinations would be complete without the inclusion of at least one winery from Northern California's Napa and Sonoma Valleys. Most of the wineries here stretch the budgetary limits and guest count of the typical destination wedding. Viansa Winery is no exception, but it is about as close to a Tuscan-style wedding as possible without putting the entire entourage on an airplane. The winery, moreover, comes highly recommended by couples who've already toasted their vows there.

Founded in 1989 by Sam and Vicki Sebastiani, Viansa Winery and Italian Marketplace is a destination winery in the Carneros grape-growing region at the entrance to the Sonoma Valley. Viansa's tile-roofed Tuscan villa sits on a hilltop surrounded by olive trees and vineyards, overlooking a ninety-acre waterfowl preserve that has drawn acclaim from environmental groups across the nation. Designed with hand-painted murals, massive beams, and Italian marble, the villa exudes Tuscan charm. A series of French doors along the left wing opens onto a circular courtyard; colorful flowerpots full of red geraniums encircle the fountain in the center and mark the perimeter. The extensive grounds are planted with Italian cypresses and stone pines.

The founders' winemaking heritage extends back more than a hundred years to Sam Sebastiani's legendary grandfather, Samuele, who journeyed from the wine-producing region of Tuscany in 1895. Sam and Vicki Sebastiani created Viansa as a way to share their love of good food, wine, and their Italian heritage, and their catering menus reflect their dedication to the marriage of wine and food. Grapes grown at Viansa (short for "Vicki and Sam") include Sangiovese, Dolcetto, and Tocai Friulano. The Italian Marketplace on the premises sells delicious specialty sandwiches and salads to complement Viansa's Italian-style wines.

Viansa hosts about seventy-five to eighty weddings per year, particularly in August and September during the harvest and grape crush season when nights are warm. The spacious circular courtyard, surrounded by grape vines and olive trees and anchored by a central fountain and massive cellar doors, provides a dramatic ceremony site. After the ceremony the wedding party and guests proceed through the candlelit wine cellar and on up to the terrace overlooking the Viansa Wetlands and Sonoma Valley for wine and hors d'oeuvres. The bride and groom are invited to share a private celebratory moment together in the cellar's Tuscan Room before the evening continues. For a gorgeous finale the reception is held in Le Mura: Linen-draped tables set with crystal and flowers are an elegant complement to the polished-paver floor and soaring white canopy overhead; multiple windows open out onto the adjacent terrace and lawn. The pavilion can serve a maximum of 200 guests, but 500 can be served with extended tenting.

Viansa Winery & Italian Marketplace
25200 Arnold Drive
Sonoma, CA 95476
(800) 995–4740 or (707) 935–2728
Special Events: (707) 935–4722
www.viansa.com

Location: Viansa Winery is on California Highway 121, fourteen minutes south of Sonoma.

Facility Fees, Amenities, and Policies: Facility fees for a Saturday (or legal holiday) wedding during the peak season from mid-April through mid-October are $10,000 with a minimum of 150 guests, although a Saturday wedding during the remaining months of the year would be $6,000 for a minimum of seventy-five guests. Friday and Sunday weddings during the peak season are $6,000 and $8,000, respectively, for a minimum of one hundred guests; off-peak fees for the same days are $5,000 with seventy-five guests. Monday through Thursday weddings any month of the year are $4,000 with a minimum of seventy-five guests.

Facility fees cover a five-hour period, from 6:00 to 11:00 P.M.; each additional half hour is priced at $850. The fee includes setup and breakdown of the ceremony, reception, and dining sites, plus 6-foot round tables for up to 200 guests. Clients are required to purchase a rental package through Viansa for ceremony and dining chairs, linens, and china and stemware for $20 to $44 per person, from simple elegance to top-of-the-line selections. The fees also include professional coordination of the rehearsal, ceremony, and menu selection. All flowers and decorations are to be kept in the elegant theme of the winery's decor. An insurance policy is required.

Catering: All food and beverages must be purchased from Viansa, which requires a food minimum of $75 per person, and a wine package minimum of $20 per person. Plated dinners are $75 to $117; buffets are $75 to $98 per person, with a minimum of 150 guests. Dinners and buffets include a choice of five hors d'oeuvres.

Wedding coordinator Marni Goodman says many couples select the combination meat and fish plates, such as the petit mignon and roasted black sea cod with tapenade, for $108 per guest. The chefs can also put together a vegetarian meal. A dessert buffet called Dolci Nuziali (wedding sweets) can be served with a selection of four treats for $10 per guest.

For a buffet the Assaggi Mondiale (world flavors) is tempting at $96 per guest, and includes three hors d'oeuvres as well as Tuscan, Asian, quesadilla, and sweet stations. Couples provide their own wedding cake, and staff coordinators provide a list of vendors.

Extras: Viansa offers a variety of unique wedding mementos such as personalized wine bottles ($38 each), Viansa logo wineglasses ($10 each), and monogrammed olive oil bottles ($14 each). Customized toasting glasses are $120 to $200 each. After-wedding treats include robusto cigars, espresso bar, and an after-dinner bar.

Accommodations: Lodging is available throughout the Sonoma and Napa Valleys.

YOSEMITE NATIONAL PARK

Yosemite National Park, California

Yosemite, a 1,177-square-mile national park in the Sierra Nevada Mountains of central California, is home to the world's largest trees, some of the tallest waterfalls, and ominous rock formations created by glaciers and other forces of nature over millions of years. Couples from all over the world exchange vows beneath such breathtaking spots as Bridalveil Fall or Cathedral Peak in what some call "the grandest of all God's temples." With a little planning, all of this can become a setting for a wedding, and given the seasonal beauty, decorations are superfluous.

Couples can marry, in the company of less than ten people, virtually anywhere in the park that is accessible, with the exception of open meadows in Yosemite, the base of sequoias, or on river banks, stream drainages, and bridges. The park also offers sixteen permit use sites for larger groups with certain date and use restrictions.

Ceremony Permit Sites in Yosemite Valley

The Merced River runs through the Yosemite Valley, and is followed on either side by two scenic drives to its impressive waterfalls, meadows, cliffs, and unusual rock formations. Sites along the drives are the easiest to reach and, therefore, the most crowded, especially in late spring and summer. Five picnic areas along these drives are open to wedding ceremonies. Most are near restrooms, but all have limited parking and require shuttle buses or carpooling. **Lower Yosemite Falls** (capacity fifty) is open year-round with a quarter-mile walk. Yosemite Falls can also be viewed from **Swinging Bridge Picnic Area** (twenty), a sandy beach on the north side of the

Merced River. **Cathedral Beach Picnic Area** (fifty), on the south side of the river, has views of El Capitan, but is closed November through April. **Sentinel Beach Picnic Area** (one hundred), with views of the Half Dome formation and Yosemite Falls, is open May through October but limited during raft season (mid-May through mid-August). A location on the old roadbed below **Bridalveil Fall** (fifty) is open all year. The wind often blows the waterfall sideways, giving it the appearance of a bride's veil.

Ceremony Permit Sites in Wawona

Wawona is a small mountain valley community within the park near Yosemite's south gate, and has approximately the same elevation, climate, and vegetation as Yosemite Valley. The **Chilnualna Falls Trailhead Parking Lot** (fifteen) is available anytime throughout the year. Ceremonies are welcome mid-May through mid-November at **Wawona Point** (fifty), a half-mile walk from the Wawona Tunnel Tree tram stop (ask the driver for trail directions). At 6,810 feet above Mariposa Grove, Wawona Point's flagstone terrace—overlooking Wawona Meadow, a golf course, and Wawona Dome—makes for a cozy wedding. No private vehicles are allowed. The short round-trip walk should take less than an hour. The **Mariposa Grove Museum Area** (ten), where 500 sequoias (Sierra redwoods) thrive, permits ceremonies mid-May through mid-November.

Other popular options, generally for late May through October, include Glacier Point (fifty), two sites in Tuolumne Meadows (fifty each), Tuolumne Lodge area (one hundred), and two areas in Big Oak Flat (thirty each). Couples can be married in the Yosemite

Community Chapel (Southside Drive) with a maximum of 125 guests. Weddings are scheduled through the chapel secretary for a ninety-minute period.

Formal receptions are prohibited in the picnic areas. The park offers three properties for catered functions, operated by its concession agency, Delaware North Company: the Ahwahnee, Wawona Hotel, and Yosemite Lodge. All three are set against the rugged beauty of Yosemite and were built to complement their environment. Outdoor weddings and indoor receptions at these sites still require a permit.

Built in 1927 of redwood and granite to blend in with the earth tones of the scenery, the castlelike **Ahwahnee** was meant to attract prominent figures into the park to assist in its preservation. Cathedral ceilings, enormous stone hearths, and floor-to-ceiling windows frame the landscape and formations. Native American decor is true to its original design, with the motif carried throughout guest rooms, public areas, and reception rooms, which accommodate 40 to 200.

The **Wawona Hotel** (1879) is California's oldest hotel, complete with wraparound balconies, Victorian cottages, and fountain. It can accommodate up to 50 guests in its sunroom and 200 on lush green lawns. **Yosemite Lodge** near the relaxing roar of Yosemite Falls offers the most casual setting, for up to 190 guests. The patios provide the ideal location for a casual reception during late spring and summer when the

water is falling. Receptions are moved inside during fall and winter, in rooms with warm wood paneling and picture windows.

National Park Service
Yosemite National Park Office of Special Programs/Weddings
P.O. Box 700
El Portal, CA 95318
(209) 379–1854
www.nps.gov/yose/

Yosemite Community Chapel
(209) 372–4831 (leave message)

Catered Reception Information for Lodges:
Yosemite Concession Services Corporation
Delaware North Company
6771 North Palm Avenue
Fresno, CA 93704
(559) 253–5673
www.yosemitepark.com

Location: Yosemite is four hours from the Sacramento, Oakland, and Reno/Tahoe airports, five hours from the San Francisco airport, and more than two hours from the Fresno/Yosemite, Merced, Modesto, and Mammoth Lakes airports.

Facility Rental, Amenities, and Policies:
The special-use permit for Yosemite's sixteen sanctioned ceremony sites is $150 for a three-hour period. A wedding within the park may be scheduled three weeks to one year in advance. The park provides a wed-

ding application form; submission must include a $50 nonrefundable fee. The wedding party and guests must also pay their admission fees upon arrival. The sites are closed to weddings on major holidays.

The ecosystems of Yosemite are sensitive and subject to human-caused erosion. The park asks that wedding groups "respect the resource and tread lightly." Parking is in designated places only and is often restricted, and wedding furniture is allowed only in the picnic areas. Even with a permit, use of these areas is on a first-come basis; the sites cannot be reserved, and park visitors will not be restricted during a wedding. It is recommended that high-traffic areas be avoided—or scheduled early or late in the day, or during low-traffic seasons, for more privacy.

Catering: In addition to submitting an application for a wedding permit, the marrying couple must also submit an application for a reception, if one is required, listing four choices for dates. Reception applications should be submitted more than a year in advance, but the date is confirmed one year ahead. Booking a wedding with DNC means complete catering service with personal attention from the professional wedding specialists to assure that no detail is overlooked. The specialists can provide lists of vendors and officiants.

Three-hour room rentals range from $300 to $1,900 for Ahwahnee, and $400 for Yosemite Lodge and Wawona Hotel, plus $200 for each additional hour. The rental fee includes tables, chairs, standard linens, china, table settings, glassware, and setup and teardown of function space. The reception rooms are for catering only; ceremonies are not permitted. A lawn rental fee and chair rental for a forty-five-minute ceremony might be assessed.

With costs of $100 to $130 a person, the Ahwahnee creates the most elegant receptions of the three properties. Average reception costs at Wawona and Yosemite Lodge range from $75 to $90 per person. Lunch and dinner buffets are also available for a minimum of twenty-five people, and range from $30 per person at Yosemite Lodge to $50 per person at Ahwahnee.

Ahwahnee has a covered terrace in the case of inclement weather, but the other locations do not have alternative options. All food and beverages must be purchased through DNC at Yosemite, and a minimum is applied to all events depending on the number of people attending. Wedding cakes are available through Ahwahnee and can be delivered to the other event sites. Cake-cutting fees per person apply.

Accommodations: Lodging is available at Ahwahnee, Wawona, and Yosemite Lodge, and rates start at $100 to $379, depending on the hotel, room type, and season. Lodging is available throughout the park.

Keep in Mind: Is there a best time to get married in Yosemite? The perfect season for waterfalls is spring (April, May, and June) during snowmelt, but not all areas of the park are accessible until a week or two into June. The wildflower bloomfest follows the waterfalls, May through July. The park is the most accessible—and consequently the most crowded—late June through September. Yosemite draws some three million visitors every year, most of whom stick close to the main park drive, so traffic and parking can become congested. The crowds diminish by fall; unfortunately, so do the waterfalls and colors. Most of the trees are evergreen, but the big-leaf maples, black oaks, and other deciduous trees tend to be showy around mid-October. While Yosemite Valley and Wawona remain accessible by car all year, some roads and park areas close around late October. Winter (December through March) is a season of snow and solitude.

ALPS BOULDER CANYON INN

Boulder, Colorado

Boulder, Colorado, at the base of the Flatirons, may be the adrenaline capital of the world. This sophisticated college and high-tech research town has tens of thousands of acres of open space and parks, 200 trails, more bicycles than people, and some of the best rock climbing and skiing in the world. And the Alps Boulder Canyon Inn is perfectly situated to take advantage of it all.

Partway up Boulder Canyon, the inn is just a few minutes west of the University of Colorado campus, Boulder's Pearl Street pedestrian mall, downtown shops, restaurants, award-winning library, and museums. What's more, patrons can walk right out their guest rooms and stroll along the paved 16-mile Boulder Creek path down the mountain, past kayaks and inner tubers negotiating waterfalls, through shady picnic areas, and on to trout ponds and to the eastern edge of the city.

The Alps Boulder Canyon Inn was originally constructed in the 1870s as one of Colorado's first resorts. Owners Jeannine and John Vanderhart converted the inn into a bed-and-breakfast and reopened it in 1993. It's now recognized as one of the West's most romantic and distinctive inns.

The inn is popular for weddings among knowing Denverites and residents of towns along the Front Range. The world has yet to discover the place as a wedding venue, by and large, but the New York Times (January 9, 2005) did report on a New Year's Eve wedding between two career runners at the Alps Inn, which epitomizes the sporty Boulder spirit. Roxanne Hawn wrote: "It was a short, raucous ceremony during which the couple's two dogs served as ring bearers and the bridegroom brandished a handker-

chief in jest. Then, as he read his vows, he wept in earnest, stopping to ask, 'Where's that tissue?' The wedding . . . wrapped up the triathletes' short off-season, giving the couple and their 95 guests an opportunity to blow off steam."

The Alps Inn, with both indoor and outdoor facilities on twenty-seven private acres, indeed specializes in such Colorado-style, family-oriented weddings and receptions. Its Web site states: "Our wedding planners are experts in creating one-of-a-kind events to exceed the expectations of even the most discriminating brides. You can trust their knowledge and experience to help you plan and organize a wonderful event that matches your personality and style." Part of that responsibility is playing host to the couple's extended families. Jeannine Vanderhart told us, "In most instances, the two sides haven't met each other prior to the wedding, and so the majority of people stay for several days and hang out getting to know one another." The Vanderharts strive to provide "a true feeling of making it more of a gathering than just an event."

Alps Boulder Canyon Inn
38619 Boulder Canyon Drive
Boulder, CO 80302
(800) 414–2577 or (303) 444–5445
www.alpsinn.com

Location: 5 miles west of the heart of Boulder off Colorado Highway 93.

Facility Rental, Amenities, and Policies: The Alps can accommodate events for up to 150 people, and although it has hosted weddings for groups involving less than 20, the average size is 75 to 125. Site fees vary with time of day, day of week, and season. Prices for daytime events (11:30 A.M. to 3:30 P.M.) for seventy-five guests are less than evening (6:00 to 10:00 P.M.) for 125 guests; Monday through Thursday are less than Friday and Sunday weddings, which are less than Saturday and holiday events. The low season is considered to be October through May, and the high season is June through September and holidays. A Monday daytime wedding in October, therefore, is $995, and a New Year's Eve evening wedding is $3,195. These site fees are set for four-hour periods, plus two and a half hours allotted for setup and cleanup. Site fees include complimentary honeymoon suite and gift package for all evening events (no matter the day of week or season), 25 percent discount on guest room rates for evening events, experienced personal event coordinator, private wedding venue, ceremony, and ample on-site parking. The inn is working on all-inclusive packages for florals, catering, and photography as of this writing.

Catering: All food must be catered by full-service, licensed, and insured caterers on the inn's preferred provider list. The inn is flexible, however, and its event planners can assist in locating other caterers who also meet the inn's standards.

Accommodations: Each of the 12 guest rooms is decorated with Mission and Arts and Crafts furnishings, stained-glass windows, and a Victorian mantel above a working antique fireplace. Most have two-person Jacuzzi or antique claw-footed tub, and French doors leading to a garden, patio, or private porch. Guests are indulged with L'Occitane bath/spa amenities and Godiva turndown chocolates at their bedside. Relax next to one of inn's massive stone fireplaces and enjoy hot spiced cider, fresh-baked cookies, and evening desserts. Rooms are $99 to $274, depending on view, size, and season.

Keep in Mind: Due to the value of the estate furnishings as well as the delicate landscaping, the inn suggests hiring professionals to supervise children during the wedding.

THE ASPEN MOUNTAIN CLUB AND THE LITTLE NELL
Aspen, Colorado

An Aspen Mountain wedding begins with a fifteen-minute, 2.5-mile ride on the Silver Queen Gondola to the summit at 11,200 feet. Panoramic views of snowcapped mountains along the way are extraordinary to say the least. Couples exchange vows on the Wedding Deck, which has the vantage point of an eagle's nest, though large enough to seat 200 guests terraced over a gentle, grassy slope. A boardwalk follows the contour of the mountaintop to the deck,

which appears to be extended beyond the bluff's edge. Returning in the evening after a reception or dinner at the Sundeck or Aspen Mountain Club, ideally bathed by a full moon, guests enjoy an equally rare view of the lights of Aspen.

A ceremony on the mountain amid birdsong and cool breezes is only the ribbon on the wedding gift that is The Little Nell. This boutique hotel, which hosts the Aspen Mountain Wedding Deck, was built in 1989 on the site of Little Nell's store, bar, and cafe, named for a silver mine and ski run, and in turn named for a "lady of the evening" of the 1890s. (Only in Colorado!) Positioned at the base of Aspen Mountain just steps from the Silver Queen, this chalet is the only ski-in, ski-out hotel in Aspen. A British columnist proclaimed the ninety-two-room inn one of the world's best for the well-groomed skier. (An in-house ski concierge will warm your boots, for instance.) The staff has a reputation for blending country inn charm with the service expected of a grand hotel.

The Little Nell's reception venues are also beautiful. The Sundeck features 30-foot ceilings, a massive rock fireplace, and copper lighting fixtures. It houses three eating establishments: a cafeteria, a sit-down restaurant (Benedicts), and a semiprivate club (the Aspen Mountain Club). The building's architecture reflects both its remote mountaintop location and Aspen's mining heritage, featuring natural wood framing and beams, a galvanized metal roof, and stone siding.

Collectively the Sundeck spaces accommodate 80 to 400, depending on the style of reception (passed hors d'oeuvres, buffet, or seated dining). It's available for evening events throughout the year, except May and October when the gondola isn't running. The Aspen Mountain Club is available breakfast through dinner in summer, and for private evening functions in winter. Because the club is exclusive, there are certain restrictions on furniture arrangement.

The Little Nell has several other venues: The new Montagna restaurant and bar (120 to 200) offers alpine cooking, fresh regional ingredients, and spectacular presentation. The Wine Room (50 to 80), a comfortable private dining room, has a stone fireplace, handmade wine bins, and rich walnut paneling. View Aspen Mountain from the Greenhouse (80 to 150), perfect for brunch under

crisp clear skies. With wrought-iron chandeliers, the Grand Salon (130 to 180) is an intimate setting for wedding receptions and rehearsal dinners. The Boardroom, the smallest venue on the property, accommodates eighteen seated guests or fifty reception style.

Aspen's celebrity reputation and tabloid chairlift scandals precede it, but it is a real town with a mining history, some great old buildings, and spectacular mountain scenery. Prices are much lower in summer when the skiing crowds thin out. It is a great summer destination for dining, hiking, biking, horseback riding, and music and dance festivals.

The Aspen Mountain Club and The Little Nell
675 East Durant Avenue
Aspen, CO 81611
(970) 920–4600
www.thelittlenell.com

Location: 1 block southwest of East Cooper Avenue (Colorado Highway 82), which becomes Main Street.

Facility Rental, Amenities, and Policies: Rental of the Wedding Deck is $500.00, or $9.00 per person, whichever turns out to be greater. A fact sheet states that room rental will apply in addition to food and beverage expenditures "unless waived by your sales or catering manager," perhaps indicating opportunity for negotiation. Additional site fees for the reception are $1,000 for the Aspen Mountain Club, and $2,000 for the Sundeck, which covers attendants for the gondola (required), bathrooms, coat check, and labor for setting up the dance floor, stage, banners, and furniture. Bartenders and chef attendants are charged for by the hour, and there are fees for cake cutting, excessive cleanup, and removal of extra furniture. Votive candles and white or beige linens are included in the fees, but there is a charge for more than three candles per table or for colored linens.

All wedding parties are required by contract to hire a wedding coordinator for at least the day of the event. More than one event may be booked at the same time at the various venues, although great care is taken to ensure the events do not conflict with one another.

Catering: Hors d'oeuvres are $18 to $24 per person. Soups (perhaps vichyssoise with crisp sweet potatoes) are $8.00 to $16.00. Salads (such as smoked duck salad with market greens and grapefruit-cumin honey dressing) cost $8.00 to $13.00. Appetizer selections (Virginia crab cake with country slaw and stone fruit relish) are $13 to $27. Plated dinner selections include seafood, poultry, beef, vegetarian, lamb, veal, and game for $26 to $46 per person, and include vegetables and starch. Combination plates are around $50 per person.

Accommodations: A standard room with a town view runs from $260 in spring to $640 during ski season. The luxuriously appointed Pfeifer Suite can be upward of $4,600. The hotel closes for one month every year, mid-April to mid-May.

Keep in Mind: Use of the Silver Queen Gondola for events at the Aspen Mountain Club, Sundeck, and Wedding Deck is permitted Memorial Day weekend through August; weekends only in September; and during ski season, November through April. The gondola must cease operations by 11:00 P.M. Fees are $750 to $850 per hour during the hours of the event in summer and winter, respectively, to defray the cost of gondola operators and ski patrol. Two attendants are required but are included in the site fee. Groups with fewer than sixty people have the option of paying the catering manager $50 per hour to remain throughout the wedding day, but larger groups must retain the services of an outside company.

Arrive a few days early to acclimate to the altitude and bring sunscreen.

BETTY FORD ALPINE GARDENS
Vail, Colorado

In the Rocky Mountains, fields of flowers replace the snow mass as a summer attraction. At 8,200 feet, Betty Ford Alpine Gardens in Vail is the highest public botanic garden in North America. The garden is a microcosm of the Gore Range Mountains on a human scale; what began as a demonstration garden in the 1980s evolved into a place for meditative gardens Rocky Mountain style. It is likely one of the most secluded spots around for a wedding ceremony—and one of the most serene.

The garden was conceived by chance when Helen Fritch offered Marty Jones, a landscape architect, a ride after his truck broke down on the side of the road. He got to talking about his grand idea to design a public garden, and Fritch said she would help. It took the better half of a decade to build, plant, and open the perennial garden area, and new areas were put in every few years. The site was named in honor of former first lady Betty Ford in 1988, "for her many contributions to the Vail Valley, our nation, and beyond."

The garden is today a canvas for Jones, Fritch, and the small army that runs the place. The first English-inspired perennial garden is still the showy entrance to the Alpine Gardens, where peonies, roses, daisies, columbines, gold-veined irises, and delphiniums surround a circular sandstone terrace and waterfall. Shaded benches face a small pond, inviting newcomers to sit even before they get started.

The Mountain Meditation Garden, with its pond and waterfall, is surrounded by Colorado blue spruce, grasses, and sedges. Narrow flagstone paths lead to hidden benches cloaked in evergreens for solitude and quiet. The path meanders up to the Alpine Rock Garden, where columbines and coralbells burst out of quartzite crevices. At the base of the wall, mat and cushion plants of the alpine tundra spread alongside the pathway, interrupted by the large upright heads of the alpine sunflower, *Hymonoxy grandiflora,* better known as Old Man of the Mountains. On the far north end of Betty Ford Alpine Gardens are the Alpine Pools, which overflow to create a 40-foot waterfall. A patio in this setting offers dramatic views of the Alpine Rock Garden and is home to more than twenty beautiful weddings each season.

Betty Ford Alpine Gardens is open from dawn to dusk. There is no admission fee, but donations are appreciated and donation boxes are located throughout the gardens. The gardens are ADA accessible, although there are no resources to supply wheelchairs.

Betty Ford Alpine Gardens
183 Gore Creek Drive
Vail, CO 81657
(970) 476–0103
www.bettyfordalpinegardens.org

Location: From east or west on Interstate 70, take the main Vail exit (176) to South Frontage Road. The entrance is located at 530 South Frontage Road in Ford Park.Most people fly in to Eagle Airport in Vail, finding it to be a better value than arriving at Denver and then driving the three hours to Vail.

Facility Rental, Amenities, and Policies: Weddings involving a maximum of one hundred people are welcome at the Betty Ford Gardens—in fact, they provide funding for future projects. The price is a donation of $1,000 for a Saturday wedding and $500 for any other day of the week. (Imagine a wedding that is tax deductible!) The grounds can be rented for wedding photography for a contribution of $400 on Saturday, and $200 on a weekday. Only two private events are scheduled per day in the gardens, and all agreements are made on a first-come, first-served basis. All equipment rented for use in the gardens must be purchased through the gardens, and staff will oversee the setup of this equipment. Weddings take place rain, snow, or shine, and staff suggests arranging indoor backup weddings through your host hotel or reception venue.

Chairs are permitted on the Rock Garden Terrace for weddings of up to a hundred guests. The small amphitheater in the Children's Garden stands ready for weddings with fewer than fifty guests. Weddings with more than a hundred guests are allowed in the Lower Lawn Area or the Picnic Pavilion by the covered bridge. Typically these wedding parties still rent photography time in the Alpine Gardens itself. Events including tents and catering in this area are available on a limited basis, and renters should allow several months for the liquor and tent permit process. All events of this nature must hire professional security, and an event manager or a member of the facility's special-events committee will manage this event on your behalf.

A reservation form for weddings within the gardens is available for download on the Web site. To reserve a date in the Lower Lawn Area or the Picnic Pavilion, check the appropriate boxes on the same reservation form and contact the Vail town clerk's office at (970) 479–2136. For use of the larger, more commercial Gerald R. Ford Amphitheater, call the Vail Valley Foundation at (970) 949–1999.

The Betty Ford Alpine Gardens is part of the multivenue Ford Park. During the summer season many events are simultaneously scheduled. Though the site is not responsible for any events planned through the town of Vail, Vail Recreation District (softball fields), and/or Vail Valley Foundation (Gerald R. Ford Amphitheater), the organizations work closely together to manage this space for the enjoyment of all. Because these are public grounds, the gardens cannot be blocked off in any way from public access unless a special-event permit for liquor service is acquired. The town of Vail might institute public parking during such events.

Catering: Often the ceremony is performed in the gardens and then the party goes elsewhere in Vail for the reception. Office staff provide a preferred vendor and reception site list and help with the long-distance coordination of the event.

Accommodations: Lodging is amply available in Vail, Colorado.

Keep in Mind: Betty Ford Alpine Gardens lies at 8,200 feet, and the altitude isn't suitable for everyone. Consider coming a few days in advance of the wedding to acclimate; bring sunscreen and a wide-brimmed hat. Water is available in the gift shop during open hours.

BUTTERFLY PAVILION
Westminster, Colorado

Holding a ceremony at the Butterfly Pavilion is like getting married in a tropical rain forest. As many as 1,200 exotic butterflies flutter about in search of nectar among more than a hundred fragrant, blooming tropical plants. If the bridal bouquet and bridesmaid dresses are colorful, a zebra long wing or paper kite might even land on one of them.

The nonprofit Butterfly Pavilion was the first stand-alone insect zoo when it opened its conservatory in 1995. The U.S. Department of Agriculture allows the pavilion to import more than 200 different species, and it imports about 28,800 individual butterflies per year. A chrysalis viewing area allows visitors to watch the amazing process of metamorphosis as adult butterflies emerge from their gem-like chrysalides. In addition to butterflies, the conservatory contains twenty-two tortoises, four turtles, two ring-neck doves, frogs, fish, land crabs, and a very large but very friendly iguana. Visitors to the pavilion have the opportunity of experiencing a tropical rain forest habitat, butterfly habitat, prairie habitat, and riparian habitat created by the Rocky Mountain Butterfly Consortium.

The Butterfly Pavilion is a 30,000-square-foot facility covering five acres in the city of Westminster. The environment is maintained between seventy and seventy-eight degrees and 60 to 80 percent humidity regardless of the weather outside. This makes it a perfect venue for a ceremony year-round if your wedding involves fewer than sixty or seventy people. Ceremonies involving 60 to 150 people and receptions can be accommodated in a new 2,000-square-foot event center. Participants have full access to all areas of the pavilion and staff members are on hand to interpret exhibits. In the summer months capacity can be effectively increased through the use of outdoor tents.

Butterfly Pavilion
6252 West 104th Avenue
Westminster, CO 80020
Special Events: (720) 974–1871
www.butterflies.org

Location: Thirty minutes from downtown Denver off U.S. Highway 36 and 104th Avenue.

Facility Rental, Amenities, and Policies: The Butterfly Pavilion offers three pricing tiers. Option A, the Ceremony Only package, is $500. This gives wedding participants access to the Tropical Rainforest for up to one and a half hours for a total of sixty people, with the use of a classroom for preparation. The price covers the $4 admission fee for each person attending the wedding.

Option B, the Ceremony Plus Short Reception/Rehearsal Dinner package, is $900. It provides access to the Tropical Rainforest for up to three hours and includes use of the special-events room with full kitchen. The special-events room

can accommodate up to 140 people standing and 120 seated. The fee covers admission for 120 people, and each additional guest costs $4.00. Due to the layout of the conservatory, only sixty people may view the actual ceremony, but additional guests may have access to the rest of the pavilion during the ceremony.

Option C, the Ceremony Plus Reception or Reception Only package, is $2,500. This option allows access to the entire Butterfly Pavilion for up to five hours, including four exhibits and three classrooms for catering needs. The event may be fully catered through the pavilion's preferred catering companies. The fee covers admission for 500 people; each additional guest costs $4.00. Event times include setup and breakdown. Again, due to the layout of the conservatory, only sixty people may view the actual ceremony, but additional guests may have access to the rest of the pavilion during the ceremony.

The wedding party may begin to set up for the event at 6:30 P.M. in summer and 5:30 P.M. in winter, although caterers can start setting up prior to the scheduled event by coordinating directly with the Butterfly Pavilion. The pavilion's professional event team can help create a wedding to suit various needs and budgets. However, setup and cleanup are the responsibility of the renting party.

Catering: Food and drink may be served in the events room. The pavilion provides a list of preferred caterers.

Accommodations: Available in the Greater Denver area.

Keep in Mind: The Butterfly Pavilion has become so popular that booking at least six months in advance is recommended.

CHAPEL AT RED ROCKS

Morrison, Colorado

What grabs the attention most when turning into the Chapel at Red Rocks parking area is the sudden appearance of gigantic slabs of rusty sandstone standing almost on end. The Fountain Formation, stained by iron oxide and thrusting into the Colorado sky, is millions of years old and is the so-called ancestral Rocky Mountains. The chapel was built to take full advantage of the dramatic views through its orientation and expansive windows. There is ceiling-to-floor paned glass just behind the altar, and no matter the time of day or season, the interactions among sunlight, shadow, and clouds on the jutting boulders creates a pageantry of color. Add to this the professional services of the chapel, and the venue is perfect for a wedding.

The chapel is located at the southeast entrance of the Red Rocks Park (and a few miles south of Red Rocks Amphitheatre), fifteen minutes west of the Greater Denver area. Visitors can explore myriad rocks, animals, and wildlife on miles of hiking trails in the area that was once the stomping ground for dinosaurs, and later the hunting and wintering grounds for Ute chief Colorow and his people.

The creators of the Chapel at Red Rocks understand the importance of location and light to photography. Not only is the architecture aligned with the best views of the red rocks, but the patios, reflecting pond, waterfalls, flowering trees, native shrubbery, and wildflowers around the chapel provide dramatic photo opportunities as well. Inside the chapel specially designed lighting above the aisle tracks on the bride during her procession, creating highlights and keeping her out of shadows for the photographs. Lighting in the chapel and the dressing rooms is true light, and is again conducive to both putting on makeup and those "getting-ready" shots. Most of the photographers on the chapel's preferred vendors list are award winning, and all have their favorite spots in Red Rocks for dramatic and romantic shots.

The chapel is spacious and will accommodate 140 guests. The interior is enhanced by the extra-high ceilings, a grandly wide aisle for the bride, and a separate side aisle for the groom. The eighty-year-old solid oak pews add warmth and dignity to the interior setting. Dressing areas are provided for the wedding parties; the bride's dressing room has full-length wall mirrors, makeup lighting, vanity, and bathroom.

The chapel has been operating for fifteen years and is owned by Kathleen DiFulvio with the assistance of a director of weddings.

Chapel at Red Rocks
905 Bear Creek Avenue
P.O. Box 306
Morrison, CO 80465
(303) 697–0270
www.chapelatredrocks.com

Location: The chapel can be reached by taking Colorado Highway 470 south to Morrison Road; from the Boulder area via Colorado Highway 93 through Golden and south to Morrison; and from downtown Denver via Interstate 70 west to CO 470 south to Morrison Road.

Facility Rental, Amenities, and Policies:
Rental for the chapel is $375–475 per hour. A two-hour period is usually enough time for

most weddings, but split time is available when needed. During the high season the last wedding on a Saturday is reserved for a two-and-a-half-hour block. Time is a commodity for the chapels, but weddings are not run back-to-back to allow for cleaning between each ceremony. The wedding coordinators can guide the couple in using their time as effectively as possible.

Several money-saving packages are available. Prices for Friday and Saturday afternoons and evenings start at $775.00 for a one-hour package for less than ten guests and range up to $1,687.50 for two and a half hours. Rates for Sunday through Thursday, in the morning, range from $675.00 for one hour to $1,437.50 for two and a half hours. These packages all include the minister, a print of the chapel, silk flowers, CD music, candelabra with candles, a wedding director, and the special lighting. The chapel provides an information packet.

As with most professional wedding venues, the chapel provides complete wedding services, and clients must use their wedding coordinators and musicians. The chapel has a Baldwin baby grand piano, musicians, and vocalists.

Catering: Receptions are not permitted on the property. The Fort Restaurant is less than two miles away from the Chapel at Red Rocks. The restaurant is a full-size adobe replica of Bent's Fort, an 1830s fur-trade post on the Santa Fe Trail. The Fort has served "early West" cuisine since 1963, featuring fine beef, buffalo, game, and seafood. Owner and founder Sam Arnold trained with James Beard and La Varenne Ecole de Cuisine in Paris. Private dining for 48 is available in Bent's Quarters as well as a number of the other 8 rooms. Lunch entrees range from $16.95 to $24.95, and dinner entrees range from $26.95 to $49.95 for up to fifty guests. Extravagant reception packages are $75 to $100. The Fort is located at 19192 Highway 8, Morrison, CO 80465-8731 (303–697–4771; Fax 303–697–9310; www.thefort.com).

Accommodations: Lodging is available in the Greater Denver area, the closest options being in Golden and Lakewood. There are a number of enchanting bed-and-breakfasts in the mountains.

Keep in Mind: Booking inquiries begin about twelve to eighteen months in advance of the wedding date, although last-minute arrangements can almost always be worked in. The best and most popular time, of course, is sunset.

CHEROKEE RANCH AND CASTLE
Sedalia, Colorado

Cherokee Ranch and Castle is an unexpected blend of fanciful, yet stately architecture, wildlife preserve, and working cattle ranch just a half hour from downtown Denver, Colorado. A local real estate tycoon built the twenty-six room mansion in the 1920s in the style of Great Britain's castles and country manors. The castle hugs a rocky bluff in the middle of thousands of open acres, which provides unobstructed views of surrounding mountains and an exclusive atmosphere for weddings.

Cherokee Ranch and Castle came into its own when Tweet Kimball, a flamboyant Texas cattlewoman, purchased it along with the adjoining land to become the seat of her Santa Gertrudis cattle operations. During her forty-five-year reign, Kimball entertained dignitaries from around the world. Guests often donned the suit of armor and clanged around the castle during her lavish parties. In the late 1990s Kimball established the Cherokee Ranch and Castle Foundation, donating the castle, the land (now protected as a wildlife sanctuary), cattle operation, and her art and furniture collections to the foundation. The foundation still maintains the castle, cattle, and preserve, and most recently began accommodating private events.

Cherokee Castle is constructed of native stone quarried on the property and hand hewn by thirty local stone masons. Architectural highlights include artistic stonework, winding staircases, towers, and gargoyles. Rhyolite columns and arches frame the entryway to the Great Hall, welcoming visitors to view an eclectic collection of European art and furnishings, and such interesting objects as an 1891 Chickering piano, the suit of armor, and a door of spears. An intimate sitting room located off the Great Hall is an ideal location for viewing wildlife and mountain vistas. Don't picture a dank and dark medieval tomb; this castle is full of light and polish.

Ceremonies take place in front of the grand carved stone gate at the Memorial Garden overlooking the castle, on the newer Veranda or Castle Court in view of Pikes Peak, on the Guest House Tower, or in front of the carved stone fireplace in the Great Hall of the castle itself. After the ceremony guests will be invited into the castle, where they may enjoy drinks and appetizers or go on guided tours of this historic landmark.

For parties of eighty or fewer, a buffet dinner may be served from the elaborate castle dining room, with the guests choosing seats anywhere on the main floor, including the

Great Hall, Foyer, Conservatory, Churchill Room, Master Suite, and Mother's Suite. In warm-weather months this capacity increases to 120 when tables may also be set on the West Terrace, in the Courtyard, and on the Guest House Tower. A musician's balcony in the Great Hall offers excellent acoustics for a trio, quartet, harp, or, of course, bagpipes. Although dance bands, disc jockeys, and dance floors are not permitted in the castle itself, the newlyweds may enjoy their first dance in the Great Hall. For parties of 150, a buffet or plated dinner may be served in the Castle Court (a large assembly area at the complex's center), or under the new seasonal tent on the Veranda. The smallest wedding the castle has hosted has been for thirty people, but weddings of this size aren't economically feasible for everyone.

The entrance to the property is along a 2-mile stretch of rugged terrain, and the parking lot is a short walk from the castle. Golf carts, limousines, and valet parking are often put into service to transport guests, who are welcomed by bagpipers.

Cherokee Ranch and Castle
6113 North Daniels Park Road
Sedalia, CO 80135-9716
(303) 688–5555
Information and Reservations: (303)
688–5555, ext. 14
www.cherokeeranch.org

Location: Daniels Park Road is 2.7 miles west of Interstate 25, just north of Castle Rock.

Facility Rental, Amenities, and Policies: The cost to rent Cherokee Castle and/or Veranda for a wedding and/or reception is $4,500 for a Saturday from mid-April through mid-October, and $4,100 for days other than Saturday. A castle wedding, any day, mid-October through mid-April is $4,100. A 20

percent discount is offered for weddings in November, January, February, and March, excluding the weekend closest to February 14. A discounted Saturday Afternoon Wedding package featuring a ceremony at the castle complex, castle tours, and afternoon food service at the Pavilion is also available. Additional time may be purchased at the rate of $600 per hour.

The rental period for weddings and receptions is seven and a half hours, which includes one and a half hours to set up catering, florals, and other services, five hours of "guest time" for the ceremony and reception, and an hour to clean up. The bridal party is given access to castle rooms in which to change, but otherwise the castle is not open to guests until the appointed time for guided tours.

Catering: The couple may hire only approved caterers, who are licensed and insured, and are familiar with the unique conditions of the historic building. These catering companies offer a variety of styles and price ranges. The castle provides twenty-seven round tables and 200 chairs to be setup by the catering company.

Accommodations: A few motels are available nearby in the Castle Rock area.

Keep in Mind: Cherokee Ranch and Castle is a museum filled with fragile and valuable antiques, humanities, and art objects. While children are not excluded from attending weddings in the castle, an adult-only function or adult supervision is strongly suggested.

DENVER BOTANIC GARDENS
Denver, Colorado

What catches the eye at the Denver Botanic Gardens is the geometry. Fields of brilliantly colored flowers offset the diamond-shaped glass-and-metal-beamed conservatory. The extensive waterway system, a connecting series of rectangular and arch-shaped pools, transitions into fresh themes at every turn. Cleverly placed whimsical posts, cement planters, sculptures, and park benches create perfect vignettes for posing or just sitting. The bride and groom would be breathless keeping up with their wedding photographer, who will want to compose images from every angle.

Some 32,000 plants cover the gardens' twenty-three acres, originating from as far away as Australia, Africa, and the Himalayas, merging European horticulture with Denver's high-altitude climate and geography.

Despite its location in a semiarid climate, Denver Botanic Gardens has become a world leader in aquatic gardening, displaying more than 450 species and varieties of aquatic plants. Collectively the gardens are truly a global achievement with a distinctively Western slant, but these are only a few reasons why this site is recognized as one of the top five botanical gardens in the United States.

As a tribute to the beauty of the gardens, the staff in charge of rentals open their books in October for the following year and immediately get about 200 calls. Most of the garden areas can be used for ceremonies, with the exception of the Japanese Garden, which is considered a sacred meditation site. The Water Garden Gazebo, the South African Plaza, the Woodland Mosaic Garden, and the

Romantic Gardens are the most conducive for an outdoor wedding with seating.

The **Water Garden Gazebo** is the most intimate wedding site in the garden, with a capacity for fifteen guests on built-in benches. It borders the Japanese Garden and is almost completely surrounded by water, with a stunning view of a flowing fountain in the Monet Garden.

The **Woodland Mosaic Garden** is a lush, private area filled with fragrant flowers, tall trees, shrubs, and a wooden trellis at the garden's center that provides a beautiful setting for up to fifty seated guests. The two brick pathways leading into the garden can be blocked off from the public during the ceremony.

The **South African Plaza** is punctuated with plants that overflow from large cobalt-blue pots. Seating around a circular water feature with aquatic plants is for up to eighty guests. The **Romantic Gardens** have a long entrance under four arches and form the largest outdoor wedding site at the Denver Botanic Gardens, seating a maximum of 150 people. This wedding site can be sectioned off from the public and can accommodate a reception for up to 250 standing. Two picturesque gazebos can be used for acoustic musicians or singers.

Gates Hall, the newest facility—serving up to eighty people seated—features high ceilings, a view of the Community Gardens, a state-of-the-art lighting system, and fifteen 5-foot round tables. Just outside the hall is the **Gates Garden Court,** which seats sixty people at tables and features the same modern lighting and view.

The gardens have two more facilities for larger weddings, **Mitchell Hall** and the **Conservatory.** Mitchell Hall, located in the Education Building, can hold 350 people standing or 200 to 250 seated at the provided 8-foot banquet tables (rounds must be rented). The room features a curtained stage and a skylight for ambient lighting. Rental of the Conservatory includes Mitchell Hall, the Tropical Conservatory, and the Lobby Court, which has skylights over the fountain. The Tropical Conservatory's centerpiece is the Cloud Forest Tree, covered with orchids and epiphytes. Limited receptions, standing only, are allowed in the Tropical Conservatory, and in all cases guests will be able to meander through it at their leisure.

Denver Botanic Gardens
1005 York Street
Denver, CO 80206
Mail: 909 York Street, Denver, CO 80206
Information Desk: (720) 865–3585;
Facility rental (recording): (720)
865–3572; Facility Rental Coordinator:
(720) 865–3590
www.botanicgardens.org

Location: From Interstate 25 take the Sixth Avenue east exit (exit 209A). Go east on Sixth Avenue to Josephine Street, take a left onto Josephine Street, go 3.5 blocks, and turn left into the Denver Botanic Gardens (free) parking lot between Ninth and Tenth Streets.

Facility Rental, Amenities, and Policies: Wedding ceremonies are generally scheduled 9:00 A.M. to 7:00 P.M. daily. Rental fees for ceremony sites throughout the gardens range from $350 and $400 for the Water Garden to $1,000 for the Romantic Gardens. The Monet Deck and the Romantic Gardens can be rented for an after-hours reception Wednesday through Friday at a cost of $750 to $1,500. The garden venues do not have backup facilities in case of inclement weather, but the couple may rent tents to cover some of the areas.

The best indoor facilities, Gates Hall and

the Gates Garden Court, are available seven days a week from $400 to $900 for four to eight hours. Mitchell Hall is also available anytime from $2,165 to $3,165 for four to eight hours. The Conservatory is available after hours, Wednesday through Friday, for $2,700. Although out of reach for the typical destination wedding, the entire Denver Botanic Gardens can be rented for $11,000 to accommodate up to 2,500 people.

Discounts apply to those weddings that rent space for both the ceremony and the reception. Fees include free admission for guests, chairs when necessary, and a changing room for the bride. Some sites may not be available year-round. Reservations are made beginning the first week of October for the following year.

Catering: Three Tomatoes Catering (and its division, Cowtown Catering, for a western-style barbecue) is the exclusive caterer for the Denver Botanic Gardens. All food is prepared from scratch according to the selections of the couple. While the caterers pride themselves in providing any style cuisine, including preparing family recipes provided by their clients, they do have a list of menu items that has won them a nod from the locals, such as scampi in phyllo, petite smoked turkey and scones, prawns wrapped in pancetta with essence of rosemary, and open-faced tenderloin with fried onions. Three Tomatoes Catering is located at 2520 West Twenty-ninth Avenue, Denver, CO 80211 (303–433–3332; Fax 303–433–3929; www.three tomatoes.com).

Accommodations: Available in the greater Denver area.

LOVELAND SKI AREA
Georgetown, Colorado

Colorado has a number of glorious ski parks and resorts, and nearly all of them cater to weddings. (Two noteworthy wedding expeditions are Winter Park Resort, with its Ski Train and Zephyr chairlift; and Keystone Resort, with a gondola that takes the wedding party to the famous Alpenglow Stube restaurant.) We loved the simplicity of Loveland Ski Area's annual "Marry Me and Ski for Free" promotion. Every Valentine's Day some one hundred adventurous couples gather at 12,440 feet for what may be the world's highest mass wedding ceremony. The event is open to couples who wish to exchange or renew wedding vows.

Couples are required to pre-register at least three days before this event. After signing in on the morning of the event, they are asked to take the twelve-minute chairlift to the top by 11:30 A.M. The ceremony starts at noon sharp outside Ptarmigan Roost Cabin at the top of Chairlift 2 at Loveland Basin. The ceremony is performed en masse and lasts approximately half an hour. At the conclusion all participants and guests ski or ride down the mountain to the reception for food, music, prizes, and spirits. In years past the reception has started at 1:30 P.M. at the base of Loveland Basin.

The runs leading back to the base area from this point are beginner and intermediate. Participants and guests must be able to ride the lift up to the top and then ski down, or ride the lift back down the hill in order to attend the ceremony. There is no transportation up or down the mountain for those who cannot ski or snowboard.

Loveland Ski Area opened in 1936 with a single rope tow, doing business as the Loveland Ski Tow Company. It was the first major ski area in Colorado to make snow in 1967 with diesel compressors used by construction crews building the nearby Eisenhower Tunnel. Loveland, on the Continental Divide, provides 1,365 diverse acres of terrain and views from the highest chairlift in the world. It enjoys an annual average snow mass of 400 inches. Base elevation is 10,600 feet, with a summit elevation of 13,010 feet, and 12,700 feet served by ten lifts carrying two to four people. The longest run is 2 miles, with slightly more than 80 percent evenly divided between intermediate and advanced runs.

Loveland Ski Area
Box 899
Georgetown, CO 80444
(303) 571–5580
www.skiloveland.com/wedding

Location: Loveland Ski Area is 53 miles west of Denver, or 12 miles east of Silverthorne, at exit 216 off Interstate 70, and should not be confused with the city of Loveland north of Denver.

Facility Rental, Amenities, and Policies: Participating couples who complete the pre-registration form on the Web site will be eligible for the two-for-one lift tickets the day of the event, which otherwise run about $50. Pre-registration ends three days before the wedding ceremony.

Couples getting married are required to obtain a valid Colorado marriage license and need to bring it with them to the ceremony to be signed. They are encouraged to dress in appropriate "ski-wedding" attire in order to compete in a best-dressed-couple contest. One year a local jewelry company provided a fourteen-karat-yellow-gold Cleopatra bracelet with a retail value of $569 for the winners.

The official florist provides decorations for the reception and has offered discounted bouquets, boutonnieres, and corsages for interested couples. These arrangements can be made to order and will be waiting for you at Loveland Ski Area the day of the event. Prices vary for bouquets, but in the past corsages and boutonnieres were only $12. Sometimes the boutonniere is included free with purchase of a bouquet. Official photographers cover the event, taking pictures of the ceremony and reception, and of couples as they ski or snowboard down the hill, as well as formal portraits. These images are usually posted on a commercial Web site for purchase by interested couples.

Catering: The reception is free for all pre-registered couples and $15 per person for guests.

Accommodations: The Loveland Ski Area is near Georgetown, Empire, Idaho Springs, and Silver Plume, where lodging, good food, and shopping are available.

Keep in Mind: The wedding will not be rescheduled because of snow or cold weather, so be prepared! The Ptarmigan Roost Cabin is located at 12,440 feet, and dressing warmly is important even on a sunny day. Necessities include layered, water-resistant clothing, ski goggles, gloves, hat (don't forget the veil!), and sunblock. To help stave off altitude sickness, avoid salty foods a week before skiing, and drink plenty of water. If you have never skied or snowboarded before, consider taking a class at Loveland.

THE MANOR HOUSE RESTAURANT

Littleton, Colorado

The Manor House Restaurant will make both the bride *and* the groom happy. For the bride, the Victorian decor and stunning views of the Ken Caryl Valley create just the right mood for the ceremony and guests. For the groom—let's admit it here and now—it's the food. As Zagat asked in 2000, "When was the last time you ate like a feudal lord?"

The Manor House Restaurant is a beautifully restored American Georgian, southern-style mansion built in 1914. During its history the lords and ladies of this manor entertained such dignitaries as Presidents Theodore Roosevelt and William Howard Taft. John Shaffer, a Chicago newspaper magnate who created the *Rocky Mountain News,* built the original 8,000-square-foot Manor House for $100,000. The house sat on a 28,000-acre ranch he named for his two sons, Kent and Carroll. Over the century, the ranchland—which ran the first Hereford cattle in Colorado—became known as Ken Caryl. As a patron of Chicago's Opera House, Shaffer engaged opera companies to perform at the Denver Auditorium and housed the cast at the manor.

This historic house was opened as a restaurant by the Peterson brothers in December 1990, with the utmost care taken to preserve the original architectural intent. The 105-foot flagpole behind the Manor House has a light at the top that was originally battery operated. The light could be seen from Denver through the saddle of the Dakota Hogback as an invitation to Shaffer's friends to "come on out." The lamppost is still illuminated.

The Manor House has two beautiful garden areas for outdoor ceremonies, and two cozy fireplace rooms for more intimate weddings, as well as private rooms and enclosed sunporches open year-round. Reception accommodations include 200 guests for a sit-down dinner, 150 for buffet, and 225 in the outdoor patio or tented area. All rentals include tables, chairs, linens, and dishes. Depending on the size of the wedding and the season, a couple can rent the entire house and grounds, or just the lower half of the house, with or without adjoining patios and tents.

The Manor House Restaurant
1 Manor House Road
Littleton, CO 80127
(303) 973–8064
www.themanorhouserestaurant.com

Location: Twenty-five minutes west of downtown Denver; 1.5 miles west of the Ken Caryl Road exit off Colorado Highway 470.

Facility Rental, Amenities, and Policies: Daytime rentals (9:00 A.M. to 3:00 P.M.) are $1,000 to $2,500, with a food and beverage minimum of $2,500 to $6,000, depending on whether the bridal party is renting half a house, the whole house, or the house and grounds. Evening rentals (after 3:30 P.M.) are $1,800 for the house to $3,000 for the house and grounds, with up to an $8,000 food and beverage minimum.

The smallest group the Manor House has accommodated is a wedding party of twelve. The minimum charge for wedding ceremonies with fewer than sixty people held at the Manor House is $500. This guarantees a private garden area, front porch, or fireplace room for your ceremony. To have a private dining room for your group, for a special evening, a $200 charge applies. These fees are contingent upon purchase of food and beverage from the Manor House and do not apply if renting a half-house package or whole-house package. These smaller packages are not available on Saturday evening during peak wedding season (mid-May through mid-September). However, discounts on the whole-house rental rate will be given during the off-season, January through April.

Catering: Called one of "the 200 most romantic and prestigious restaurants in America," the Manor House lets wedding guests dine like presidents, industry chiefs, and opera divas. If ordering from the menu, may we suggest starting with escargots and Stilton cheese, or Manila clams steeped in white wine and habanero aioli. The lobster pasta and the chateaubriand of beef tenderloin with shiitake mushrooms look good.

Hot and cold hors d'oeuvres start at $3.50 per person, with a $21.00-per-person price on groups serving just hors d'oeuvres. Buffets, including brunch, lunch, and dinner, start at $40 to $58 per person and include such entrees as baked stuffed salmon with a wild mushroom duxelle wrapped in puff pastry. Lunches, with a minimum of twenty orders, are $25 to $28 per person; dinners are $30 to $40. Dessert is chef's choice; if you have your own cake delivered, the cutting fee is $1.50 per person.

Accommodations: Lodging is available in the Greater Denver area, the closest options being in Lakewood and Golden.

RED ROCKS PARK AND AMPHITHEATRE
Morrison, Colorado

The Red Rocks Park and Amphitheatre 15 miles west of Denver is considered the eighth geological wonder of the world. Hundreds of musicians—from Asia to ZZ Top—have played in the natural arena bordered by two rusted monoliths the height of Niagara Falls: Ship Rock and Creation Rock. Over the past 250 million years, give or take, gradual earth movement slowly raised the great sandstone ledges from the prehistoric ocean floor to form the acoustic walls of the amphitheater, some sloping as much as ninety degrees, others tilting backward. Concertgoers enjoy a panoramic view of the Denver skyline with the Rocky Mountains at their backs.

The rock formations began as an entertainment venue in the early 1900s when John Brisben Walker produced a number of concerts on a temporary platform between Ship and Creation Rocks. In 1927 the city of Denver purchased the Red Rocks area from Walker and began planning an amphitheater on the foundation he had laid. Labor and materials were funded by the Civilian Conservation Corps (CCC) and the Works Progress Administration (WPA). After the first annual Easter sunrise service took place there in 1947, the 10,000-capacity Red Rocks Amphitheatre began attracting big-name entertainers to its stage. More recent concerts have been broadcast on PBS, including those by John Tesh and Yanni.

The new 30,000-square-foot Burnham Hoyt Visitor Center provides a different kind of venue for weddings, which includes an unlikely blend of rocks and rock stars. The center was built at the top of the amphitheater seating, but beneath the surface, out of the line of sight for concertgoers and performers, thus preserving the look and feel of the 1941 venue. The center offers interactive, educational displays featuring the geological and musical history of Red Rocks, as well as a short film that documents the people, the performers, and the physics that create this spot's essence. The Performers Hall of Fame showcases many historic performances. The visitor center is accessible for people with disabilities and is open seven days a week.

Red Rocks Park has several venues appropriate for weddings. The **Rock Room** in the visitor center, accommodating 200 to 250, was built around a red rock formation that actually serves as an altar for some ceremonies. Sliding glass doors lead to the **Lower Terrace** (accommodating 200 to 300-plus), and the view of the valley from the terrace serves as a breathtaking backdrop for ceremonies and receptions.

The **Ship Rock Grille** can be closed for an informal reception for sixty to one hundred, and has an adjoining patio (with a view) for outdoor seating, cocktails, and staging between events. The **Sierra Room** is used as a backup in case of inclement weather, for which Denver is famous, and larger events can take place on the **Upper Terrace** overlooking the amphitheater.

The Pueblo-style **Trading Post** on the road below the amphitheater offers an intimate garden-framed lawn for ceremonies and barbecues, with an up-close view of the valley and the red rock formations in the vicinity. It can accommodate

150 to 225 for standing receptions and seated dinners.

Since the visitor center opened in spring 2003, the park has booked about 200 events per year, of which 60 to 80 have been weddings.

Red Rocks Park and Visitor Center Special Events
18300 West Alameda Parkway
Morrison, CO 80465
(303) 697–6047
www.redrocksonline.com

Location: Red Rocks Amphitheatre is located in Red Rocks Park near Morrison, 15 miles west of Denver.

Facility Rental, Amenities, and Policies: Ceremonies without receptions are held at the Trading Post garden for $495.00, plus a rental fee of $2.00 per chair. Ceremonies with receptions are based on food and beverage minimums: $1,500 for the Grille, and $5,000 to $6,000 for the Rock Room, Trading Post, and the Upper Terrace, for a four-hour event. Minimums for the Lower Terrace are calculated per event.

Catering: The Red Rocks Park and Amphitheatre is operated by the City and County of Denver Department of Theaters and Arenas, which has an exclusive service contract with ARAMARK Corporation for private event planning and catering. Seated luncheons and buffets are $14.50 to $26.50 per person. Dinner buffets run $38.50 to $48.50 per person, and dinner entrees $22.00 to $42.00 plus up to $6.25 for various salads. The Red Rock Moonlight Buffet, at $38.50 per person, includes roasted pear and Maytag blue cheese salad, achiote niçoise salad, sun-dried tomato and fresh rosemary potato salad, seasonal vegetables, chilaca chile seared salmon with pesto cream, carved adobo breast of turkey with avocado aioli, and cheesecake or mini pastry assortment. ARAMARK also offers "build-your-own" buffets for $35 to $55 per person, as well as a variety of specialty and carving stations. Culinary attendants and extra wait staff are an additional fee.

Extras: Valet parking by several private companies is available for an additional fee, except during concerts, when the wedding party and guests must use the same parking as concertgoers.

Accommodations: Lodging and campgrounds are available in the Greater Denver area.

Keep in Mind: The amphitheater's busy concert season is from the end of May through September. October is the most popular month for weddings and books out early. It is possible to book a wedding on the day of an amphitheater event, but not necessarily recommended. If an alternate date is not acceptable, the couple might consider booking a morning wedding and afternoon reception on event days. If the park's management books an event after a wedding has been booked, ARAMARK will attempt to reschedule the wedding or refund the deposit. The Ship Rock Grille cannot be booked for a private event on the day of a concert. Private booking is examined on a case-by-case basis. The Red Rocks Park and Amphitheatre is also used as recreational area for bikers, hikers, and the like.

ANDREWS MEMORIAL CHAPEL
Dunedin, Florida

Andrews Memorial Chapel is a tribute to early-Victorian church architecture, to the local shipbuilding industry, and to the rich Scottish American heritage of the founding fathers of its home in Dunedin, Florida. Dunedin (pronounced *done-ee-din*) became one of Florida's chief seaport and trading centers early in its history, thanks to a dock built to accommodate schooners and sloops as well as to the ingenuity of pioneers from Georgia and Scotland. At one time Dunedin had the largest fleet of sailing vessels in Florida.

Florida's sacred relationship with the water is evident in the construction of Andrews Memorial Chapel, which was hand-crafted from 1886 through 1888, using the shipbuilding techniques of the era. Crafted of native heart pine, the nautically shaped beamed ceiling, styled like a ship's hull, was completely hand carved. A carpenter, believing that only God can build a perfect church, left one beam unfinished. The chapel has two foyers with Gothic archways leading into the sanctuary. The pews, also hand carved, are 17 feet long, and the Tiffany-style stained-glass window over the pulpit is original.

The story of Andrews Memorial Chapel begins with the 1876 construction of an earlier structure located on what is now a cemetery. While that first chapel was being built, the son of congregant John Andrews died riding to meet his fiancée during a violent storm. Andrews donated $200 toward building costs, provided the chapel would be named in his son's memory.

When the population of the area moved closer to downtown Dunedin, a new chapel was built on the corner of Scotland and Highland Streets ten years after the original church was built. This new chapel—the one we know today—carried the Andrews

Memorial name. Andrews Memorial Chapel was moved in 1926 to make way for the First Presbyterian Church of Dunedin. The old Andrews Memorial was preserved, though it was moved two more times, passed around like an elderly aunt. Facing demolition in 1970, it was given to the newly formed Dunedin Historical Society provided the society paid for yet another move. The city of Dunedin permitted the chapel to be moved to its present location near the entrance of Hammock Park. The building was literally cut in half in order to be moved, and restoration began in 1974. At that time the chapel was added to the National Register of Historic Places, and it is now nondenominational.

We spoke with the delightful Linda Sanders, who has worked for the chapel for eight years and does everything regarding weddings—including "pushing the Hoover around." One year the officiant (and close friend) passed away about an hour before the ceremony was to start. Sanders found someone else to officiate, and the wedding commenced on time without the bride and groom knowing what had transpired.

After recent renovations, Sanders says the chapel, though "beautiful before, is now extraordinary." Wedding parties number from four (with Sanders serving as witness) to full capacity. The chapel hosts as many as six weddings on a weekend, and it is recommended that these be booked a year in advance. One woman loved the chapel so much, she married there four times!

While Dunedin has a small-town image, it is actually a bustling city of 37,000 residents, and there are plenty of wedding vendors in the area. One of the oldest towns on the west coast of Florida, it has a wooded and subtropical setting with nearly 4 miles of picturesque waterfront, a relaxed lifestyle, and activities for all tastes and ages. Dunedin's quality of life is linked to its appreciation of its diverse and colorful past, and to the country that helped shape its future, Scotland. In commemoration of its ancestral ties, Dunedin chose Stirling, Scotland, as its sister city.

Andrews Memorial Chapel
1899 San Mateo Drive
P.O. Box 2393
Dunedin, FL 34698
www.andrewsmemorialchapel.com

Location: Just minutes from Clearwater, take Bayshore Drive (Alternate U.S. Highway 19); turn east onto Mira Vista Drive, then north onto San Mateo.

Facility Rental, Amenities, and Policies: The fee for a three-hour wedding and one-hour rehearsal is $428 with tax. The seating capacity is approximately 130 people on twenty-one pews. A pump organ, keyboard, unity candle stand, and flower pillars are available. The chapel caretakers state unequivocally—and this is emphasized in block letters—that the bride and groom designate someone to be in charge of cleaning up after the ceremony. No alcohol is permitted, and the staff asks couples not to have a receiving line, which delays the use of the chapel for the next party and wastes electricity by letting the air-conditioning escape through open doors.

Catering: Catering is not permitted at the chapel, but the staff suggests Bon Appetite Restaurant (150 Marina Plaza, Dunedin, FL 34698; 727–733–2151; Fax: 727–738–2811), located at the Best Western Yacht Harbor Inn. Bon Appetite is a four-star restaurant with casual dining waterside, fine dining, and a banquet and catering staff. Choice of prime rib or the chicken Oscar stuffed with crabmeat is $27 per person, for example.

Accommodations: The Best Western Yacht Harbor Inn (150 Marina Plaza, Dunedin, FL 34698-5703; 727–733–4121; Fax: 727–736–4365) is a waterfront resort on Florida's west coast. Located at Dunedin's Marina Plaza, the Inn overlooks beautiful St. Joseph's Sound and offers vacationers a friendly port with immediate access to the open Gulf. Each of the hotel's 55 rooms face the water, and most rooms include kitchen facilities. Charter boats are available at the marina for sightseeing and for gulf deep-sea fishing. Rooms start at $85.

CASA DE SOLANA
St. Augustine, Florida

Recommendations for Casa de Solana as a wedding destination came from several sources. As with most places in St. Augustine Antigua, history and romance converge here. But antiquity and beauty aren't the only reasons so many couples have begun their married lives on the property over the years. The attraction, more specifically, is the hospitality of owner and innkeeper Joe Finnegan. Finnegan, with his wife, Margaret, also owns the St. Francis Inn, claimed to be the nation's oldest continuously operated inn, and has built a reputation in St. Augustine as an excellent innkeeper for the past twenty years.

Casa de Solana Bed & Breakfast Inn takes its name from the original owner, St. Augustine native Manuel Lorenzo Solana. When Spain traded Florida to Great Britain in exchange for newly acquired Havana in 1763, Don Solana was one of only eight men—all mounted dragoons of the Spanish army—who was permitted to remain in St. Augustine. He stayed during the twenty-year British period helping to settle Spanish property claims, including some of his family's holdings along Aviles Street. Many St. Augustine natives today can trace their lineage back to Don Manuel Solana; one account describes his home as a place where Native Americans received kindness and protection.

That tradition of hospitality continues.

Records show a tabby house on the Casa de Solana site as early as 1764. Solana constructed the part of the house that is now the bed-and-breakfast between 1803 and 1820. As is typical of most of St. Augustine structures, the house was built of coquina stone, and remnants of its original construction are still visible, including pegged beams, colonial windowpanes, double-crossed doors, and handmade bricks. A 6.5-foot wall, built during the British period, runs along Aviles Street and the south side of the property, creating the peaceful courtyard where weddings take place.

Casa de Solana's new De Palma House, designed with weddings in mind, is open to the inn's private-walled courtyard. Mary Mitchell's Room, on the first level of the De Palma House, boasts state-of-the-art features camouflaged by historic decor. It can accommodate seated dinners or buffets.

At Casa de Solana a courtyard ceremony, coupled with a reception in Mary Mitchell's Room, can involve up to thirty-two people. If a larger wedding is desired, a reception for up to seventy-five people can be held at the nearby St. Augustine Art Center or Llambias House and Garden following a courtyard ceremony at Casa de

Solana. St. Francis Inn (800–824–6062; www.stfrancisinn.com) is perfect for small weddings of up to sixteen people and includes a dressing room and reception areas.

As St. Augustine enthusiast Kellie Sharpe said, "The only thing wrong with having your wedding at the inn is you would also want to stay there, and that would negate you arriving in a horse-drawn carriage for the ceremony."

Casa de Solana
21 Aviles Street
St. Augustine, FL
(888) 796–0980
www.casadesolana.com

Location: In the historic district 1 block from the Atlantic Ocean.

Facility Rental, Amenities, and Policies: Each wedding at any of the venues is so unique, Finnegan does not offer fixed wedding packages. He and his staff sit down with each bride and groom to customize their wedding. Prices vary depending on group size, menu selections, lodging, and individual requests. However, in a telephone interview, he did tell us that the average wedding numbers fourteen to twenty-five people, and weddings with reception aver-

age a reasonable $2,000 to $3,000, although one or two weddings have reached $25,000. Most of the weddings are small, and ceremonies start at around $250.

Catering: Weddings at the Finnegan properties include the following options: rehearsal dinner, location for a ceremony, wedding officiants, catered reception (seated or buffet style), full or limited bar, and contacts for music, flowers, and photographer. They will even bake the wedding cake!

No outside catering is allowed.

Accommodations: Casa de Solana has 10 guest rooms (9 if Mary Mitchell's Room is used for your function). If a weekend wedding includes more than nine guests, then lodging is required for guests for a minimum of two nights. For smaller weddings (up to nine people), lodging is required only for the bride and groom. If the group can fill more than half of the inn's rooms, the marrying couple is required to book the entire inn. Many of these guidelines can usually be waived for midweek weddings with no Saturday involved. (With reasonable guest room rates starting at $119 to $250 and a two-course breakfast, who wouldn't want to stay here?) No lodging discounts are given for weekend weddings (since the inn would be booked in any event).

CASA YBEL RESORT

Sanibel Island, Florida

Casa Ybel came into being by happenstance. Back in 1889 the Reverend George Barnes's boat became stranded on Sanibel Island off Florida's western coast. Turning shipwreck into fortune, he claimed 480 acres on which he built Sanibel's first home, church, and cottage, which he named The Sisters honoring his two daughters. The Sisters cottage evolved into a thirty-room inn, eventually becoming Casa

Ybel Hotel, and a full-service resort by the 1920s. One daughter married a resort guest, and as a wedding gift he built her a grand waterfront Victorian home named Thistle Lodge. The lodge drew a number of celebrities and statesmen of the day, including their Fort Myers neighbors Thomas Edison and Henry Ford. After Thistle Lodge became run down, new owners re-created the building not far from its original site in 1979, but it remained the social heart of the island community. Originally a wedding gift, this Casa Ybel's restaurant today hosts 200 weddings a year.

Sanibel Island lies just far enough off the trampled touristways to remain pristine yet easily accessible, and the locals keep it that way with more than 70 percent pre-served. The J. N. "Ding" Darling National Wildlife Refuge (named for a 1930s editorial cartoonist) protects the habitat of the alligator, manatee, bald eagle, river otter, roseate spoonbill, and more than 200 other bird species. Sanibel's east–west orientation catches shells washed up from the Caribbean, earning it a reputation as the shelling capital of the United States.

Casa Ybel Resort itself is situated on twenty-three acres fronted by lawns and a natural, shell-studded sand beach. In its early life as a resort, guests hunted, fished, collected seashells, and strolled down a stretch of beach then known as the Grand Boulevard. Over the century owners pre-served Casa Ybel's corner of the island as a sheltered retreat. Upholding its long-standing reverence toward nature, Casa Ybel main-tains its own sanctuary, where cormorants, ibises, ospreys, pelicans, sanderlings, and other birds come to feed and rest in Florida's friendly climate. Now owned by the Shellabargers family, the resort is among the top spots to stay in the world.

Most of the weddings at this rustic, his-toric place tend be casually elegant. Whether you choose as your backdrop the private, shell-carpeted beach, the beachfront lawn, or the gazebo overlooking the lagoon, the staff at Casa Ybel Resort can create an inti-mate dream wedding. Weddings can range from 7 to 300, or even just 2.

The Intimate Wedding Package was designed to accommodate twenty or fewer guests and includes an officiant to perform the ceremony, elegant torches or columns to demarcate an altarlike area, a bridal bouquet and boutonniere, a champagne toast, and a selection of four-course dinners. Staff will arrange a Utica poled canopy, gold Chavari chairs, and a royal runner for the occasion.

For larger weddings the catering and coor-dination team draws on years of experience to help the couple in the selection and realiza-tion of the ultimate wedding and reception theme. Plated and buffet wedding dinner packages include the ceremony site, cere-mony chairs, champagne toast, three-hour open bar, and wedding cake. Receptions take place in an upper-story room of the lodge where guests can view the Gulf through large windows, or beneath a tent on the lawn. October, November, March, and April are the busiest seasons, but no time is slow. The contract mentions a $500 backup ceremony fee in case of inclement weather, but it has never been enforced. Jessica Pasek, a sales coordinator on staff, said she wouldn't dream of charging guests to come in out of the rain.

Casa Ybel Resort
2255 West Gulf Drive
Sanibel Island, FL 33957
(800) 276–4753 or (239) 472–3145
www.casaybelresort.com
www.casaybelweddings.com

Location: Twenty minutes from Fort Myers Airport, with a $3.00 toll on Sanibel Causeway.

Facility Rental, Amenities, and Policies: Packages are all-inclusive and cost is determined by the catering and the number of people involved in the wedding event.

Catering: Buffet and plated dinners are $125 to $160 per person and include a choice of three butler-passed hors d'oeuvres for the cocktail reception, three salads, soups, vegetables, and three entrees. Carving stations can be added to any of the buffet packages.

A $160-per-person buffet might consist of butler passed char-grilled shrimp skewers, lobster medallions with osetra caviar, and wild mushroom strudel; tropical fresh fruit, handpicked spinach salad with caramelized onions, baked apples, dry salt ricotta and house-made lemon-leek vinaigrette, and Thistle Lodge's own Caesar salad; Asian barbecued duck with hoisin sauce and crispy noodles, mustard-crusted salmon with red wine butter sauce, and roasted tenderloin of beef carved by a chef. Save room for the premium wedding cake accompanied by a rich assortment of chocolate truffles.

Accommodations: Casa Ybel Resort has 114 one- and two-bedroom suites with living room, fully equipped kitchen, and screened terrace or balcony views of the Gulf. Suites start at $275 per night. The resort also offers time shares.

Keep in Mind: Winters are mild (average daytime temperatures in the seventies and eighties) and it rains just enough to keep the islands lush. Summer temperatures, ranging from the eighties to low nineties, are tempered by cooling sea breezes and brief afternoon showers, followed by more sunshine and glorious sunsets.

EDISON AND FORD WINTER ESTATES

Fort Myers, Florida

Inventor Thomas Edison said, "I find out what the world needs, then I try to invent it." If necessity is the mother of invention, then Florida must be its inspirational father. It is at his Florida chemical laboratory that workers helped Edison in his research on goldenrod as a source for natural rubber. The laboratory is part of the Edison and Ford Winter Estates, and the weddings that take place here are equally inspired by their environment along this lush riverfront property.

Thomas Edison first fell in love with the acreage on the Caloosahatchee River in 1885. He and a friend, Ezra Gillilland, built mirror homes—the Seminole Lodge and the Mangoes—next door to each other, with a laboratory installed on Edison's estate. Edison purchased the Mangoes in 1906 for use as a guest cottage. His lifelong friend Henry Ford, the legendary automobile maker, stayed there frequently until he bought it from Edison in 1915. Edison and Ford spent many winters working, talking, and even relaxing together—if you can believe it—in tropical southwestern Florida.

As Edison said, there is only one Fort Myers, and ninety million people are going to find out about it. Perhaps he was referring to the natural beauty of the area, or perhaps the revolutionary work he and Ford did there together. Whatever the case, when you visit Seminole Lodge and the Mangoes, you enter a world unlike any you have ever seen. The furnishings and architecture of these gracious, rambling buildings are reminiscent of a bygone era. Circling the homes are large overhanging porches, which, combined with French doors on the first floor, provide a cool breeze through the home at all times. The electric chandeliers, "electroliers," were designed by Edison and handmade of brass in his own workshop.

Edison's tropical botanical garden, one of the most complete in America, contains more than 1,000 varieties of plants imported from all over the world, including African sausage trees and a banyan tree that was a gift from Harvey Firestone in 1925. Edison was interested in the various products and by-products of the plants, which he used in many of his scientific investigations. His wife later planted roses, orchids, and bromeliads, among others.

Ford's home is situated on three and a half acres of prime waterfront property with a beautiful view of the Caloosahatchee. Wedding ceremonies are conducted among a forest of mature trees, including a citrus grove and a natural aisle of royal palm trees. An assortment of bamboo, pine, oak, and many others provide a beautiful Old Southwest Florida tropical paradise. From the simplest ceremony to the grandest, wedding locations include the Royal Palm Allée, Moonlight Garden, Coconut Garden and Lily Pond, Riverside Garden, and Banyan Tree and Garden Café. The staff work closely with the bride and groom to match the location to the type and size of the event.

The Edison and Ford Winter Estates, joined by a walkway, encompass the two historic homes, the laboratory, a museum housing Edison's inventions, a museum store, a garden shop, an outdoor cafe, and three electric launches for cruising the river.

Edison and Ford Winter Estates
2350 McGregor Boulevard
Fort Myers, FL 33901
(239) 334–7419
Special Events Department: (941) 461–2686
www.edison-ford-estate.com

Location: On the Caloosahatchee River off Cleveland Avenue in Fort Myers.

Facilty Rental, Amenities, and Policies:
Rental of the Ford Estate for an outdoor ceremony and reception is $3,000 for up to 400 people. The rental fee includes use of the Ford grounds the day of the wedding for four hours, 6:00 to 10:00 P.M.; a wedding rehearsal on the Ford property the evening before the wedding, usually 5:00 to 6:00 P.M. unless otherwise booked; and use of the Edison and Ford Winter Estates property for the purpose of a formal portrait sitting (scheduled through the special-events department). The ceremony-only rental package is for two hours, 6:00 to 8:00 P.M., and is scaled at $250 for ten people or less, $450 for eleven to thirty people, and $1,500 for more than thirty-one people. This package includes everything included the four-hour wedding and reception package. The estates exist for the benefit of the public, which may place constraints on use of the property as well as effect its availability for a wedding. There also may be additional costs. Staff members are available to protect the estates' facilities and contents, answer questions, and help coordinate, but will not be available to carry equipment or be involved in preparation, setup, or teardown of the event. These tasks must be provided by the couple. A million-dollar liability insurance policy is required, and the couple might also need to hire extra security for larger events. Security, a housekeeper, a

groundskeeper, an electrician, and staff representative of the estates will be on hand during the event.

Extras: Guests are given free admission to the Edison and Ford Winter Estates on the day of the wedding, and the bride and groom receive two annual passes to the estates as a wedding gift.

Catering: Catering and rentals for furniture, tents, and the like are handled through an approved vendor list.

Accommodations: Available in the Fort Myers area.

Keep in Mind: No parking is available at the Ford property itself, and only vendor vehicles are permitted at the Ford Home. Guests may park at the Edison and Ford Winter Estates' lot and walk to the Ford Home.

HISTORIC BOK SANCTUARY
Lake Wales, Florida

Historic Bok Sanctuary, with its meandering gardens and hidden Singing Tower, has been characterized as a storybook place, but the stories are personal. Some couples marry at the sanctuary because it was where their grandparents had spent their first date. Others visited with family, friends, and on school field trips, and always considered it a very special place. One mother gave her daughter as a wedding present an album of pictures taken of her at the sanctuary over the years.

Perhaps it is fitting, then, that the gardens were donated as a gift of appreciation by Dutch immigrant Edward W. Bok to the American people. Born in 1863, Bok had come to this country at the age of six, and eventually became an influential editor of the *Ladies' Home Journal,* Pulitzer Prize–winning author, humanitarian, philanthropist, and advocate for world peace and the environment. In the 1920s, after his retirement, he set out to create an Eden in Lake Wales, enlisting the expertise of landscape architect Frederick Law Olmsted Jr. (son of the creator of New York's Central Park). The result is subtle, almost ethereal: The bark-chip-covered paths through the woods invoke reflective moments; the vistas are contemplative and softly romantic. In his book *The Other Orlando,* author Kelly Monaghan said of architect Milton B. Medary's magical Singing Tower with its sixty-bell carillon: "It's as if you have come upon a magical remnant of an ancient city in a storybook land, part cathedral, part castle keep."

Couples are given a choice of three natural settings within the sanctuary for their wedding: The White Garden, St. Francis Garden, and Exedra. The tower is visible above the trees from the **White Garden,** and the reflection pool can be seen behind the lush green foliage and delicate white blossoms. Four benches located in this garden invite guests to sit, and a canopy formed by tall shade trees and various palms creates an atmosphere of sheer beauty and tranquility. Just a short stroll from the education and visitor center, **St. Francis Garden** has two benches, and is bordered by a carpet of colorful blooms on one side and towering live oak trees on the other. Azaleas burst forth a sea of bright colors at their peak, providing a vibrant background to the wedding ceremony and photographs. The **Exedra,** a semicircular seating area, is located on the western edge of Iron Mountain, the highest point in peninsular Florida. This charming structure is built of the same marble as the tower and stands opposite an overlook that offers spectacular views to the west. Given as a gift by Edward Bok's neighbors in Mountain Lake, it offers seating for ten people on either side. This green lush area has large shade trees.

A choice of three wedding times is offered, and all ceremonies must begin at exactly one of these times: 9:00 A.M., 11:00 A.M., and 1:00 P.M. Consider timing the ceremony to begin or end with the playing of the carillon preprogrammed music: The minute-long Scherzo (Suite III for carillon) is played before each hour strike; "For the Beauty of Earth" is played at 9:00 A.M.; "Chartres" at 11:00 A.M.; and "How Great Thou Art" at 1:00 P.M. Musicians and a cappella singers may be brought in, but not amplified.

Couples may also wish to time their wedding with the blooming of their favorite flowers: Brazilian plume and impatiens bloom year-round. Spring weddings are popular, especially when the azaleas are in bloom, along with cape honeysuckle, gardenias, japonica camellias, nun's orchids, and magnolias. Autumn is also popular, when American beautyberry, golden rain tree, java glorybower, salvia, sasanqua camellias, and wildflowers bloom. American holly, calla lily, camellias, flame vine, and pansies play in winter. Summer flowers are also beautiful, but this is not a popular season for weddings because of the heat and humidity. Many of the one hundred weddings performed at Bok Sanctuary every year are for couples from the United Kingdom, where they love their gardens.

Historic Bok Sanctuary includes an exhibit hall and museum, the Carillon Café (seating eight patrons) and gift shop, and the Pine Ridge Preserve Trail. It is adjacent to Pinewood Estate, also open to tours.

Historic Bok Sanctuary
1151 Tower Boulevard
Lake Wales, FL 33853
(863) 676–1408
www.boksanctuary.org

Location: Fifty-five miles southwest of Orlando off U.S. Highway 17A, also called Burns Avenue.

Facility Rental, Amenities, and Policies:
Fees are $300 for weddings involving ten people or fewer, $500 for eleven to fifty people, and $800 for fifty-one to one hundred. (Numbers include the wedding party.) The fee includes admission for the wedding party and guests, and a one-year duo membership as a newlywed gift. A host guides guests to the setting and remains during the ceremony. A private bridal salon is also provided. Transportation from the parking area is available for the bride and her attendants, as well as for the elderly and physically challenged. A maximum of ten chairs will be set out for these more frail guests. The fee also includes the photography opportunities within the sanctuary before or after the ceremony. (If the couple marry elsewhere, they may do their photography at the Sanctuary for an $80 fee.) The couple is offered the opportunity to conduct a rehearsal by appointment only, and will receive complimentary admission for up to fifteen people for the rehearsal.

Having a wedding at Bok Sanctuary precludes the need for arches, runners, potted plants, and candles, and therefore these are not permitted. As with all natural environments, great care must be taken to not damage the setting.

Catering: Alcohol and receptions are not permitted at Historic Bok Sanctuary. Less than ten minutes away is the legendary Chalet Suzanne Restaurant overlooking Lake Suzanne. The Bavarian–themed chalet was built by the Hinshaw family more than seven decades ago and sits on a sprawling seventy-acre estate surrounded by orange groves. The chalet is flanked with courtyards, fountains, turrets, spires, and steeples. The wedding meal includes the restaurant's signature broiled grapefruit with chicken liver canapé and cream of romaine soup, choice of chicken Suzanne, baked sugar-cured ham, or king crab Thermidor, and wedding cake. Chalet Suzanne is located at 3800 Chalet Suzanne Drive, Lake Wales, FL 33859 (800–433–6011; www.chaletsuzanne .com).

Accommodations: Some lodging is available in the Lake Wales and New Haven area.

Keep in Mind: The Historic Bok Sanctuary was hit hard by Hurricane Charlie in August 2004, but thanks to an army of volunteers was able to reopen a month later—though complete reconstruction has been a slow process.

HOYT HOUSE
Amelia Island, Florida

Amelia Island, named for the daughter of King George II of England, is one of America's few remaining unspoiled island paradises—population fewer than 60,000. The birthplace of the shrimp industry, Amelia is the northernmost of Florida's Atlantic barrier islands, just half an hour from the Jacksonville airport. The island is 18 square miles of white sand beaches, hundred-year-old moss-covered oaks, and 40-foot sand dunes. Magnolia-lined streets are home to dozens of stately mansions preserved right down to the tiniest detail. Among them is Hoyt House Bed & Breakfast Inn—we're talking rocking chairs on wraparound porches, lazy ceiling fans, down quilt comforters, shade trees, breezes from the ocean just blocks away, and complimentary wine and cheese in the late afternoon. The inn is located in the historic district with many fine restaurants within a short walking distance.

Built on Centre Street in 1905, this modified, pale yellow Queen Anne, with its tall bay windows, was modeled (on a smaller scale) after the Rockefeller "Indian Mound" Cottage on Jekyll Island. Banker Fred Hoyt and his family resided here until his death in 1925. Only two more owners occupied the mansion until 1992, and today it is operated by Ron and Holli Franzese. Over the past century each owner worked to preserve the authentic and beautiful detail of the mansion's original architecture. Inside, inviting rooms show off antique and reproduction furniture; walls are painted in rich hues.

An acre of gardens and spacious lawns, with gazebo, terrace, and bandstand, become host to tastefully elegant wedding celebrations. Indoor events take place in yesteryear surroundings of the parlor and formal dining room, complete with beautiful linen, china, and glassware. Whether you wish to share an informal service in the garden with a few friends and family or prefer a more formal service followed by dining and dancing under the stars, the staff can customize your event.

The gardens can accommodate up to sixty guests seated, and up to a hundred for a cocktail party or standing reception. Indoor events provide seating or cocktail/buffet service for twenty. Amelia Island enjoys tropical weather most of the year, which means generous amounts of sun and rain are always factors to be considered. For protection against the elements and peace of mind, tents are required for all table-and-chair events and those with thirty or more guests. The gazebo and bandstand are wired for musical instruments or sound system; outdoor amplified music may be played until 10:00 P.M. A grand piano and a CD stereo system are available for indoor use until 8:00 P.M.

Hoyt House
804 Atlantic Avenue
Amelia Island, FL 32034
(800) 432–2085 or (904) 277–4300
www.hoythouse.com

Location: Hoyt House is in Fernandina Beach, exit 373 off Interstate 95, across the Intracoastal Waterway on the Thomas Shave Bridge.

Facility Rental, Amenities, and Policies: Hoyt House offers several packages that provide the basic structure for the event, to which the bride and groom may add custom elements such as tents, tables, linen, dishes, fans, or lighting for an outdoor event; flowers and decorations; photography; music, catering, or event planning; and a ceremony officiant.

The Celebration House Party package is $5,000 for groups of thirty to fifty. It includes unlimited use of the garden for outdoor seating, ten guest rooms with two nights' accommodations for up to twenty guests, and two Hoyt House bathrobes for the bridal couple. The Small House Party package is $2,550 for ten to thirty people, and includes three hours' use of the garden, five guest rooms for two nights for up to ten people, and champagne for the bridal couple.

The Hoyt House has smaller packages for intimate garden weddings in the company of just a few friends. For a wedding involving seating for up to twenty guests for two hours in the garden and gazebo area, the fee is less than $700; a one-hour wedding with no seating is $450, plus $15 per person for a cake-and-champagne reception ($75 minimum) if preferred. The use of the Hoyt House parlor and dining room for three hours is $450 ($350 if the ceremony is outdoors). This includes place settings, table linen, and glassware for twenty guests. A lovely wedding-and-honeymoon package for just the bride and groom costs less than $1,000. It includes a private ceremony performed by a local officiant, bridal bouquet and groom's boutonniere, champagne in the garden, a restaurant gift certificate, and two nights' accommodations in the Superior Suite (based on availability).

Event consultants on staff are available to discuss all details, from menu planning to makeup and hair. However, the Hoyt House recommends that a couple planning their wedding long-distance retain a professional wedding consultant.

Catering: The staff can assist with catering, or couples may provide their own professional caterer. After reservations are booked, Hoyt House staff can obtain pricing for catering upon receipt of a fully planned menu, service plan, and confirmation of the number of invited guests. Guests may be served banquet or buffet style, at specialty food stations, by waiters with passed trays, or at a sit-down meal.

Extras: Hoyt House can provide a welcome supper for wedding guests, a river cruise, fishing and golf outings, or even a caricature artist as part of a celebration.

Accommodations: The couple may be required to rent a minimum number of two-night guest room accommodations at the Hoyt House depending on the size of the wedding party. This provides some space and privacy for a bridal party the evening before the ceremony, as well as changing areas for bride, groom, and their

attendants; it also gives guests access to restroom facilities while they are on the grounds. The 10 guest rooms are $139 to $209; 3 of them have space for a third person for $35.

LITTLE PALM ISLAND RESORT & SPA
Little Torch Key, Florida

A wedding on Little Palm Island would be such a fantasy come true, the bride and groom must seriously consider leaving everyone else at home. The entire island is but five and a half acres, and accessible only by boat. Twenty-eight thatched-roofed bungalows (plus two expansive suites) are scattered throughout the island, each with landscaping ingenious enough to preserve the illusion of complete solitude. The pitched roof is not just a clever theme hotel design; authentic thatch and bamboo are layered so thickly that even hurricane rain cannot penetrate. Yes, these are huts, but four-star huts nonetheless, embellished with British Colonial, Polynesian, or Indonesian decor.

President Harry Truman chose the island for his winter White House, through his contact with the island's owner John Spottswood, a sheriff, state senator, and proprietor of Key West's only radio station. It was Newton Munson, the island's first inhabitant, however, who planted the 250 Jamaican tall coconut palms that form the island's profile, which became a set for the Warner Bros. film *PT-109*. Truman's fishing camp evolved into a resort in 1988. Patrick Collee purchased the resort in 1995 and, through his financial investment and vision, turned it into the highly acclaimed

tropical retreat it is today. The resort now includes a restaurant; bar; two pools (one outdoor with small waterfall, one indoor); a health club and spa; in-room massage; extensive water sports equipment and rental; a courtesy van from the Key West or Marathon airport; and ferry service to and from the mainland.

It isn't surprising that Little Palm Island Resort books about 150 weddings every year. Weddings are limited to forty guests, maximum. If more than forty guests are desired, the couple is asked to reserve the entire resort for a minimum of three nights. (Children under sixteen are then welcome in this event.) A special boat can be arranged for $400 to transport a party of more than twelve guests who are not staying at the resort.

The island's white sand beach on the western end is perfect for a sunset ceremony. The Zen Garden nestled among the towering palms, Oriental foliage, and rock pools makes for a private ceremony. The thatched-roofed gazebo at the island's northern end is a tropical version of a traditional wedding chapel, and an ideal location for a private celebratory dinner for two. The west-facing Sunset Dock stretches out over the Atlantic and doubles as a long processional aisle with room for seating.

Little Palm Island Resort & Spa
28500 Overseas Highway
Little Torch Key, FL 33042
(800) 3–GET–LOST or (305) 872–2524
www.littlepalmisland.com

Location: At the western end of Newfound Harbor Keys where the Gulf of Mexico meets the Straits of Florida; it's a fifteen-minute motor yacht ride from the resort's station on Little Torch Key.

Facility Rental, Amenities, and Policies: The resort's wedding packages include a guarantee that yours will be the only ceremony on the island that day, as well as an "Island Official" to perform the ceremony. Wedding packages range from $1,495 to $3,895 plus tax, and increase according to such included elements as a bridal bouquet and groom's boutonniere, a wedding cake for two, champagne, engraved champagne flutes with the couple's names and wedding date, a photographic package of prints and CD, and a ninety-minute video. The Sunset Sail package is what it sounds like—a ninety-minute ceremony voyage on the Atlantic. The package includes photography, a bottle of Taittinger Brut La Française champagne, and a platter of fruit and cheese on board. The cruise is limited to the bride and groom and two witnesses.

Reading between the lines, the packages appear to emphasize intimate ceremonies just for two, but each can be customized. Keep in mind that Little Palm Island is already a lush, tropical location, and extravagant bouquets or decorations would be overkill.

Catering: Created by the island's talented pastry chefs, the cake menu—even just for two—includes seven mouthwatering choices, such as a wedding cheesecake

decorated with light buttercream piping to look like a traditional wedding cake. For those who want to buck the vanilla wedding-cake tradition, there's rich dark chocolate genoise, layered with raspberry puree, decorated with white icing—but there are plenty of vanilla choices, too. If customizing or expanding a wedding cake included in a package, there is an additional charge of $95, plus $20 per extra portion.

As for catering, if the wedding party involves fewer than fifteen people, dining would be selected from the menu. Larger groups must have a prearranged menu; three- and four-course plated dinners or the Wedding Buffet are $95 to $110 per person.

Extras: The resort has negotiated several photography, videography, and music packages with area vendors.

Accommodations: 28 thatched-roofed bungalows (at $865 to $1,145 per night) all have ocean views, Jacuzzi tubs, hammocks, and private, outdoor, bamboo-screened showers. There are some modern conveniences, such as a very slow Internet connection, but no televisions, telephones, or children under the age of sixteen—this is, after all, Paradise.

Keep in Mind: The official hurricane season is late June to mid-November. Full refunds are given in the event of a National Weather Service hurricane watch or warning that causes wedding cancellations. The best time to book a wedding is late winter, early spring. June tends to be busier despite the heat and humidity. For a weekend wedding March through June, it is best to book six months in advance. Mosquito repellent and long sleeves might be necessary on the island's breezeless south side, but that is a small price to pay for Paradise.

MARIE SELBY
BOTANICAL GARDENS

Sarasota, Florida

Marie Selby Botanical Gardens is still reeling over the 2001 Schimmel wedding. Sarasota, Florida, resident Stephen Schimmel had brought in more than 2,000 additional flowering plants, an orchestra, and a gospel choir for his stepdaughter's wedding. Guests later enjoyed hors d'oeuvres under the banyan trees before moving to a catered seven-course dinner that included stone crab, duck, and rack of lamb in the Activity Center. (Schimmel, it is said, loves his food.) Pleased with the setting, Schimmel and his wife, Rosalba Schimmel, endowed the botanical gardens with a sizable donation to construct a glamorous wedding pavilion trimmed in stained-glass flowers. State-of-the-art heating, lighting, and acoustics, and a stunning view over Sarasota Bay, have made Schimmel Pavilion one of the most celebrated wedding venues in Sarasota.

Called the "supernova in the constellation of botanical gardens," the bayfront tropical gardens are the draw, where koi ponds, massive banyan trees, and gazebos create an exotic setting. The gardens also feature an open-air and under-glass museum of more than 20,000 colorful plants. The pride-and-joy showpiece is a living collection of more than 6,000 orchids, many of which were collected in the wild by the gardens' research and conservation scientists on more than 150 rain forest expeditions.

For brides and grooms the most difficult decision is not whether to have their wedding at Selby Gardens, but rather *where* in the gardens to set it. From the Gazebo at the tip of the eight-and-a-half-acre penin-sula, across the great lawn and along the waterfront, to the lovely Colonial-style museum, the scenery is breathtaking.

Any outdoor area of the gardens may be used for a wedding ceremony provided care is taken to preserve the surrounding flora. A map of the grounds shows as many as ten acceptable sites, but the most popular areas are the Gazebo, the Schimmel Wedding Pavilion, the banyan trees, and the bayfront adjacent to the mansion.

Most outdoor ceremonies begin after 5:00 P.M. when the gardens close to the public. Receptions are generally held in the Great Room of the Activity Center, however, which is available for rental anytime from 9:00 A.M. to 11:00 P.M. This air-conditioned room is 360 square feet and has 60 feet of windows facing west for spectacular bay and sunset views. It seats approximately 200 people at round dinner tables, or up to 300 people theater style. The Great Room is usually booked on weekends more than a year in advance.

The Mansion Museum, formerly known as the Christy Payne House, is a unique example of eclectic southern Colonial architecture primarily used for display of botanical prints. The downstairs portion is perfect for small receptions and dinners of up to fifty people after 5:00 P.M.; there are two main rooms, each with a sunporch and an outside patio.

Staff suggest booking about a year in advance for weekend weddings (some weddings book two years out), although there's much more flexibility for weekday weddings. Selby Gardens is a popular venue for marrying couples from England and Japan.

Marie Selby Botanical Gardens
811 South Palm Avenue
Sarasota, FL 34236
(941) 366–5731
www.selby.org

Location: 8 blocks south of Main Street off U.S. Highway 41 in Sarasota.

Facility Rental, Amenities, and Policies: Rental fees for the Schimmel Wedding Pavilion vary depending on the day of the week and whether the rental is for a ceremony, reception, or both. The range is from $1,080 for a Monday-through-Thursday ceremony, to $4,385 for a ceremony and reception on a Friday or Sunday evening. Rates for the Gazebo, banyan area, Oak Grove, and Activity Center are similarly scaled. Fees range from $800 for a Monday-through-Thursday ceremony, to $3,250 for a ceremony and reception on Friday or Sunday. Holidays carry a different fee scale. Rates include the use of the gardens, a preferred vendor list, coordination of event-related deliveries, a staff person on site during the event, white folding chairs for ceremonies, chairs and tables for indoor receptions, and signage. Dressing rooms will be provided for one hour, if available.

One and a half hours is allotted for the ceremony, and four and a half hours for receptions and dinners. Additional time is billed at $200 per hour. The site allows extra time as needed for bridal preparation, guest arrival and departure, and setup and cleanup.

Security must be provided by the couple after hours. There is ample parking for as many as 220 vehicles. Wheelchairs are provided with advance request.

To preserve and maintain the lawns, tents are limited to a certain size, and restrictions apply. However, the facility does recommend making alternate plans in the case of inclement weather.

Catering: Caterers not on the preferred list must provide insurance certificates and damage waivers. Alcohol must be handled through a licensed caterer.

Accommodations: Available in the Sarasota area.

ST. AUGUSTINE HISTORIC SITES
St. Augustine, Florida

You become part of St. Augustine's long and intricate history when you marry in one of her elder houses or at the fort near the sea. That history begins with tribal settlement, and continues through French occupation, followed by Spanish and British tug-of-war for colonization. Pedro Menendez de Aviles, in Spain's final attempt to conquer the region, arrived on scene on the Feast Day of St. Augustine in 1565. As governor of Las Floridas (land of the flowers), newly appointed by the king of Spain, Menendez came ashore with 600 soldiers and settlers near a Timucuan Indian village, which he fortified and named in honor of the saint. With the help of a hurricane and clever military maneuvers, Menendez defeated a nearby French garrison and its fleet. He then set to building the town and establishing missions to the Indians for the church. Thus St. Augustine was founded forty-two years before the English colony at Jamestown, Virginia, and fifty-five years before the Pilgrims landed on Plymouth

Rock in Massachusetts, making it the oldest permanent European settlement on the North American continent. Control seesawed among various countries until Florida finally became the twenty-seventh state in the Union in 1845.

Fast-forward to 1885 when Henry Flagler, enticed by the city's temperate climate and eclectic culture and architecture, began to turn St. Augustine into a winter resort and playground for rich northerners. A co-founder of the Standard Oil Company with John D. Rockefeller, he built two lavish hotels and a railway, as well as a hospital, a city hall, and several churches. St. Augustine's era of prestige and prosperity ended in 1914, but the effects are still evident today. Its delightful historic district comes alive with locals and tourists setting out on foot and horse-drawn carriages along cobblestone lanes to explore significant landmarks. Some come to be engaged or married at the old inns, houses, and other historical sites.

Historical Society Properties

The **González-Alvarez House** is hailed as St. Augustine's oldest continuously occupied residence, the only survivor of repeated raids by the English and pirates. The house seen today evolved from a two-room structure built between 1702 and 1727, but an earlier dwelling stood on the site in the 1600s. The house was rebuilt using coquina (limestone composed essentially of shell and coral) from nearby Anastasia Island, and the material is still an integral part of the old house. Tomas and Francisca González were the first people of record to live at this address until England took possession of St. Augustine in 1763, when all Spanish residents were ordered to leave. The Peavettses bought the house in 1775 and rebuilt it to their tastes, adding a second story with a shingled roof for their living quarters and a tavern downstairs in the old living area. They accumulated land, slaves, and money, but when Joseph Peavetts died in 1786, his widow's new husband lost much of their wealth to gambling. The house was auctioned to the highest bidder, Geronimo Alvarez, baker for the government hospital.

Visitors began touring what was already being billed as America's oldest house in 1892 by an entrepreneur. The house museum exhibited evidence of the Spanish, British, and American occupations of St. Augustine. The St. Augustine Historical Society, which had formed in 1881, purchased the house in 1918. In 1970 the U.S. Department of the Interior designated the house a National Historic Landmark, and it became the nucleus of the Oldest House Museum Complex.

The St. Augustine Historical Society refurbished the downstairs portion of the house to look as it did when González had owned it, with simple tabby floors and sparse furnishings. Upstairs, visitors see the influences of the other owners: Mary Peavetts's reading parlor and the table in the dining room set for an Alvarez meal.

Behind the traditional garden walls, a common feature of Spanish communities, find a tranquil place for repose (and weddings). Native plants and those introduced by generations of Spanish, British, and American colonists mingle in this subtropical garden. Stately live oaks festooned with moss and resurrection fern dominate the scene, along with southern red cedar, crepe myrtle, banana, fig, sweet and sour orange, and several palm varieties. Redbrick walkways and arched loggias invite a slow stroll and reflection on what it might have been like to live here. Add the *clip-clop* of horses' hooves as the sightseeing carriages pass by, and the illusion is nearly complete.

The society is also steward of the **Fernández-Llambias House** on St. Francis

Street. Named in part for its first owner of record, Pedro Fernández, its date of origin is unknown. The house changed hands and dimensions a number of times before the Llambias family took possession in 1854. Restored in 1954, the antique charm of the Fernández-Llambias House and garden provide a picturesque setting for weddings or receptions. It is equipped with a large catering kitchen and restrooms.

The **Garden of St. Francis Park,** located just across the street from the Fernández-Llambias House, is another popular venue for weddings. The green oasis features a coquina well and fountain, flowering plants, tropical plants, and orange trees. There is also an arbor covered with blooming jasmine.

Castillo de San Marcos

Integral to St. Augustine's history is Castillo de San Marcos on Mantazas Bay, with its elaborate double drawbridge entrance. Now a national monument, the Castillo served as the city's outer defenses for many years and now serves as an reminder of the might of the early Spanish empire in the New World. Built of the ubiquitous coquina over a twenty-three-year period (1672 through 1695), the walls of the fortress remained impenetrable through 300 years of enemy shelling and violent storms.

Weddings are popular here, but with nearly 700,000 annual visitors, certain restrictions apply. Ceremonies (and no receptions) may be conducted only on the North Green near the seawall, but not inside the Castillo itself, in the Water Battery, in front of the Entrance Station, or near the visitor parking lot.

Mission of Nombre de Dios

The Mission of Nombre de Dios originated with the founding of the city of St. Augustine, when Menendez landed and proclaimed the site for Spain and the church. Father Fran-cisco Lopez de Mendoza Grajales, chaplain of the expedition, presented a wooden cross to Menendez, who knelt and kissed it. It was on these grounds that Father Lopez celebrated the first parish Mass. He then began the work of America's first mission. This site still serves as a place of worship today. The mission preserves a number of historic features, including a beautiful outdoor altar, called the Rustic Altar, at the northern end of the Prince of Peace Votive Church. Ceremonies may be held at the Prince of Peace Votive Church, the Rustic Altar, and Our Lady of La Leche Chapel. As with all Catholic churches, weddings are arranged through the help of each couple's local parish.

St. Augustine Historical Society
271 Charlotte Street
St. Augustine, FL 32084
(904) 824–2872
www.staugustinehistoricalsociety.org

Location: The St. Augustine Historic District.

Facility Rental, Amenities, and Policies: The González-Alvarez House garden is a popular site for weddings and can accommodate up to 250 guests. The fee is $636 with tax. Restrooms, a gallery for the use of the bride and her attendants, and free parking are available. The Fernández-Llambias House also rents for $636 with tax, while the fee for the Garden of St. Francis Park is $150.

Catering: Check with St. Augustine Historical Society for approved catering companies.

Castillo de San Marcos
1 South Castillo Drive
St. Augustine, FL 32084
Recorded Message: (904) 829–6506

Visitor Information: (904) 829–6506, ext. 234
Permits: (904) 829–6506, ext. 246
www.nps.gov/casa
Permit Information and Application: www.nps.gov/casa/home/permits/htm

Location: The Castillo is located on A1A in downtown St. Augustine.

Facility Rental, Amenities, and Policies: Only one ceremony is permitted per week, and only on Saturday after 5:00 P.M. unless it's a holiday or special-event weekend. The ceremony may not impact the park resources in any way, or interfere with visitor use. The application is downloadable from the Web site, and must be sent along with a $50 nonrefundable fee at least a month in advance. The wedding party and guests also pay entrance fees.

Mission of Nombre de Dios/Shrine of our Lady of La Leche
27 Ocean Avenue
St. Augustine, FL 32084
(904) 824–2809
www.missionandshrine.org

Location: The Mission of Nombre de Dios is located off San Marco Avenue (on A1A).

Facility Rental, Amenities, and Policies: For information about requirements and to schedule use of ceremony facilities at the mission, call the Cathedral-Basilica of St. Augustine at (904) 824–2806 or visit their Web site at www.thefirstparish.org.

Catering: Dozens of unique restaurants are sprinkled throughout St. Augustine, ranging from quaint cafes to four-star dining establishments, with many restaurants serving as attractions themselves.

Accommodations: Area accommodations are plentiful and range from splendid resorts to charming bed-and-breakfast inns.

SUNKEN GARDENS
St. Petersburg, Florida

The Sunken Gardens drop 15 feet below street level. That's because a hundred years ago the site was an ancient lakebed. George Turner Sr., a plumber, came up with the idea to purchase the six-acre lake and drain it using an elaborate maze of clay tiles. The result was a rich muck soil ideal for his gardening hobby. He filled the bed with lush tropical gardens, ponds, and waterfalls. Local gardeners, inspired by the unusual leaves and glorious flowers, enjoyed strolling through the garden after church on Sunday so much that by the early 1920s, Turner was charging a nickel for tours. Three generations of Turners continued the plumber's vision until 1999, when the city of St. Petersburg purchased Sunken Gardens with funds from a voter-approved tax.

As St. Petersburg's oldest living museum, this century-old garden is home to more than 50,000 tropical plants and flowers—500 species in all. Today the garden still models the senior Turner's original vision of a botanical paradise. Demonstration Japanese, cactus, and butterfly gardens have been added as "walk-through encounters." The site offers horticultural programs, guided tours, and orchid and butterfly festivals.

Since 1935 couples have exchanged vows amid dancing butterflies in the Butterfly Garden, or under a canopy of 200-year-old shade trees in the Oak Pavilion. Brides and their attendants make their grand processional over a bridge into the historic Wedding Lawn. Some of the oldest Cuban royal palms and bougainvillea in the Southeast provide towering backdrops for wedding photography. Guests are amazed by the contrast between the rapid pace of the metropolitan city outside the gardens and the tranquil atmosphere within their vine-covered walls.

Until 2004 weddings at the Sunken Gardens were relatively simple affairs. Now with the availability of an indoor banquet facility, wedding celebrations can be much more elaborate if desired. The 1926 building was occupied by the Coca-Cola Bottling Company in the 1940s, and was purchased by the Turner family in 1967 to house the World's Largest Gift Shop and the King of Kings Wax Museum. The city recently restored the building to its original Mediterranean Revival style, and it is the new home for Great Explorations, a children's science museum. Receptions are held in the second-floor Garden Room, which is illuminated with natural light through an expansive glass wall. Overlooking the exquisite butterfly garden, this special space was refurbished with its early history in mind, creating a loftlike feel with high, wooden ceilings and metal beams.

Ceremonies without receptions are still welcome, however. Sunken Gardens hosts fifty to sixty weddings a year and recommends booking about a year in advance, but depending on availability, couples might be able to get in sooner. The destination wedding aspect is beginning to pick up, with most of the couples coming from Canada and England. The largest wedding on premises to date has been for 175, and the average small wedding is for 10 to 20 people.

The gardens are fully wheelchair accessible, and the Garden Room does have an elevator.

Sunken Gardens
1825 Fourth Street North
St. Petersburg, FL 33704
(727) 551–3106
www.stpete.org/fun/parks/SGprivate rentals.htm

Location: Near Crescent Lake Park at Fourth and Eighteenth Streets.

Facility Rental, Amenities, and Policies: With the exception of the Fountain Plaza, couples may conduct their outdoor ceremonies from 10:00 A.M. to 4:00 P.M. at the following locations: the Oak Pavilion ($650 for up to seventy-five guests), the Butterfly Garden ($850 for up to 150 guests), and the Wedding Lawn ($1,250 for up to 200). After 5:00 P.M. couples may exchange vows in the Fountain Plaza, tucked just inside the gardens' entrance ($500 for up to fifty people). Other locations are available for evening ceremonies when renting the entire facility from 5:00 P.M. to midnight for $2,300.

The Oak Pavilion is also a lovely place for daytime passed hors d'oeuvres and cocktails before 4:00 P.M., again for $650 for seventy-five people. The Oak Pavilion is also available for evening events, 5:00 P.M. to midnight, but only with the rental of the entire outdoor gardens for $2,300. The Garden Room seats 150 to 175 guests, depending on setup, and is available for rental for $1,250 from 9:00 A.M. to 4:00 P.M., or 5:00 P.M. to midnight.

For the ultimate ceremony and reception, the Garden Room and the entire outdoor gardens can be rented from 5:00 P.M. to midnight for $2,950. A 20 percent discount applies to all events booked Monday through Thursday.

Catering: Sunken Gardens does not have a wedding coordinator, but staff will do all they can to help plan a smoothly run event, and will provide a preferred vendor list that includes some of the finest catering in the area.

Accommodations: Available in the Greater St. Petersburg area.

'TWEEN WATERS INN
Captiva Island, Florida

Wedged between the Gulf of Mexico and the Pine Island Sound on the narrowest part of Captiva Island, 'Tween Waters Inn is a bit of Old Florida. At a time when Gulf-front property is sold to hotel ventures at a premium, 'Tween Waters Inn chose to preserve and refurbish its historic cottages. Nostalgia is only one draw for visitors; there's also a marina, a beach, and some of the best seashelling in Florida. All rooms have a view of water. Everyone is made to feel welcome at 'Tween Waters—from families with children to couples on a weekend getaway wedding. The entire resort has been owned by the same company since 1973, and is very much a family-oriented business.

The inn opened in 1926 with just one cottage; today there are eighteen. Six of the oldest cottages have been renovated and named for some of the influential people who had called them home. One such resident was J. N. "Ding" Darling, an editorial cartoonist and conservationist who made 'Tween Waters his winter home in the 1930s, and his cottage features his artwork. The cottage named for President Theodore Roosevelt has an outdoorsy theme in honor of his fishing trips. Aviator Charles Lindbergh's cottage has a bomber leather sofa, and the cottage named for his wife, Anne Morrow Lindbergh, is decorated in feminine, creamy yellow and blue hues. She visited often while writing *Gift from the Sea*. All of the cottages contain period furnishings and fixtures, including paddle fans and heart-pine floors.

'Tween Waters Inn hosts about 200 weddings per year. Most of the ceremonies take place on the beach owned by the resort. The inn offers three romantic locations overlooking turquoise Gulf waters, on 6 miles of pristine, shell-strewn white sand beaches. Ideal for spectacular year-round sunsets and sensual barefoot ceremonies, the beach creates a beautiful reception setting as well. Captiva Island is less than 5 miles long and 0.5 mile wide, and the inn itself is on a thirteen-acre strip of that thin slice of island. During peak seasons the beach may be too crowded for a beach ceremony, in which case the Garden Terrace is a lovely alternative.

The inn has half a dozen reception sites. The Old Captiva House dining room (capacity 120 to 160), with hardwood floors and Victorian decor, conveys a nostalgic Florida ambience. French doors open to spectacular views of the Gulf from the balcony of the spacious and elegant Wakefield Banquet Room (50 to 120). The Garden Terrace and Sunset Room (twenty-five to fifty each), adjoined through white French doors, are booked together for most events. The garden is a lush, tropical alfresco setting amid lattice-covered arbors of bougainvillea, a sparkling fountain, and stonework floor. The Oasis Poolside Bar and Grill (25 to 120) is casual and fun for island-style entertaining for a tropical welcome, rehearsal gathering, barbecue, or luau party. The Canoe and Kayak Club (twenty to fifty) is a waterfront cafe with an air-conditioned dining area and open-air covered deck overlooking the bay and marina.

'Tween Waters Inn
15951 Captiva Road
P.O. Box 249
Captiva Island, FL 33924
(800) 223–5865 or (239) 472–5161
Sales: (800) 223–5865, ext. 453
www.tween-waters.com

Location: About an hour from Fort Myers Airport with a $3.00 toll on Sanibel Causeway.

Facility Rental, Amenities, and Policies: The flat-cost, no-options fee for a beach ceremony is $300 for one hour for up to 20 people, and $300 for a reception with up to 160 people, but certain restrictions apply. Because the beach is often crowded on weekends during the peak season, the beach may not be used for a ceremony unless booked along with a dinner reception or as a package.

The inn offers two intimate ceremony packages (the Bougainvillea and the Jasmine) and two ceremony packages with a private reception on the premises (the Orchid and the Bird of Paradise). The Bougainvillea and the Jasmine packages are $600 and $800, respectively, for up to ten guests. The packages include a beach location for the ceremony, an officiant to sign and file the marriage license, a choice of fresh bridal bouquet and groom's boutonniere, limited wedding coordination, witnesses if needed, and a pair of tropical tiki torches for a beach altar. The packages also include a coupon for a wedding dinner in the Old Captiva House or Crow's Nest restaurant for the bride and groom, and 10

percent off their accommodations (some restrictions apply). The larger package includes chairs, cake, and champagne for ten guests, plus $5.00 for each additional chair, glass, or cake serving.

The Orchid and the Bird of Paradise packages are $500 and $700, respectively. These packages offer the same amenities as the Bougainvillea and Jasmine, but allow for up to twenty-five people. The cost of the reception is additional.

Catering: Facility charges for the dining areas range from $700 to $1,600; they're booked for three or four hours depending on the room. The Oasis Bar and Grill and the Canoe and Kayak Club rent for two and three hours, respectively, for $400. Facility charges include use of event space, standard linens, china, flatware, stemware, round tables, chairs, portable bars, accessory tables as needed, setup/breakdown, and banquet staffing.

Accommodations: The 18 cottages form the historic core of what's now a 138-unit vacation resort with swimming pools, docks, and tennis courts. The spacious hotel rooms and apartments are in three modern buildings on stilts; they all have screened balconies facing the Gulf or the bay. Rates are seasonal, dependent on view and decor, and include continental breakfast. A standard room ranges from $150 to $260; a suite, $210 to $585; a cottage, $190 to $650. Cottages require a two-night minimum stay.

Keep in Mind: Terry McParland, director of sales, said rates tend to rise 5 to 10 percent every year, but not always across the board. The peak months are April, May, and October, when they conduct thirty-plus weddings, sometimes six a weekend. The inn does offer midweek discounts on weddings, and sometimes weekend discounts in the slow season (August and September).

WEDDINGS ON WATER

Clearwater, Florida

A ceremony on a floating chapel might sound a bit gimmicky at first, yet such a venue combines the best of all destination wedding worlds—charming chapel, ocean breezes, beaches, proximity to a tourist area for great wedding vendors, restaurants, lodging, and, above all, mobility. What bride-on-the-go wouldn't love to move a country chapel to a beach?

Weddings On Water accomplishes all these things. Touted as America's only floating wedding chapel, this 60-foot, fifty-ton barge hosts ceremonies on the calm waters of Florida's west coast. The floating chapel is anchored in Clearwater Harbor on Florida's Intracoastal Waterway in the Tampa Bay area. Most ceremonies take place next to a tropical island in the calm intracoastal waters, but the chapel can be brought to many places accessible by water, including seawalls and waterfront properties.

The chapel blends the amenities of a traditional church with the advantages of being at sea. Though built of steel, it looks like a pristine whitewashed wooden chapel with pitched blue roofs and steeple. Instead of walking around chapel gardens, guests walk along the decks to enjoy the nautical experience. Cathedral ceilings, pew seating, and elaborate stained-glass windows behind the altar add ambient charm and beauty, while several large windows provide magnificent views of the water and the coast in all directions. The chapel is air-conditioned and has a total capacity of 125 people.

Janet Henderson, president of the company, and her husband saw the floating chapel concept on the Gold Coast of Australia and decided they wanted to replicate the idea in Florida. Once built, the chapel was certified by the U.S. Coast Guard in September 2004 and launched its maiden wedding voyage a few days later. Henderson wrote, "It has been quite a unique experience getting our operation up and floating!"

On the day of the wedding, the bride and her entourage board the chapel and are taken out to the calm waters of Clearwater Bay while they prepare for the ceremony. They have full use of the chapel as well as the comfortable bridal sanctuary, complete with bathroom, seating, and large mirrors. For the commencement of the ceremony, the groom, groomsmen, and guests are transported to the chapel aboard a double-deck ferry.

Other Area Options

Honeymoon and Caladesi Islands. Honeymoon and Caladesi Islands lie just off the coast in the area and are both worthy destinations and potential ceremony locations. Honeymoon Island State Park is less than a five-minute drive from the mainland and offers a natural getaway for boating, swimming, fishing, picnics, and nature exploration. Caladesi Island State Park, accessible to the public by ferry from Honeymoon Island or by private boat, has consistently been named one of Florida's top ten beaches. Along the Dunedin Causeway to Honeymoon Island, within the protected waters of St. Joseph Sound, you will find all the classic sun-and-fun activities. Weddings On Water is affiliated with The Dolphin Encounter on Clearwater Beach and the Caladesi Island Ferry connecting Honeymoon Island State Park and Caladesi Island State Park.

Weddings On Water
200 Seminole Street
Clearwater, FL 33755
(866) 466–0969 or (727) 466–0969
www.weddingsonwater.com

Location: Home port is on the Intracoastal Waterway a few blocks north of downtown Clearwater, Florida, west of North Fort Harrison Avenue.

Facility Rental, Amenities, and Policies: Weddings On Water offers multiple packages that cater to wedding parties of varying sizes. Packages range from $575 (for up to twenty guests) to $1,500 (for up to one hundred) Monday through Thursday. These packages increase around $500 for weddings that take place Friday through Sunday and holidays.

All weddings include the use of the chapel for one to one and a half hours, starting at the time the chapel leaves the port. The Platinum package ($1,500 to $2,000) includes transportation for guests aboard the *Clearwater Express* to any suitable port from the Belleair Causeway to the Dunedin Causeway. Also included in the packages are a nondenominational ceremony performed by the captain in dress whites, silk flower arrangements, the use of a silk flower bouquet and boutonniere if desired, and a videotape of the wedding. Music is coordinated through a high-quality sound system. Although these features are included, couples are welcome to decorate with their own flowers, provide their own music, or bring any certified person of their choice to officiate the ceremony. Also included in the pricing is a rehearsal during the week prior to the wedding, and the assistance of consultants to help coordinate all the elements of the event. Every ceremony can be personalized.

"Walk-ons"—weddings with fewer than ten guests—are also welcome for $350. The same amenities are included in the price, with the exception that the ceremony is performed by a notary, and the chapel doesn't leave the pier.

Catering: Receptions aren't permitted on the floating chapel, but Weddings On Water suggests Belleview Biltmore Resort, Cabana Club Grill & Bar, and Island Way Grill in the Clearwater, Florida, area.

Accommodations: Lodging is available in the Clearwater/Tampa Bay area.

CHOTA FALLS
Located near Atlanta, Georgia

The mountains of northern Georgia are blessed with an abundance of waterfalls. Chota Falls is a 150-acre private family estate and wedding facility; its name is a Cherokee word meaning "that place to the north of where waterfalls flow into a green valley." Chota Falls is indeed replete with waterfalls, ponds, streams, meadows, and a mountaintop overlook with views of three states. Blessed with unrivaled natural beauty, the estate affords visitors miles of secluded paths and trails that meander alongside pristine mountain creeks.

Chota Falls has several unique gathering areas, and ceremonies are welcome in all structures and outdoor venues throughout the year. The **Treehouse at the Upper Falls,** a large shaded deck in the midst of rhododendron and mountain laurel, is equipped with a bar, refrigerator, fire pit, and bathhouse that all overlook the beautiful Upper Falls. The Treehouse, easily accommodating fifty guests, is a favorite setting for a rehearsal dinner, bridal luncheon, or romantic wedding ceremony where at night tree lights beautify the rushing waters of the falls and creek. The **Vineyard Overlook** is a spacious deck situated high atop a vineyard hill, with panoramic mountain views of the valley and creek below, and can accommodate fifty to eighty guests.

The most recent addition to Chota Falls is the **Vineyard Wedding Chapel,** which functions as a year-round Georgia mountain wedding venue. This new yet antiqued chapel adds to the Tuscan theme of hillside vineyards among mountain vistas. Artfully crafted stonework creates a picturesque scene of gardens, fountains, sitting areas, and reception or pre-function tented patio. Chota Falls's representatives are particularly proud of the chapel's bridal dressing area, which is outfitted to coordinate large wedding parties. Eighty to a hundred guests can dance away the hours under tall white tents above the patio's charming stone garden and fountain area.

The multilevel **Stekoa Creek House** includes the Chota Creek Pub, two large tented flagstone patio areas, and an upstairs room with adjacent terrace for indoor, climate-controlled functions.

Chota Falls today hosts an average of forty weddings every year. Couples tend to spend what they would for a wedding at home, or much less, but expenditures include five special events over three days and two nights as well as lodging in a honeymoon suite and eight guest rooms for family and close friends. Chota Falls's signature event is a 15-foot bonfire in the valley, lit after the rehearsal dinner.

Chota Falls
Located near Atlanta, Georgia
(706) 490–2071
www.chotafalls.com
(Note: Address not listed for privacy.)

Location: Chota Falls is located approximately ninety minutes north of Atlanta near the town of Clayton in Rabun County, Georgia, and is a two-hour drive from the Atlanta airport.

Facility Rentals, Amenities, and Policies: Chota Falls's collage of packages starts with the Grand Country Wedding ($15,900), which covers the site fees for a wedding ceremony for one hundred guests, indoor or outdoor wedding reception facility, rehearsal dinner facility, bridal luncheon facility, and farewell brunch facility. It also includes three nights in the Honeymoon Suite, as well as accommodations for up to twenty-two in eight guest rooms for two nights.

The Mountain Wedding ($10,900) includes a ceremony and a reception for as many as one hundred guests for eight hours. The Intimate Country Wedding ($7,900) covers facility rental for as many as fifty guests for eight hours. The Sunday Afternoon Wedding ($5,900) includes a five-hour event for fifty guests from 4:30 to 9:30 P.M. (Date restrictions do not apply to this package.)

The Small Weekday Wedding package ($3,600) covers three and a half hours for twelve guests Monday through Wednesday anytime of year, plus such additional amenities as a night's stay in a honeymoon suite, minister, and a small reception.

Only the Grand, Sunday, and Sunday Afternoon Wedding packages are available during prime weekend dates of April through July 4 and August 26 through mid-November. The Mountain and Intimate packages are available mid-November through March, and July 10 through August 25. Other intermediate packages are available. Facility fees include choice of ceremony site (Upper or Lower Falls, Vineyard Wedding Chapel, the Vineyard Overlook, or lakeside), wedding coordinator time, setup and teardown of event (including tents), staging and sound system, tables, linens, settings, white padded folding wedding chairs, and elaborate decorations. Additional guests may be added to any package for an additional small fee. Other events, such as a rehearsal dinner, can be added to any package.

Catering: Several excellent regional caterers are available for every dining need, including breakfast, lunch, dinner, hors d'oeuvres, and cakes. Prices begin at $7.00 per person for breakfast, $10.00 for lunch, and $20.00 for dinner. A local wine shop and local package store are available to assist in arranging beverage needs. There is no additional service charge for beverage setup (other than any bartenders hired by the couple).

Extras: Ministers, entertainers, photographers, and horse and carriages are available locally. The bonfire (provided by Chota Falls staff) is available for $100. Outdoor areas can be tented for around $4,000.

Accommodations: Chota Falls is able to provide rooms for approximately twenty-four guests at the estate. The Mountain View Lodge at Chota Falls ($700 per night) has five bedrooms, each with a private bath, as well as futon sofas that can sleep an additional seven guests. The Orchard House ($300 per night) has two bedrooms, each with a bathroom, private entrance, and porch. The Vineyard View Room, or Honeymoon Suite, is furnished with a king-size bed, a wood-burning fireplace, and a Jacuzzi tub. The Bunk House ($150 per night) is a spacious, one-room studio ideal for a family of four or a groom and his groomsmen. The Laurel Loft ($100 per night) is a smaller one-bedroom/one-bath suite with a bar and microwave. All accommodations require a minimum two-night stay. Clayton has well-furnished hotels, a charming bed-and-breakfast, and a golf resort.

Keep in Mind: Chota Falls is a private facility. Guests arriving at the estate must have a Chota Falls escort and are asked to call for an appointment to be met at the gate.

HAWAII STATE BEACHES AND PARKS
Hawaiian Islands

Hawaii is probably the most popular wedding destination in the United States, and fast becoming one of the most expensive. The number of marriage licenses issued in Hawaii has more than doubled in the last ten years; not only are more locals getting married, but so are the increasing numbers of mainland couples. Hawaii is particularly popular among the Japanese, many of whom obtain their license in their home country and conduct a wedding on one of the islands for good luck—and the pictures.

At the beginning of this steep uptrend, the larger resorts were hosting as many as six ceremonies a day; staff said they "felt like Las Vegas." After the initial excitement wore off, however, the resorts turned themselves into full-service wedding shops and raised their site fees significantly. Packaged weddings allow resorts to control the quality of their suppliers. Higher prices mean fewer weddings, of course, but also more time to concentrate on the brides.

It's a seller's market for weddings in Paradise, but it is possible to cut costs if a couple is willing to do the legwork. Ceremonies in Hawaii's state and county beaches and parks are permitted at no cost, but couples must fill out some paperwork to obtain the necessary permits. Public beaches will be crowded, particularly in peak seasons, but the hidden beaches are not published on the Web. It might pay to hire a local wedding coordinator to advise on the best locations and help cut through the red tape. Many wedding planners are also marriage license agents, and ministers and nondenominational officiants do it all. The good news about the latest resort price hikes is that many wedding planners have reoriented their markets toward lower-end weddings. Planners might charge $500 or more for their well-earned services; they also offer all-inclusive packages that include the site, ceremony officiant, flowers, photography, and celebratory refreshments.

Here is a list of beaches where couples may marry for free or with a permit:

Maluaka Beach Park or Beach, adjacent to Maui Prince Hotel in Makena, South Maui. A large, manicured grassy park beneath coconut trees with the beach and ocean in the background with stairs down to the spacious beach. Weddings are performed on a grass peninsula cliff lined with a lava rock wall.

Makena Cove Beach, South Maui. Located past Big Beach between two residences, it is hard to find without the minister as a guide. Free, but limited to ten guests.

South Makena Beach, South Maui. Near Makena Cove Beach. There's no limit on guests but it's a popular spot, so others may be getting married at the same time.

Makena Surf Beach, South Maui. Located in front of the Makena Surf condominiums in Makena. Cement walkways lead to a tropical garden past an ancient Hawaiian *heiau*. This is a private location for small groups, and is free.

Ulaua Beach, Wailea, South Maui. On the south end of Stouffer Wailea Beach Resort. Weddings are performed on the grassy hill with Haleakala, the 10,000-foot volcano, or the ocean in the background. The site is free, but popular with surfers and scuba divers.

Paulauea Beach ("White Rock"), Wailea, Maui. South of the Kea Lani Hotel, this large white beach has 180-degree views of Kaho'olawe, Molokini, and the western Maui Mountains. This is not a beach that is publicized by hotels, so it can be private.

Kapioloani Park, Oahu. On Kalakaua Avenue, this is ideal at sunset. Wedding photographs will have Waikiki Beach and Diamond Head in the background.

Lanikai Beach, Oahu. Tucked in a residential neighborhood on the lush windward side of the island, this secluded beach is usually crowd-free, especially on weekdays.

Hanalei Beach, Kauai. One of the most dramatic spots on the North Shore, with white beaches and Bali Hai cliffs.

Hapuna Beach State Park, Big Island. Near Mauna Kea and Hapuna Prince Resorts, this beach is endowed with white sand and emerald water. It's free.

Hawaii Volcanoes National Park, Big Island. Small weddings can be performed on overlooks with scenic views of the crater, or in forested areas for a $50 permit plus entrance fees, with some restrictions.

For a *Getting Married* Brochure and Licensing Agents Lists:

Honolulu Marriage License Office
State Department of Health Building
1250 Punchbowl Street
Honolulu, HI 96813
(808) 586–4545 or (808) 586–4544
www.state.hi.us/doh/records/vr_marri.html

For Park Permit Requests:

Hawaii Volcanoes National Park
Attention: Aleta Knight, Management Assistant
P.O. Box 52
Hawaii Volcanoes National Park, HI 96718
(808) 985–6027
www.nps.gov/havo/manage/weddings.htm

Facility Rental, Amenities, and Policies: To use a state park or state beach park, contact the district office of the state Divisions of Parks on the island where the ceremony is to be held and request a special-use permit for a wedding ceremony: Oahu, P.O. Box 621, Honolulu, HI 96809, (808) 587–0300; Big Island, P.O. Box 936, Hilo, HI 96721, (808) 974–6200; Maui, 54 South High Street, Suite 101, Wailuku, HI 96793, (808) 984–8109; Kauai, 3060 Eiwa Street, Suite 306, Lihue, HI 96766, (808) 274–3444.

Use of county beach parks may not require a permit, although a park facility such as a pavilion will need a permit. Most permits require a refundable custodial deposit. For more information on use of county parks, contact: City and County of Honolulu (the entire island of Oahu): 650 South King Street, First Floor, Honolulu, HI 96813, (808) 523–4527; Big Island of Hawaii: 25 Aupuni Street, Hilo, HI 96720, (808) 961–8311; Maui: 1580-C Kaahumanu Avenue, Wailuku, HI 96793, (808) 270–7389; Kauai: 4444 Rice Street, Lihue, HI 96766, (808) 241–6660.

Catering: Receptions are generally not permitted in the parks and beaches. Check with the wedding officiant for recommendations of nearby reception sites.

Accommodations: Available on all of the islands. Bed-and-breakfasts tend to be the best buy.

Keep in Mind: May and June were once Hawaii's peak season, but now wedding bells ring in fall, especially among the Japanese and mainlanders. However, there is no bad time to marry in Hawaii. Watch for shifting low-season discounts. When selecting one of Hawaii's six main islands for a ceremony site, take into account the character of each. The Big Island is mostly rural, less crowded, but has greater driving distances. Oahu has a lively nightlife; its famous Waikiki Beach is great for kids of all ages, though crowded and overbuilt. Maui has surpassed Oahu's nightlife and is the winner for sheer variety of activities, though expensive. (Don't forget your JUST MAUI'D T-shirts!) Kauai is for the adventurous and admirers of beauty, but with fewer dining options. They say that Lanai is for lovers, but what Hawaiian island isn't?

MAUNA KEA BEACH HOTEL

Kohala Coast, Hawaii

For a sunset ceremony in Hawaii, consider the Third Tee on Mauna Kea Beach Hotel's golf course on the Big Island. Seriously. The Third Tee is situated high on an ancient lava bluff among coconut palms and sculpted fairways overlooking the rolling blue surf of the Pacific Ocean. The golf course setting, on the island that tourism has all but forgotten, ensures that your wedding will be virtually private and absolutely memorable.

Perhaps a Big Island wedding might be unexpected, but returning vacationers and savvy celebrities know this is the place to get away from it all. Hawaii proper is larger than all its sibling islands combined, leaving plenty of elbow room for visitors to soak up the scenery and culture without all the crowds. Although spectacular in its own right, with rain forests, lava fields, and award-winning salt-and-pepper beaches, it isn't the tropical-island-and-nightlife fantasy that is Oahu or Maui. For that reason this is the island less traveled.

Back in the 1960s Laurance S. Rockefeller's RockResorts built the Mauna Kea Resort on a golden crescent of sand. Rockefeller's internationally acclaimed architectural firm succeeded in blending modernism with Japanese naturalism. The hotel is eight stories high with two mirror-image structures, one facing the ocean, the other facing its namesake volcano.

Winding paths meander past gardens, koi ponds, and restaurants that look like Buddhist temples.

This is a luxury hotel of sophistication and comfort, but new hotels have eclipsed the resort with more modern architectural style and amenities. None, however, matches its beach, mature landscaping, and clublike character, and none pays the same gracious attention to guests.

Mauna Kea Hotel (along with its sister property, Hapuna Beach Prince Hotel) hosts 200 weddings a year. The Mauna Kea offers seven outdoor and two indoor ceremony and reception venues, but the golf course remains its most popular, although course activity restricts ceremonies to evenings. The **North Pointe Lawn** is a large area on the north end of the hotel's grounds with expansive views of the beach and Kauna'oa Bay. The ceremony is staged on the lava stone patio, while the lawn provides ample room for a reception or dinner. For a setting steeped in Hawaii's multicultural heritage, consider the **North Garden**'s symmetrically arranged lawns, lava rock paths, and tropical foliage. At the top of a grand staircase, a massive seventeenth-century granite Buddha sits beneath a bodhi tree, its folded hands often holding an orchid offering, and its belly black with good-luck rubbing.

HAPUNA BEACH STATE PARK

The Big Island is the youngest of the chain of Hawaiian Islands, and therefore some of the black beaches have not yet been pumiced white. Next to the Kauanaoa (Mauna Kea) Beach, the Hapuna Beach State Park might be the most beautiful in all Hawaii. Some who marry at Mauna Kea Beach Resort prefer to lodge at the Hapuna Beach Prince Hotel.

Set among mature, indigenous strands of keawe and naupaka, the **Luau Grounds** are said to be the most authentic of its kind on the Big Island. An existing stage, bar, imu (underground oven for roasting pigs), and buffet lend themselves naturally to a wedding celebration (except on Tuesday during the resort's weekly luau). **South Pointe Lawn,** adjacent to the beach at the southern end of the property, is perfect for larger parties set among a grove of coconut palms and junglelike vegetation. The **Manta Ray Lookout** at the water's edge, in a human-made circular lava outcropping, allows wedding guests to view manta rays in the sea below by night; by day there is no spot closer to the ocean. For gatherings of thirty or fewer guests, the **Garden Terrace** is ideal. The patio is just off **The Garden Room,** which has terraced dining levels with floor-to-ceiling sliding glass panels that present panoramic views of the resort. With hardwood floors and original art by its namesake, the **Lloyd Sexton Gallery** suits formal gatherings or seated dinner events. (It may serve as a backup in the unlikely event of inclement weather.)

On occasion, and with prior written approval, **The Batik** and **The Pavilion at Manta Ray Point** restaurants may be secured for private events.

Mauna Kea Beach Hotel
62-100 Mauna Kea Beach Drive
Kohala Coast, HI 96743
(808) 882–7222
Weddings and Special Events Coordinators:
(808) 882–5466
www.maunakeabeachhotel.com

Location: On Hawaii, the "Big Island," 28 miles north of Kona Airport on Queen Kaahumanu Highway.

Facility Rental, Amenities, and Policies: To marry at the Third Tee, or anywhere else at Mauna Kea, the bride and groom must purchase one of four all-inclusive wedding packages. On-staff wedding coordinators take care of all the details, from hiring the ceremony officiant to arranging the appointment to obtain the marriage license. The couple must stay at the resort a minimum of three nights, and preferably book a year in advance. Summer months are best for nice weather, but May and September offer discount room rates.

The packages run $2,400 to $4,800. All are based on a maximum of twenty-five people and include the ceremony site, officiant, basic photography, a white floral lei or *haku lei po'o* (head lei) for the bride, and a woven *maile lei* for the groom. Succeeding packages increasing in price include: a chilled bottle of champagne, two Mauna Kea Resort keepsake champagne flutes, a wedding cake for two with fresh flowers at the ceremony site, professional musicians (solo or duo), salon treatments for the bride and groom, a Hawaiian wedding certificate, and a videography package.

Catering: Reception prices are subject to change, but some items on the specialty buffet menu, at $15 to $30 per person for a minimum of forty people, look tempting: tempura bar, sushi counter, Peking duck, and Chinatown wok station.

Accommodations: Rooms at Mauna Kea Beach Hotel run from $370 for a mountain-view standard room to $1,600 for a one-bedroom ocean-view suite.

PRINCEVILLE RESORT

Princeville, Kauai, Hawaii

When one imagines a wedding-turned-honeymoon in Hawaii, one undoubtedly pictures the blue-green Bali Hai cliffs against the palm-lined beaches of Kauai, made popular by so many films. Called the Garden Isle, Kauai is the most mature of the Hawaiian Islands; it's had plenty of time to manufacture its rugged interior and pumice clean its sandy perimeter. The North Shore, in particular, is an enchanting jumble of steepled mountains, waterfalls, sea caves, snorkeling reefs, and hidden beaches, much of it encompassed by the Hanalei National Wildlife Refuge. The Princeville Resort, taking full advantage of this setting, terraces along a twenty-three-acre ridge facing Hanalei Bay. With such commanding views (that mountain in the background is Bali Hai), it is no surprise that Princeville Resort is Kauai's most popular venue for weddings.

The panoramic view from the lobby, adorned in dark green marble and heavy chandeliers, may be the most dramatic from any hotel in the state. The lobby is actually on the ninth floor; elevators take guests down to their rooms or the beach. Most first-timers rave about such embellishments as the door chime, dimmer switches, bedside control panels, original oil paintings, oversize bathtub, and liquid-crystal bathroom doors that switch from clear to opaque. There are no lanais, but no worries—large windows allow you to admire the view even from the bathtub. Three restaurants, including the renowned La Cascata, offer excellent cuisine.

In the mid-1800s the resort property began as a sugarcane plantation owned by a colorful Scotsman named Robert Crichton Wyllie. After a summer visit by Queen Emma and her young son, Prince Albert, in 1860, Wyllie renamed the estate "Princeville." The property changed hands a number of times after Wyllie's death before it was commercially developed in 1985.

Princeville Resort hosts some 300 weddings per year, many of them Japanese, at one of four sites. **Hanalei Beach** and **Kamani Cove** offer magnificent ocean and mountain views. **Makana Terrace** commands spectacular views of Hanalei Bay and the waterfall-laced mountain of Na Molokama. Meaning "gift" in Hawaiian, Makana is indeed a gift of treasured memories for years to come. Or walk down the aisle along the **Bay Terrace,** featuring a reflecting pool and mountain and ocean views. This location provides both indoor and outdoor venues for a wedding ceremony and reception.

Princeville Resort
5520 Ka Haku Road
Princeville, Kauai, HI 96722-3069
(800) 826–4400 or (808) 826–9644
www.princeville.com

Location: Princeville is on the north side of Kauai.

Facility Rental, Amenities, and Policies: Resort wedding coordinators offer four fantastic wedding packages, beginning with the *Ku'uipo* (my sweetheart) package at $2,450. This includes the wedding site on the property, a ceremony officiant, a hand-tied bridal bouquet, a groom's boutonniere, a Hawaiian wedding certificate,

KAUAI ACTIVITIES

Active honeymooners and wedding guests can venture into the Na Pali Coast, featuring caves, secluded beaches, waterfalls, tropical foliage, and vistas that rise 4,000 feet from the ocean. Most day hikers turn around after about 2 miles. Or they view the coast from a twin-hulled catamaran or kayak, try a day of surfing in the punishing waves of Hanalei Bay, or simply float around inside of the reef and enjoy the colorful show in the underwater world. (Caution: Winter swells can be dangerous.) Less exhausting—though much more expensive—is exploring the interior from the vantage of a helicopter charter.

Better yet, sun at the resort's secluded beach, whether it be napping, taking long walks, shelling, or snorkeling. Take advantage of the treatments offered by the Princeville spa, preferably beachside where the sound of the surf and cool trade winds provide a perfect complement to the treatments. Most noteworthy is the lomi lomi treatment, passed on from generations of Hawaiians.

a bottle of champagne, and a 6-inch gourmet wedding cake. The *Aloha Pau'ole* (eternal love) package for $3,475 adds a white lattice archway adorned with florals, a Hawaiian *maile lei* for the groom, a professional photographer (twenty-four color photos in an album), a solo musician (Hawaiian or classical guitarist or flutist), a koa-framed Hawaiian wedding certificate, and assistance with the marriage license appointment.

For larger groups the Princeville Wedding package, at $5,400, includes the above-mentioned amenities, plus standing florals and railing bouquets with tulle, fifty chairs with white covers, a white runner, a larger photography package (thirty-six photos), videography, Princeville champagne glasses, a two-tiered stacked gourmet wedding cake, an enchanting candlelight dinner for two (oceanside setting or private terrace), and breakfast for two in the privacy of the couple's room.

The *Ali'i Nui* (royalty) package, for $8,400, includes all the amenities in the Princeville Wedding package as well as twenty-five more white covered chairs, a three-tiered wedding cake, an even larger

photographic and video package, champagne and chocolate-dipped strawberries in the room, a special couple's massage at the Princeville health club and spa, and three nights' luxury ocean-view accommodations for the wedding couple to include daily breakfast for two in Café Hanalei. The Royalty Wedding package is available January 4 through December 19. Functions held on most observed holidays are subject to an additional labor fee.

Catering: Four-course romantic dinners for two can be added to the package for $410 with a forty-eight-hour reservation. All wedding packages are set, however; no substitutions or credit will be given for unused package items, and restrictions may apply. Check with the resort for larger catering packages.

Accommodations: Choose from 252 rooms and suites, all with spectacular views of the Pacific Ocean, Hanalei Bay, or Na Molokama Mountain. Prices for a standard room, depending on the view, range from $465 to $695; suites are $820 to $5,000.

SEAWATCH RESTAURANT

Wailea, Maui, Hawaii

Wedding guests will congratulate you for finding the Seawatch Restaurant at Wailea. Their surprise will begin the moment they catch sight of the foliage, ponds, and cascading waterfalls clustered around the main entrance, and continue as they walk toward chairs set up on the wedding knoll overlooking the calming ocean. Knowing how relatively cost-effective this site is for Maui, you will be smiling all the way to the altar.

The Seawatch Restaurant itself is located on the Wailea Gold and Emerald Golf Courses, but it is no standard clubhouse. The interior is framed by giant fan palms and banana trees. Dining areas flow into one another, each complemented by soft pastel upholstery and whitewashed oak tables and chairs. Two murals by Big Island artist Arthur Johnson, capturing the vivid natural hues of the surrounding views, adorn the walls of the Grill. Maui's own Jan Kasprzycki's large paintings, with their brilliant colors, are displayed throughout the restaurant. Giant glass doors are open most of the time to coax in the gentle trades. Those who prefer dining alfresco love the lanai where the views are as delicious as the food—Maalaea, Molokini, Kahoolawe, Makena, humpback whales (in season), astounding sunsets, the seemingly infinite shades of green reaching up Mount Haleakala.

A primary attraction of the Seawatch as a wedding venue is its grounds—so many choices for setting up a circle of white chairs. The **Upper Wedding Knoll,** a grassy area near the restaurant, offers palm trees, a bougainvillea hedge, and partial views of ocean, the extensive greens of the golf course, and beyond. The **Lower Wedding Knoll,** on the opposite side of the hedge, presents a fuller view of the ocean, with the islands of Molokini and Kahoolawe in the background. The private **Lower Lawn** near (but below) the main dining room is surrounded by palm trees, with views of the ocean, neighboring islands, the golf course, and Mount Haleakala. Bordered by a low, hedge-lined fence for privacy, the Lower Lawn has a seating capacity of up to seventy people, making it an intimate setting for a wedding reception or cocktail party.

Wailea Vistas is a large grassy area at the peak of the Wailea golf course above the restaurant, with views of Haleakala, Makena, Molokini, and Kahoolawe, and is expansive enough for as many as 1,000 guests. The immense flat, grassy area of **Molokini Lookout** has the same panoramic ocean views and was specifically designed for wedding celebrations.

The **Upper Pond** is ideal for nestling groups of up to forty people near a landscaped water feature; the sound of cascading waterfalls enhances this semiprivate setting. The **Lower Pond,** also situated along the beautiful water feature, is part of the outdoor dining area and provides for an intimate setting for smaller wedding parties, showers, and bridal luncheons. Arrangements can be made to set up tables in the main dining room or on the lanai for smaller parties.

We spoke with Susan Jencks, who was cordial and professional. She will help arrange a wedding, large or small, casual or formal, and prefers, if possible, to conduct all arrangements via e-mail to keep a running record.

The Seawatch became an instant favorite from the day it opened in late January 1994. Much of the credit belongs to the kitchen staff, now headed by chef Todd Carlos, the grandson of a Greek immigrant who owned three restaurants. Always influenced by the sea, Carlos loves his work, and also loves to find new ways to put ingredients together. One of his signature dishes is macadamia nut crusted opakapaka (pink snapper) on Molokai purple sweet potatoes with lemongrass butter sauce. The Seawatch is the fourth Maui restaurant in seven years for the team of Roy Dunn and Mike Hooks, proprietors of two Koho Grill & Bar locations and The Plantation House Restaurant at Kapalua. They have also just recently opened their newest restaurant, Beach House, located in Koloa, Kauai.

Seawatch Restaurant
100 Wailea Golf Club Drive
Wailea, Maui, HI 96753
(808) 875–8080
www.seawatchrestaurant.com

Location: On the Gold Golf Course in Wailea, Maui, south of Kihei and north of Makena.

Facility Rental, Amenities, and Policies: Wedding ceremony site fees for the knolls and the vista areas are $225 to $850 for thirty chairs. Additional chairs for all sites are $3.00 each. With a cocktail reception on the Vista or Lookout sites, the fee starts at $1,500 for up to thirty guests, plus a food and beverage minimum of $1,200. The setup fee for the Upper Pond is $200 for up to forty guests; there is no fee for the Lower Pond area. The fee for the Lower Lawn for less than fifty guests, including the bar, is $400; $450 for more than fifty. The reception setup fee includes tables, chairs, serviceware, white linens, bar, and staff. Additional fees may be charged for special requests, plus tax, gratuity, and a service charge.

If you are planning a large event, the expansive restaurant is available for exclusive use in the evening. The open-air lanai and Lower Lawn will accommodate cocktail parties or wedding receptions. Buy-out of the entire restaurant requires a food and beverage minimum of $10,500, plus $50 to use existing seating, or $1,000 if a complete breakdown and reset with banquet round tables is necessary.

Catering: Parties with fewer than fifteen guests may order from the restaurant's regular menu; dinner entrees on the restaurant's menu are $25 to $34. (Vegetarian and children's menus are available.) Passed canapés, chafers, and platters are $3.50 to $10.00 per piece, with a minimum of twenty-five pieces; banquet meals are $44.00 to $63.00 per person, plus $7.00 for champagne or dessert. All wedding cakes are to be ordered directly through Maui Wedding Cakes.

Accommodations: The Grand Wailea Resort, Four Seasons Hotel, and the Fairmont Kea Lani Resort are in the immediate area.

CHRETIEN POINT PLANTATION

Sunset, Louisiana

Brides who book their weddings at the Chretien Point Plantation get to be Scarlett O'Hara for the day. A wedding here is a step back into the architecture and gentility of the Old South. "I think we're fabulous at spoiling and ta-ta-ing our brides," said manager Lynley Jones. "We try to out-think their every need and wish. Our plan is to have the bridal party arrive at the mansion, get dressed, and go!"

Situated on twenty secluded acres and just a fifteen-minute drive from Lafayette, Louisiana, the Chretien Point Plantation is a preserved vignette of the past. The plantation's ramp knee staircase and fan light windows were copied from Tara in the movie *Gone with the Wind*. Built in 1831 on the banks of the Bayou Bourbeaux by Canadian Hypolite Chretien and his Spanish-born wife, Felicite Neda, the twelve-room brick mansion was the centerpiece of a 3,000-acre cotton plantation. Elements of French Colonial, Early Classical, and Adam architecture—which features upper and lower galleries, arched windows, and Tuscan columns—combine to make the Chretien Point mansion unique. The interior of the house was designed such that all of the main rooms open onto the upper and lower galleries (porches), which allows the cool breezes to freely flow during southern Louisiana's tropical summers.

Like Tara, Chretien Point had its day in the Civil War. On October 15, 1863, the Battle of Buzzard's Prairie was fought on the grounds of the plantation, with Union forces occupying the lower floor of the mansion. Battle reenactments are held on the property annually, during a weekend of teas, storytelling, and demonstrations by docents in period costume.

Formal tours of the plantation are conducted daily, and special historical events are scheduled throughout the year. The plantation holds regular ghost tours and candlelight ghost dinners overseen by the family matriarch, Felicite Neda Chretien, whose portrait hangs in the dining room. Visitors to the plantation have reported seeing several different ghosts, such as a robber, Union and Confederate soldiers, and a young female cousin who had all died on the property.

Museums and fine dining are just ten minutes away in Lafayette, the capital of Cajun country. Lafayette's first settlers were exiled French Acadians from Nova Scotia in the late 1700s. Acadian Village, which is a museum of early Acadian houses, a blacksmith shop, a general store, and a chapel, best illustrates Lafayette's settlement history.

Chretien Point Plantation
665 Chretien Point Road
Sunset, LA 70584
(800) 880–7050 or (337) 662–7050
www.chretienpoint.com

Location: Sunset is half an hour north of Lafayette on Interstate 49. After leaving I–49 at exit 11, follow the highway signs at each turn to the plantation.

Facility Rental, Amenities, and Policies: The rental fee for the plantation grounds and mansion for a three-hour event is $1,200 for up to 100 guests, $1,500 for up to 200, and $2,000 for 200 or more. This fee includes uniformed butlers; white chairs; buffet, cake, guest book, and cake tables; silver serving trays, coffee service,

serving trays, cake plate, punch bowls, and champagne buckets.

A staff consultant is assigned to the couple to assist in the planning, design, and preparation of the ceremony and reception. The consultant can coordinate the officiant, cakes, photographer, florist, and musicians from a list of referrals, as well as the in-house catering and service.

The mansion is open for preparation, dressing, and early photography for one and a half hours prior to the commencement of the ceremony. The bride and her photographer may schedule a one-hour photo session during open hours (10:00 A.M. to 5:00 P.M.) several weeks prior to the wedding day. The couple may also schedule a one-hour rehearsal the afternoon prior to the wedding, although another date may be requested.

Catering: Buffets, butler-passed hors d'oeuvres, and plated meals are all prepared in house for the reception. Italian, Mediterranean, and seafood with a Cajun flavor dominate the menu options, although tempting arrays of meats and sides are available. Buffets range from $30 to $50 per person, while seated dinners are $20 to $80 per person. Beverage service starts at $6.95 per person for punch, champagne, and soft drinks, ranging to to $19.95 for the premium open bar. Couples are free to contract with a baker directly, but may wish to take advantage of the wedding and groom's cakes made exclusively for the mansion. The staff prepare a complimentary send-off picnic, complete with a chilled bottle of champagne and two plates generously filled with tastes from all items served at the reception.

Extras: Tents for the reception or ceremony rent from $750 to $1,400. Horse-drawn carriage rental is available for $375 for the bride's arrival and the wedded couple's departure. The mansion also offers 20 percent off the retail price on wedding invitations, stationery, shower invitations, napkins, and wedding favors.

Accommodations: Weddings beginning after 4:00 P.M. must rent the entire mansion overnight for $925. This includes the 5 guest rooms and a full plantation breakfast served the following morning. (Summer couples usually skinny-dip in the pool after midnight, we're told.) Couples not renting out the entire mansion should be sure to spend their wedding night in the "Prime Minister's Suite" (the honeymoon suite), which features a Jacuzzi tub with chandelier and a full breakfast. The remaining 4 rooms can be negotiated for other guests, but Jones says it makes more sense to rent out the entire mansion for exclusive use. Guests otherwise will be politely asked to leave once the three-hour site rental period ends with "last call."

The 5 bedrooms, with names like Plantation Office and Magnolia Room, are all tastefully appointed with period beds and armoires. Rates range from $175 to $250 per night, and include a full plantation breakfast and a tour of the mansion upon check-in. French and German languages can be accommodated if notified in advance. Tennis, hiking, and swimming (in season) are available on the grounds. Guests not staying at the mansion will be able to book rooms in Opelousas or Lafayette.

Keep in Mind: The Gulf of Mexico generates hot, humid weather in summer. Peak bridal season for Chretien Point is March through May and September through November. It's best to book as far in advance as possible.

NOTTOWAY PLANTATION RESTAURANT AND INN

White Castle, Louisiana

John Hampden Randolph completed the wedding-cake-white Greek Revival mansion on the Nottoway sugar plantation in 1859. It was one of more than 300 mansions bordering both sides of the Mississippi from Baton Rouge to New Orleans. The story goes that in 1862, a Union gunboat opened fire on "the white castle," but one of its officers recognized Nottoway as a place he had previously visited and promised to spare the mansion if Randolph's wife, Emily Jane, would invite him back after the war. Although the film *Gone with the Wind* was set in the northern hills of Georgia, Nottoway served as inspiration for Tara. Scarlett O'Hara fashioned her dress from drapes similar to those still hanging in the Randolph study.

This 100-mile "River Road" was the richest area in America, but during the Depression most of the mansions that weren't destroyed during the war fell into ruin; only a few dozen are left standing. Many have opened their ornate doors to overnight guests who wish to sleep where Confederate soldiers once slept, rock on verandas pocked by Union bullets, and set their weddings in the genteel opulence of antebellum aristocracy. Thanks to a wealthy Australian who stayed at the Nottoway in 1985 and loved it so much that he bought it, it is the largest surviving mansion in the South (at 53,000 square feet).

Of all of the sixty-four rooms, perhaps the one that speaks most eloquently of a bygone era is the grand White Ballroom. Graced with Corinthian columns, triple archways, and plaster frieze work, the spacious ballroom is still one of the many enchanting features of the mansion. It is easy to picture couples in period dress waltzing in and out of the huge guillotine windows to enjoy the view of the Mississippi. The Randolphs designed the room with the weddings of their seven daughters in mind, and six were married here. Ceremonies usually take place in the White Ballroom, while receptions are held in Randolph Hall or the Camellia and Magnolia Rooms, and each carries certain size and catering restrictions.

Misty Palermo, event sales coordinator, said weddings at Nottoway "typify the tradition of great southern hospitality." The staff handle forty weddings per year with couples from all over the United States and as far away as Hong Kong. The largest wedding included 500 guests; the smallest involved just the bride and groom.

Chef Johnny "Jambalaya" Percle, so nicknamed by Dr. John, one of the musician celebrities he has worked for, heads the staff in the preparation of all meals at the Nottoway. His salty background began with cooking gumbos for his father's hunting camp and continued through an apprenticeship offshore with a former army cook; he's also catered to such celebrities as the Neville Brothers, Diana Ross, and the Rolling Stones.

Nottoway Plantation Restaurant and Inn
30970 Highway 405
P.O. Box 160
White Castle, LA 70788–0160
(225) 545–2730
www.nottoway.com

Location: Between Baton Rouge and New Orleans on the Great River Road.

Facility Rental, Amenities, and Policies: A ceremony and reception in Randolph Hall (70- to 250-guest capacity) is $2,000, or $1,200 for a reception without a ceremony. A ceremony and dinner in either the Camellia or the Magnolia Rooms (fifty to one hundred) costs $1,500, or $700 for a reception alone. Package fees in various rooms include a thirty-minute ceremony and three-hour reception, and require a $3,800 minimum food and beverage purchase.

Ceremony rental fees include twelve chairs, and each additional chair, if approved, is $4.00. Two guest rooms are available for changing. Fresh floral arrangements and matching candelabras are provided. Reception fees include setup, cleanup, cake cutting, china, glassware, linens, silverware, service staff, and a bridal basket of champagne, fruit, cheese, and crackers after the reception.

The bride and groom are responsible for retaining a minister or officiant, entertainment, photographer/videographer, cakes, and florist for the wedding party from Nottoway's contact list. Nottoway's wedding coordinator will work with the couple on all wedding details. The ceremony begins after 6:30 P.M.; guests are invited to arrive thirty minutes prior and walk about the mansion. Photography can take place in any room or gallery as long as no tour group is present.

Catering: The Iberville, Cornelia, and Magnolia hors d'oeuvres packages are $26.95 to $31.95 per person, and each includes six or seven hot items (perhaps Chef Johnny's Cajun Two-Step) and four or five cold items (say, almond chicken with black olives and grapes). The Randolph is $33.95 for 100 to 250 guests and begins with a round of beef or plantation glazed ham, plus a choice of nine hot and five cold items. The Paddlewheel is $37.95 for 15 to 250 guests and begins with steamship round of beef, pineapple honey glazed ham served with onion and poppy seed breads, and a paddlewheel of imported cheeses, fruit, and vegetables. Plated dinner entrees are $27.95 to $31.95 with choice of salads and starters.

Accommodations: The Nottoway has 11 guest rooms and 3 suites, ranging from $115 to $275 depending on room and number of occupants. All rooms include sherry, a guided tour of the mansion, wake-up call with hot coffee, juice, and sweet potato muffins, and a full plantation breakfast. The bridal suite has three rooms with Victorian queen bed, parlor, breakfast area, sleeper sofa, Jacuzzi, and private pool.

Keep in Mind: Guided tours are offered from 9:00 A.M. to 5:00 P.M. seven days a week, excepting only Christmas Day. Some of the rooms are integral to the public tours, which restricts check-in and check-out times.

ASTICOU INN
Northeast Harbor, Maine

Asticou Inn, at the doorstep of Acadia National Park, is in Northeast Harbor on the "quiet side" of Mount Desert Island. Augustus Chase Savage built the inn in 1883 on a hill overlooking the harbor to meet the great lodging demands of the "rusticators," those

wealthy urban refugees who flocked here in summer to enjoy the island's beauty. The country inn soon became renowned for its charm and hospitality. Named in honor of a local Penobscot chief, Asticou Inn itself is not rustic; it bespeaks an understated sophistication—in a Maine way—and is as comfortable as your grandmother's house.

This classic resort beckons with relaxed strolls through graceful flower gardens, good Down East dining, and warm, attentive service. Restored to its turn-of-the-twentieth-century style, the inn re-creates the charm of a bygone era. Sit with cocktails on the deck and watch sailboats bob at anchor as the sun sparkles off the deep blue water, or as the moon turns the harbor to liquid gold. Across the road, trails wind deep into Acadia National Park.

Mount Desert Island is anything but a desert. Much of the island is included in Acadia National Park, encompassing more than 47,000 acres of granite-domed mountains, woodlands, lakes and ponds, and ocean shoreline. Such diverse habitats create striking scenery and make the park a haven for wildlife and plants. Today the park offers scientific, educational, and recreational activities unparalleled along the East Coast. Hike to the top of Cadillac Mountain to enjoy a spectacular sunrise over Frenchman's Bay, or explore some of the quieter, more secluded mountain paths. Bike along more than 40 miles of the tree-lined carriage roads that wind over hillsides and near glassy lakes.

The elegant Asticou Inn offers beautiful grounds and gardens for a ceremony. The extensive lawns are perfect for a tented reception, and can accommodate 750 guests—although the inn does many destination-size weddings for 100 or fewer, and Sunday weddings ranging from 30 to 50. The dining room can host a formal reception or rehearsal dinner, and for weddings of fifteen to fifty, the inn offers a room that overlooks the water. Across the street are the Asticou Azalea Gardens for wedding photographs, particularly mid-May through mid-June for spring blooms. Impeccably manicured, with Oriental themes, the Azalea Gardens were created by Savage and now owned by the Island Foundation.

Asticou Inn has hosted weddings for more than a century; from the moment they step through the door, the bride and groom will know they're in capable hands. We spoke with the inn's assistant manager, Tom Weverstead, who told us he prefers the "high-maintenance" bride who knows exactly what she wants. (One year the bride's father ran the wedding from folders with tabs for *every* detail—that might have pushed Weverstead's otherwise affable personality.)

The Asticou Inn
P.O. Box 337
Northeast Harbor, ME 04662
(800) 258–3373 or (207) 276–3344
www.asticou.com

Location: Follow Maine Highway 3 south onto Mount Desert Island.

Facility Rental, Amenities, and Policies: Saturday weddings require a minimum of one hundred people. Pricing varies depending on the number of guests, rental, food, alcohol, and whether it is a tent or dining room event. Evening weddings in July and August must be held in a tent so that the full-service dining room is available for inn guests. The inn offers different-size tents to accommodate as many guests as desired. Tent options include a white cathedral tent with clear windows overlooking the harbor, food tent for buffet or kitchen annex, bathroom tent with deluxe stalls and washstands, parquet dance floor, heating if needed, cocktail tent, electrical services, and lights. Smaller tents are available for rehearsal dinners in the Begonia Garden. A $300 fee is assessed to close down the restaurant for a large reception, if preferable to a tented reception, and there is an additional $500 setup fee for a ceremony.

Catering: Asticou Inn offers a variety of menu choices, including the Downeast Lobster Feast Reception for $36 per person, which also features fish chowder, Maine mussels, clams, roasted prime rib au jus, native corn on the cob, boiled red bliss potatoes, and Maine blueberry pie with ice cream. Two dinner buffet menus include a soup and salad choice, choice of two or three entrees, and carved meat for $44 to $56 person. A three-hour Hors d'Oeuvres Reception is offered for $38 per person and includes a variety of passed items, such as chilled main crab salad in phyllo shells and rilletes of duck with blueberry chutney in phyllo, and a carving station with the chef presiding over herb and pepper crusted tenderloin beef or ballotine of turkey with lemon apple chutney.

Extras: The bride may choose to arrive via limousine, water taxi, or horse-drawn carriage. Flowers, beauty services, photographers, videographers, cakes, ceremony music, disc jockeys, officiants, and churches are displayed on Asticou Inn's Web site.

Accommodations: In addition to the main inn, Asticou Inn offers several guest houses: Cranberry, Bird Bank, and Blue Spruce overlook charming gardens, while the more contemporary Topsiders have parlors with balconies that overlook the harbor. The Asticou Inn offers the Modified American Plan (breakfast and dinner) as well as the European Plan (deluxe continental breakfast buffet). The spring season, May 20 through June 30, offers European Plan pricing, ranging from $95 for a single with bath to $200 for a suite; the summer season, July 1 through August 31, offers Modified American Plan pricing, ranging from $199 for a single with bath to $402 for the suite, as well as a European Plan option at $150 to $325; the fall season, September 1 through October 16, offers European Plan prices of $90 to $230.

The inn will reserve a block of 20 rooms for wedding guests for $2,500 until ninety days prior to the event, at which time they will be released. Guests should be advised to book their rooms as soon as possible.

Keep in Mind: Asticou Inn is open mid-May through mid-October only, with May and June being the peak months for weddings. Book about a year in advance.

LONGFELLOW'S WAYSIDE INN
Sudbury, Massachusetts

Anyone who grew up in New England fondly remembers Longfellow's Wayside Inn, and more than likely attended a party in the inn or a ceremony in the Martha-Mary Chapel on the property. At least 400 couples participate in this slice of colonial history every year. The inn has served as a "hous of entertainment" since 1716, when it was a tavern in David Howe's one-up, one-down home (circa 1688). Howe's Tavern thrived by way of the busy coach traffic to and from the cities of Boston and Worcester. The tavern was passed down through three generations of Howes between 1746 and 1861, and it evolved in scope and size as each left his mark on the "hous." One innkeeper was Ezekiel Howe, a lieutenant colonel in the Revolutionary War who led the Sudbury Minute and Militia to battle in Concord in 1775. In 1861 relatives closed the inn to overnight accommodation, renting the small rooms out to itinerant farmers for lengthy stays and its hall out for dances. The Howe innkeeping business would not thrive again until a wool merchant from Malden, Massachusetts, showed new interest in 1897.

In the meantime Henry Longfellow had visited the Howe Tavern, and based his 1863 book of poems, *Tales of a Wayside Inn*, on a group of fictitious characters who regularly gathered at the old Sudbury tavern. Lyman Howe, the inn's third-generation owner, was the character featured in "The Landlord's Tale," where Longfellow penned the immortal phrase, "Listen my children and you shall hear, of the midnight ride of Paul Revere." Edward Rivers Lemon, an admirer of antiquities, purchased the inn in 1897 as "a retreat for literary pilgrims," capitalizing on the interest generated by the widely read poet. Lemon renamed the old Howe Tavern Longfellow's Wayside Inn and operated it with his wife, Cora, until his death in 1919.

Cora Lemon sold the inn in 1923 to automobile manufacturer Henry Ford, who would eventually have the most visual impact on the Wayside Inn site. During his tenure he moved the one-room Redstone School to the grounds; built the Grist Mill; and, after acquiring some 3,000 acres around the inn, developed a trade school for boys, which operated until 1947. He created the nonprofit status that the inn operates under today, and was its last private owner.

Ford built the white-steepled Martha-Mary Chapel in 1940, dedicating it to his mother-in-law, Martha Bryant, and his own mother, Mary Ford. The nondenominational chapel was built from the large pine trees uprooted by the infamous hurricane of 1938 in the area where the chapel now stands. A miniature version of the First Parish Church located in Bradford, Massachusetts, the Martha-Mary Chapel has long been recognized as a South Sudbury landmark, from the gilded banner weather vane atop the stark white spire to the elegant Irish crystal chandelier above the humble pews.

Many brides choose to have their wedding photographs taken at the Wayside Grist Mill, located on the grounds of the Wayside Inn Historic Site near the chapel. The lush Longfellow Garden is also an ideal spot for wedding photos in summer.

Longfellow's Wayside Inn
72 Wayside Inn Road
Sudbury, MA 01776
(800) 339-1776 or (978) 443-1776
www.wayside.org

Location: Longfellow's Wayside Inn is an eighth of a mile from U.S. Highway 20 near Sudbury.

Facility Rental, Amenities, and Policies: Weddings at the inn are held in the nondenominational Martha-Mary Chapel through all four seasons. The chapel seats 150 guests, including three rows in a raised balcony that overlooks the altar. The rental fee for the chapel was not disclosed, although published sources have shown around $600.

Catering: Receptions are offered in the inn's private dinning rooms. The Colonial Wedding Buffet is $31.95 per person, and the Bountiful Wedding Buffet is $57.95 per person, both with a minimum of thirty guests. The Wayside Wedding Menu runs $36.95 to $49.95, and main course selections might include filet mignon with brandy mushroom sauce ($45.95 per guest); roast native turkey, sausage, bread crumb stuffing, and giblet gravy ($38.95); and mustard herb crusted roast rack of lamb ($49.95).

A Wayside Inn Wedding with reception includes candles, bridal linen, wedding cake, silver cake knife and server, champagne toast, bride and groom toasting glasses, fresh flowers, guest book, room charges, and wedding consultation services.

Extras: The bride and groom can be transported from the chapel to the Wayside Inn by traditional horse and surrey for a small additional fee. Contact the inn for local vendor information.

Accommodations: The inn's 10 intimate guest rooms are all individually decorated and interspersed with country antiques. All have a private bath, air-conditioning, and telephone. There is a sitting room reserved for the exclusive use of guests, and a bountiful country breakfast is included with each night's stay. Reservations are recommended well in advance. Nightly rates are $96 to $120 single occupancy and $122 to $155 double occupancy.

WHITE ELEPHANT
Nantucket, Massachusetts

Originally a booming whaling port, Nantucket has changed little since the seventeenth century. Nearly half the island is preserved as conservation lands and the town as a historical district. Consequently the island still has wide swaths of clean sand framed by grasslands that hug the shoreline, while freshwater ponds, salt marshes, and cranberry bogs characterize the interior. Seaside cottages and old-fashioned lamps still line the streets, but where great whaling ships once waited to set out on hazardous journeys, pleasure boats now find safe harbor in one of the finest docking facilities in the world. On the north shore Nantucket's chowder houses, stately inns, boutiques, and art galleries propel its more modern industry. Weddings on this photogenic toy island would be worth the short trip across the water.

One of the more popular places for weddings is in front of Brant Point, a quaint lighthouse considered the doorway to Nantucket. Beaches are also popular, particularly Jetties Beach, where groups of six people or less won't need a permit to assemble. One couple even married on the steps of a bank on historic Main Street. Few venues on the island will permit larger weddings, however. One exception is the White Elephant, with elegant packages for groups of 25 to 75, and up to 700 on the lawn.

The White Elephant, a sail-in hotel alongside Nantucket's magnificent harbor, is just minutes from unique boutiques, restaurants, and museums. The dream of a Nantucket socialite, the hotel began as an eclectic mix of cottages in the 1920s, which islanders referred to as "Mrs. Ludgwig's White Elephant." Now a misnomer, the White Elephant has evolved into a premier hotel that offers an unexpected blend of island charm and elegant amenities. Rooms (distributed among one building and twelve cottages) are big and airy—indeed, the most spacious on Nantucket, with country-chic decor. Most offer harbor views. The best way to characterize the White Elephant is casual sophistication—it is acceptable for bridesmaids to wear flip-flops (designer, of course) under their Vera Wang gowns.

Nantucket's population on this tiny elbow of an island (14 miles long by 3 miles wide) swells to 40,000 in summer, joined by thousands of visitors who crowd the narrow cobblestone streets every week. For this reason the White Elephant is available for a few select wedding parties in early May and late October. As part of the exclusive Wedding Weekend, wedding parties may reserve the entire facility so that family and friends can enjoy privacy and the dedicated attention of the staff. During late spring, summer, and fall, smaller, more intimate weddings for thirty to fifty people may be accommodated in the sunroom and foyers, with a ceremony and cocktail reception outside on the Harborside Terrace adjacent to the sunroom foyer. The private Ivory Room can host wedding parties for up to fifty. More options for larger weddings exist at the White Elephant's sister property, Harbor House Village. A couple might want to even shoot for April, when Nantucket is a sea of daffodils.The White Elephant has no strict rules on bookings; if space is available, the hotel can be very flexible.

White Elephant
50 Easton Street
P.O. Box 1139
Nantucket, MA 02554
(508) 228–2500
Reservations: (800) 445–6574
Catering Office: (508) 623–2400
www.whiteelephanthotel.com

Location: Nantucket Island is 30 miles off the coast of Cape Cod, Massachusetts. It is accessible year-round by flights from Boston, Providence, New York/Newark, Chicago, Washington, DC, and Philadelphia. Regular ferry service is available from Hyannis, Massachusetts.

Facility Rental, Amenities, and Policies: A harbor-view wedding at White Elephant carries a facility rental fee of $1,000. The rental includes votive candles on banquet tables, white cotton twill and sandalwood

cotton twill linens with white cotton napkins, use of a silver wedding-cake knife and server, and framed nameplates. The fee does not include special linens, chairs, lighting, or floral arrangements.

Catering: The White Elephant's chef and catering team will tailor menu selections to create a customized reception. A sampling of the plated menu includes a meal of roasted prime rib with Yukon gold mashed potatoes for $65 per person; seared sea scallops with lobster sauce, or roasted beef tenderloin with truffled mashed potatoes and seasonal vegetables, for $85 per person; or pan-seared veal chops with wild mushroom sauce for $105 per person. The White Elephant also offers a wedding brunch for $52 per person. Food and beverage minimums do apply, and there is an additional fee for each buffet chef and each bartender.

The White Elephant can offer a specialty cake for a small function, but elaborate wedding cakes should be sought from outside vendors. There is a $3.00 plating fee for cakes brought in from outside.

Accommodations: The White Elephant has 53 elegantly decorated rooms, which offer a mix of single bedrooms and two-bedroom suites, many with a working fireplace. Lodging prices vary with the season. Garden- and harbor-view king guest rooms are $225 to $600; garden- and harbor-view suites, with a king bedroom and sitting room, are $275 to $700.

Keep in Mind: The island is reachable by small plane or a high-speed ferry, but those in the know suggest that the best way to slide into its slow tempo is to take the hypnotic freight vessel. It is also advisable not to take a car to the congested island; rather, rent a bicycle and pedal along the island's many bike paths.

CHAPEL OF LOVE,
MALL OF AMERICA

Bloomington, Minnesota

Only in America can a mall become a tourist destination, and a chapel within a mall become popular for weddings. Chapel of Love in the Mall of America would not be for everyone, but for 300 to 400 couples a year, weddings at the chapel are marriages of convenience. Think about it—everything the couple needs for a full wedding is right at hand. The Chapel of Love even operates its own boutique for the wedding gown, attendant dresses, and all the apparel and ceremony accessories a couple could desire, as well as its own florist and photography studio. The women in the wedding party can get their hair and makeup done at any of a number of salons while the men shop for suits or rent their tuxes. The mall will have the rings and the perfect strappy heels. The reception can be held at one of more than a dozen restaurants, and afterward guests can ride the spiraling roller coaster in the mall's Camp Snoopy amusement park.

When Mall of America opened in 1992, it was an unprecedented mix of retail and entertainment, offering visitors—forty-six million every year—the chance to shop their favorite stores as well as see a movie, meet a celebrity, visit an aquarium, or build a LEGO castle. The Mall of America filled a seventy-eight-acre vacancy left by the Twins and the Vikings when they moved from Met Stadium in Bloomington to the Metrodome in downtown Minneapolis. The mall has since become a treasure for the entire state of Minnesota, and a destination for everything from family vacations to weekend getaways and even honeymoons. Tourists from Canada, England, Sweden, Ireland, and Japan come to take in the sights and capitalize on sales-tax-free clothing.

The Chapel of Love was the creation of MaryAnne London, who got the idea when she saw a wedding chapel in a Detroit strip mall in 1994. She took the idea for an elegant wedding chapel to Mall of America administrators, who loaned her fixtures for the store through their program that helps new retailers get their businesses off the ground.

All ceremonies are performed by ministers in the privacy of the tastefully decorated chapel, with floral baskets decorating white walls and white pedestals on either side of the altar. These professionals are happy to perform a Christian, spiritual, or civil ceremony, making each wedding personal and unique. The maximum capacity is seventy people. The chapel also boasts Weddings to Go, which offer wedding planning and personnel for off-site weddings.

Since its opening in the mall, the chapel moved to its new location on the third floor next to Bloomingdale's to feature a selection of bridal apparel including gowns, shoes, veils, gloves, and purses. The chapel also sells candles, guest books, cake toppers, jewelry, garters, invitations, novelties, and favors. The boutique has informal bridal, flower girl, first communion, and special occasion dresses as well, which can be viewed on the Web site.

Chapel of Love
345 East Broadway
Mall of America
Bloomington, MN 55425
(800) 299–5683 or (952) 854–4656
www.chapeloflove.com

Location: In the Mall of America next to Bloomingdale's.

Facility Rental, Amenities, and Policies: The chapel is open 365 days a year and offers six packages tailored to budget, guests, and time frame. The Dream Wedding is the most economically priced ceremony, and includes the wedding couple and a maximum of two guests. The couple has use of the chapel for twenty minutes, romantic background music, and an officiant. This package is offered for $299, Monday through Thursday; $349, Friday and Saturday; and $449 on Sunday. The most exclusive package is the Premier, which hosts a maximum of seventy guests for sixty minutes and includes a pre-wedding and on-site consultant, a dressing room, unity candle, garter, champagne glasses, and bottle of champagne.

This package is offered for $699, Monday through Thursday; $749, Friday and Saturday; and $849 on Sunday. Holidays have an additional fee of $75 on every package.

Catering: Receptions are not permitted at the Chapel of Love, but numerous reception sites and restaurants exist in the immediate area. Check with staff for recommendations.

Extras: Couples are allowed, based on availability, to come early or to linger after the ceremony for a fee of $25 per fifteen-minute interval. The chapel also has floral arrangements and photographers available at an additional fee.

Accommodations: The highest rated in the area is the new 257-room Crowne Plaza Hotel (5401 Green Valley Drive, Bloomington, MN 55437; 952–831–8000). It is located near Minneapolis–Airport West just ten minutes away from the Mall of America and rates are $109 to $159.

Keep in Mind: The shortest time between booking a wedding and performing a ceremony has been about thirty minutes, but bear in mind that the chapel books about five to ten ceremonies per week.

HELI USA AIRWAYS: LAS VEGAS TO THE GRAND CANYON WEST RANCH
Las Vegas, Nevada, and Meadview, Arizona

Many travelers to the American Southwest want to see it all in one trip: Las Vegas, the Grand Canyon, and perhaps a dude ranch. If there's time, some would also like to squeeze in a wedding. Heli USA Airways provides *all* of the above—literally!

Nigel Turner, president and CEO of Heli USA, has been operating helicopter tours of the Las Vegas lights and the Grand Canyon rim for more than sixteen years. He discovered that visitors want a taste of casino nightlife, but then want to experience the remoteness, adventure, and beauty of the Grand Canyon in Arizona, as well as a western cattle ranch. The company acquired a working cattle ranch in 2002, thus putting it in the unique position of being able to provide a dozen or more tour options. Three of these options are for weddings.

Grand Canyon National Park, a World Heritage Site, encompasses nearly 1.25 million acres on the Colorado Plateau in northwestern Arizona. Incised by the Colorado River, the canyon is 6,000 feet deep at its deepest point and 15 miles at its widest. To drive between Las Vegas and the Grand Canyon (a five-hour trip), you have to slip through the eye of the needle that is Hoover Dam. Bumper-to-bumper traffic may dash your awe at this engineering feat, but Heli USA tours will restore it. The Chariots of Fire tour, for instance, flies over Lake Mead and Hoover Dam before descending below the rim of the Grand Canyon. The return journey includes panoramic views of Iceberg Canyon, the Valley of Fire, and the Bowl of Fire, and concludes with a cruise down the dazzling Las Vegas Strip.

Heli USA's Grand Canyon Ranch West is a 106,000-acre working ranch on the western end of the canyon near Meadview, Arizona. One helicopter tour option is the Grand Canyon Helicopter and Sunset Adventure. After a forty-five-minute flight, passengers are taken by horse-drawn wagon along the Old Mormon Trail through the Joshua tree forest. At the ranch house they enjoy a western-style dinner and cowboy entertainment around a campfire, then return by car through the floodlight lit Hoover Dam. Other tour options include staying at the ranch overnight in authentic tepees or private pine cabins sheltered by Spirit Mountain. Patrons may also drive to the ranch for a stay.

Having flown more than 800,000 passengers, Heli USA Airways claims an exceptional safety record. The company flies only million-dollar A-Star Executive Helicopters—the preferred sightseeing helicopter worldwide—and boasts the largest fleet of them in the western United States. All are faster than Bell Helicopters and feature climate control, high-load capacities, and forward-facing seats for unrestricted viewing. (Because of weight restrictions, heavier passengers may be asked to purchase an extra ticket.)

Heli USA Airways also operates helicopter tours in Oahu and Kauai, Hawaii.

Heli USA Airways
McCarran Executive Air Terminal
275 East Tropicana Avenue
Las Vegas, NV 89109
www.heliusa.com

Grand Canyon Ranch West
3750 East Diamond Bar Ranch Road
Meadview, AZ 86444
www.grandcanyonranch.com
Reservations: (800) 359–8727 or (702) 736–8787

Location: All Heli USA Grand Canyon and Las Vegas helicopter tours depart from the Las Vegas Executive Air Terminal at McCarran International Airport, just minutes from the Strip. Grand Canyon Ranch West is forty minutes from Las Vegas by helicopter, only two and a half hours from Las Vegas by car, and "a little longer by horseback."

Facility Rental, Amenities, and Policies: The Grand Canyon Ranch Wedding option tours the canyon, and then lands at the ranch. The couple and their wedding party are taken to the ranch house by buggy, or to a vista overlooking the canyon's rim for the wedding ceremony, champagne, and cake. The return flight includes views of the Strip. The package is $2,450 for five people; that would include the bride, groom, ceremony officiant, one or two witnesses, and a photographer. Additional guests, for a maximum of twenty-four people in the wedding party, cost $285 each. Flight time and ranch time are each one and a half hours. This tour has five daily departures.

The Grand Canyon Wedding Flight tour takes the couple farther and deeper into the canyon. The ceremony is conducted at the exclusive New Water Springs located on the Grand Canyon Plateau, with panoramic views of the canyon's North Rim. The couple celebrate with champagne toasts and cake before returning to Las Vegas, touring Iceberg Canyon, Valley of Fire, and the Strip along the way. The package is $2,450 for five people in the party, including officiant, plus $285 per additional guest. Flight time is one and a half hours, with a forty-minute ceremony intermission. There are five departures daily.

Couples marry in flight over Las Vegas in the Cupid's Night Ceremony tour package. During this tour the helicopter cruises past the space beam of the Luxor Pyramid, the Statue of Liberty in front of New York–New York, the fountains of Bellagio, the old gambling area of Fremont Street, and downtown. This flight is $695 for five people, including minister, plus $72 per additional passenger for a maximum of thirty guests. The flight leaves at dusk; allow two hours.

All wedding flight packages include limousine transfers to and from the couple's hotel, driver's gratuity, officiant's fee, a 12-inch rose bouquet for the bride, a rose boutonniere for the groom, a 6-inch wedding cake, and champagne. The $50 cost of the marriage license is not included. All tours can be booked on the Heli USA Web site.

Catering: Call or see the Web site for catering add-ons.

Extras: Heli USA works with the staff at Candlelight Wedding Chapel; for additional services such as photographer or videographer, contact the chapel at (800) 962–1818 or (702) 735–4179 in Las Vegas, and refer to the Heli USA tour code.

Accommodations: Lodging is available on the Las Vegas Strip or the Grand Canyon West Ranch.

LITTLE CHAPEL OF THE FLOWERS
Las Vegas, Nevada

Las Vegas, Nevada, with more than 130,000 ceremonies every year, is the birthplace of the destination wedding and the quickie-wedding chapel, running the gamut from drive-though nuptial windows to Elvis ministers. We first discovered the Little Chapel of the Flowers on the Internet. Basing our opinions on the images, packages, and details featured on the Web site, we thought this to be among the nicest chapels in Las Vegas. Admittedly, we had our reservations and preconceived notions, but upon visiting the property we were pleasantly surprised by how elegant the little chapels really are.

Little Chapel of the Flowers, with more than fifty years in the business, is on Las Vegas Boulevard South between the traditional older casinos on Freemont—where the gambling began—and the Strip. Mind you, this is not the nicest section of the city, but it is fifteen minutes from the courthouse and probably just as far from most couples' hotels. Once they enter the parking lot, perhaps in their own limo, they will be enchanted by the miniature chapels and tiny garden complete with wishing well, bridge, and gazebo, all enclosed by tall shade trees and fencing. The chapels are quite small, but then do they need to be large? Each is simply decorated in a motif to match its name: Victorian (seating thirty guests) is draped in soft blues, with white and antique accents; Magnolia (seating twenty) is painted in a bold yellow with southern lines; and La Capella has dark wood pews (seating seventy) and a Merlot-colored Venetian plaster treatment on the walls. Ceremonies are also conducted at the gazebo in the shadow of the property's first little white traditional chapel. Seating is arranged in white chairs for up to twenty guests.

Weddings are scheduled no less than thirty minutes apart per chapel, and the staff of forty keep it all running smoothly. We witnessed four or five wedding parties coming and going during our brief visit, and there was never a sense of crowdedness or rushing. In fact, the entire production moved along like clockwork—or, more cynically, like a conveyor belt. No one looked stressed or impatient, although some came early enough to wait on the porch while the ceremony scheduled before them was being conducted—no peeking! (Little Flowers offers a "first look" service in which the bride is hidden until her time to walk down the aisle.) Once the ceremony is over, couples are whisked around certain posing points on the property by a photographer. We spoke to a photographer, coordinator, and limo driver and found all to be friendly and willing to talk to us—as they continued their work, which they clearly loved doing. One just-married couple we spoke to, from Dublin, Ireland, were pleased with the way the minister kept the ceremony fresh. (They also marveled at Las Vegas's springtime weather.)

The reservations department is separated from the wedding chapels to allow hostesses and wedding coordinators to concentrate on each wedding rather than answer phones and book future weddings during the ceremony. Each minister meets with the couple beforehand to personalize the event and add any special touches. (Some changes require prior approval from the wedding consultant; check at the time of booking.)

Little Chapel of the Flowers
1717 Las Vegas Boulevard South
Las Vegas, NV 89104
(800) 843–2410 or (702) 735–4331
www.littlechapel.com

Location: North of the Strip and south of Freemont Street.

Facility Rental, Amenities, and Policies: The Little Chapel of the Flowers offers a plethora of wedding plans that range from $195 to $995. All packages include chapel fee, coordinator, traditional wedding music, and candle-lighting ceremony. Flowers and photographs are included with every package, and are easily coordinated by the on-site floral and photo shops. Flowers are usually selected online, or in person a day or two prior to the wedding. Selections range from a single rose and a boutonniere in the smallest package, to a cascade or colonial presentation, plus two single-rose presentations or corsages and two boutonnieres for attendants in the largest package. Photographic packages range from nine 4x6 prints in the smallest package, to thirty prints and two DVDs of the ceremony in the largest package. Live Internet broadcasting of the ceremony is included in all packages beginning at the $295 level. Photos will be ready for selection usually the day following the wedding. (One complaint from former clients is that package expansion options are expensive.)

Minister fees are not included in the package, but a donation of $60 is suggested and an envelope is handed to the couple after the ceremony for this purpose (along with an envelope for the suggested $35 tip to the limo driver). Limousine service is included in every package but the smallest. A reception with a champagne toast and small cake or chocolate-covered strawberries in a small garden with water feature is extra, but reasonable.

Weddings are not just confined to the Las Vegas Boulevard chapel complex. The Eleganza Perfecta package, at $6,000, adds three nights' accommodations at the Hilton Grand Vacations club on the Strip, limousine service from the airport, salon services for the bride, a cake, champagne, and City Lights Tour by helicopter for the couple. The $1,295 package includes a helicopter tour

of the Grand Canyon; for an additional $1,400, a couple can marry on the Grand Canyon floor, along with two guests, minister, and photographer or videographer. Those who want to see more will be able to view live weddings in progress from the Web site. Couples can reserve a wedding and order all of the components directly online, including a wedding gown and tuxedo package.

Catering: Weddings and receptions can also be conducted on Lake Las Vegas aboard the yacht *La Contessa*. The $5,000 package includes a three-hour cruise with catered buffet and a beautiful cake for fifty guests. Other yacht options begin at $1,000.

Accommodations: Select from dozens of hotels along Las Vegas Boulevard. Two of the closest are the Stratosphere and the Sahara hotels, both within half a mile. The Sahara Station is the northernmost along the monorail that travels south to the MGM Grand.

THE RIDGE TAHOE
Lake Tahoe, Nevada

The Washoe Indian tribe called Lake Tahoe "the jewel of the Sierra" or "lake of the sky," and referred to it as their legendary birthplace. The sapphire-blue lake is the highest of its size in the United States and the largest alpine lake in North America. The water is so pure and clear that a 10-inch cake plate can be seen at a depth of 75 feet. This makes it a 264-square-mile mirror reflecting the deep blue sky or the red sunset.

Lake Tahoe is one of the most breathtaking areas of the West, and one that has for generations attracted Native Americans looking for sanctuary, miners looking for silver, businessmen looking for casino wealth, or

marrying couples looking for simple tranquility. The lake is almost completely surrounded by mountains—the Sierra Nevada and the Carson Range. More than 70 miles in circumference, it's ringed with ski resorts, casinos, lake and mountain communities, and, of course, wedding venues and services galore.

Our pick was the Ridge Tahoe, primarily because of its accessible Web site, simple wedding packages, reviews, service, and unique mountaintop altar. The resort is near enough to South Lake Tahoe for dining, shopping, and casinos, but far enough away to partake in the quiet mountain serenity. The view of the lake is obstructed by the mountains, but the views of the mountains themselves more than compensate.

The Ridge Tahoe hosts seventy to eighty weddings every year, May through October. As many as ten are conducted per weekend during the peak months of July, August, and September. The Ridge Tahoe offers two inclusive packages set in the Grand View Garden area, and one lake-view package.

The Grand View Garden offers sweeping views of Tahoe Mountains and the Carson Valley from 7,500 feet in elevation. Perched on a rounded grassy ridge beneath old-growth pine trees, an outcropping of granite boulders forms a natural altar. The bride can walk down a brick-inlay aisle with as many as 150 friends and relatives seated on either side. Vows take place on a rock-lined brick patio against the boulder "altar," and the area is accessible via a staircase.

The Ridge Tahoe
400 Ridge Club Drive
P.O. Box 5790
Lake Tahoe, NV 89449
Weddings and Catering: (775) 588–3553, ext. 4605
www.ridgetahoeresort.com

Location: About an hour from the Reno-Tahoe Airport, the Tahoe Ridge is at the southeastern tip of Lake Tahoe, near the Nevada-California state line, south of Nevada Highway 207.

Facility Rental, Amenities, and Policies: The smaller, intimate wedding package, priced at $1,000, accommodates twenty to forty people in the Grand View Garden area and includes nondenominational minister; a hand-tied bouquet with half a dozen roses, garden flowers, foliage, and ribbon; a double rose boutonniere for the groom; a one-hour photography package of eighteen 5x7 photos placed in an album; a two-tiered wedding

cake; and a decorative marriage certificate.

The larger wedding package, priced at $2,900, accommodates 50 to 150 people. It includes expanded floral, photography, and cake components. Besides the bouquet and groom's boutonniere, the wedding party also receives flowers for the maid of honor and best man, corsages and boutonnieres for the parents, and a floral arch for the ceremony. The three-hour photography package includes thirty-six 5x7 prints in an album. As for the wedding cake, topped with a fresh floral arrangement, the couple chooses the icing, filling, and flavor.

For those who have their heart set on a lake wedding, the Ridge Tahoe can arrange ceremonies at various locations at the water's edge, based on availability. The Lakeview Collection, at $1,800, is designed for parties of twenty to one hundred people, and package amenities are identical to the intimate package listed above. Transportation from the resort to the site relieves the stress of late arrivals and confusing maps. The transportation to the lake-view sites in this package is priced for twenty-two people; add $10 per additional person.

Site fees for the ceremony and reception (usually held in the Valley View Room) are not included in the packages because they vary according to the season and number of guests, but range from $100 to $1,000. All packages require a minimum of twenty people, and all wedding ceremonies must accompany a reception on the property. The Ridge Tahoe requires a $2,500 minimum purchase in food and beverages on Friday and Saturday nights. However, couples are not restricted to the packages and may design their own weddings, using their own vendors—even the talents of their relatives. The packages were designed for ease and simplicity.

Catering: Reception dinners and buffets range from $21 to $36 for such favorites as chicken Anna and wild mushroom ravioli, with chocolate mousse or cheesecake for dessert. Groups of nineteen or fewer are charged an additional $50 service fee.

Extras: Among its fabulous amenities, the facility has a private gondola to transport passengers directly to the slopes of Heavenly Ski Resort.

Accommodations: The Ridge Tahoe is a full-service hotel and condominium resort and spa, offering all the amenities of a first-class destination resort. The one- and two-bedroom condominiums have a spacious living room, full kitchen, and gas fireplace, for $175 to $450. The Ridge Tahoe, associated with the family of Ridge Resorts, all local, also offers a health club, indoor sports complex, indoor/outdoor swimming pool and Jacuzzis, racquetball courts, shuttle to casinos, full-service spa with massage therapy and facial treatments, restaurant, deli, and market on site.

Keep in Mind: According to California state law, vehicle chains are required in winter.

THE WEDDING CHAPELS AT BELLAGIO
Las Vegas, Nevada

Las Vegas has passed through several costly phases in the past few decades, from Sin City to Family Theme Park, and back to clandestine naughtiness (*What happens here, stays here*). Some casinos, born during the family phase, attempted to disguise gambling activities with fantasy facades and lighting set to perpetual twilight. Bellagio is different. Named for an Italian lake village, Bellagio is reminiscent of a grand European casino hotel; its $2 billion Tuscan design successfully, and opulently, integrates its multiple facets, and it will transcend marketing strategies for some time to come. Yes, this is the hotel with the dancing fountains, but these add to the elegance of Bellagio's style, and are not just (remarkable) appendages like the Eiffel Tower across the street or the Statue of Liberty a few blocks south.

Most of the hotels in Las Vegas offer decent wedding chapels, and their packages are detailed on their Web sites. But these facilities are often built on second-floor conference and ballroom wings. The rooms are fully decorated to look like chapels, but when couples burst through the doors in all their newly wedded joy, they land in a nondescript hallway, perhaps next to the fitness room. Bellagio's two chapels (South and East) are also in the conference room wing, but they border gardens far away from the sights, sounds, and smoky smells of the casino. That's real light coming through the stained-glass windows. After the ceremony couples can immediately step out onto either the Grand Patio or Monet Patio or down into the courtyard for photographs. Six pools (two with fountains) are geometrically set in a neoclassical Roman garden, crowded with pillars, statues, greenery, and archways. Italian opera is piped in over the sound system, and that sky overhead is not a painting. Bellagio's Conservatory and Botanical Gardens is just across the courtyard, presenting another photo opportunity. The glassed-in Conservatory is stuffed full of flowers and exotic plants, which change every couple of months to reflect the season.

Las Vegas wedding entrepreneurs have thought of every gimmick in the book for weddings. A pirate delivers the rings on Treasure Island, and a Klingon stands witness on the bridge of the Starship *Enterprise.* You can recite vows on a gondola at the Venetian, or marry on the Eiffel Tower observation deck, or in one of two chapels of the Stratosphere's observation deck 837 feet above ground—then take a rooftop roller-coaster ride. Bellagio's gimmick is so elegant, it barely counts as one. Forgoing the chapels, couples can exchange vows on the Terrazza Di Sogno, the two-tiered balcony overlooking the hotel's signature eight-acre lake. At just the right moment, when the couple kisses, the fountains burst to life to the musical orchestration of their choice. Most choose "Con Te Partiro" by Andrea Bocelli and Sarah Brightman.

The Wedding Chapels at Bellagio
3600 Las Vegas Boulevard South
Las Vegas, NV 89109
(888) 987-3344 or (702) 693-7700
www.bellagio.com

Location: Between Flamingo and Harmon.

Facility Rental, Amenities, and Policies: Bellagio offers seven wedding packages, starting at $1,500 and crescendoing to $15,000. Even the most basic package (available 10:00 A.M. to 5:00 P.M., Monday through Thursday only) includes half an hour of chapel time, a wedding officiant, a bouquet and boutonniere, photography, videography, a bottle of sparkling wine, chocolate, and a custom wedding certificate. As each package passes through the higher dollar marks, more time is allowed in the chapel, flower decorations are increasingly more stunning, the photography and videography packages become much larger, and the champagne, chocolate, and extra touches grow more

exquisite. Individually priced upgrades are available for all package items.

Limousine service to and from the courthouse is added to the $1,800 Deluxe Wedding package. The Bellagio Wedding package adds Beverly Clark champagne toasting flutes, a bottle of Dampierre champagne, and complimentary buffet for two at Bellagio for $3,800. The $6,300 Millennium Wedding package adds six pew runners with floral sprays and one candle each, two mouth-blown, hand-designed crystal toasting flutes, a bottle of Dom Pérignon, and mini spa services.

The *Il Sogno Di Vita* ("dream of life") package truly brings it on at $10,500. The limo shuttles the couple not only to the courthouse, but also from the airport. Photographic coverage is extended to more than three hours for an 8x10 story album; hair updo, makeup application, and nail buffing are included as well. The couple dine in Bellagio's Circo or Picasso restaurant, are entertained at Cirque du Soleil's *O,* and then spend their wedding night in the Penthouse Suite with lake view. The $15,000 *Cosa Bella* ("the beautiful thing") package adds a bottle of Cristal in two Waterford crystal flutes, couples massage, a second night in the penthouse, champagne breakfast in bed, and, of course, even more glorious flowers and photography. (The penthouse suite is $800 per night.)

Bellagio offers the first Jewish wedding package we've seen. The *Ani L' Dodi* ("my beloved") package, for $6,000, includes Rabbi fee; use of Bellagio's custom huppah, kiddush cup, and prayer shawl; huppah decoration with flowers and tulle on poles and center; and mazel tov glass keepsake with lace bag. Photography, champagne, and floral components in this package are comparable to the other packages. Jewish ceremony components can also be added on to any package for around $1,100.

The Terrazza Di Sogno Wedding package is an $1,800 upgrade ($1,200 in the hot summer months) to any of the other packages. The Bellagio even offers a package for proposing on the terrace for $1,200 (reserved with the chapels).

Wedding hours Sunday through Thursday are 10:00 A.M. to 6:00 P.M.; Friday and Saturday, 9:00 A.M. to 10:30 P.M.

Catering: Check with the resort for reception catering packages.

Extras: Bellagio offers keepsake accessories by Beverly Clark, a nationally known bridal expert, such as guest books, ring pillows, champagne glasses, and flower baskets. Photography, videography, and floral upgrades are available on all packages.

Accommodations: Bellagio has 3,005 rooms and suites, starting at $139 to $499. Discounts are given on rack room rates for couples marrying at the Bellagio chapels or terrace.

Keep in Mind: The state of Nevada requires one witness present during the ceremony, and the Wedding Chapel coordinators are not authorized to perform this duty, so a witness should be secured for elopements.

CONGRESS HALL
Cape May, New Jersey

With the largest collection of Victorian houses, shops, inns, and gaslit B&Bs in the United States, Cape May became a National Historic Landmark District in 1976, and in 2004 was voted an American Dream Town. Cape May is an American dream for weddings, too!

At the southern tip of New Jersey, Cape May is the mystical point where the Atlantic Ocean meets the Delaware Bay. (The cape became an island when a canal was created in the early 1940s.) Even before America had won its independence, Cape May was evolving into the country's first seaside resort. Visitors arrived by steamboat, and soon ballrooms, music pavilions, and hotels—one of the earliest being Congress Hall—were constructed to accommodate the influx of tourists.

Majestic Congress Hall, with its prominent position overlooking the Atlantic Ocean and Old Glory waving over its entrance, is an integral part of American history. Presidents Ulysses S. Grant, Franklin Pierce, and James Buchanan all vacationed here, and President Benjamin Harrison made Congress Hall his summer White House. Composer John Philip Sousa conducted concerts on Congress Hall's lawn with his Marine Corps band, and composed the "Congress Hall March" in its honor.

Congress Hall began life in 1816 as a sparsely decorated boardinghouse. It was destroyed by fire in 1878 and rebuilt the following year—out of brick instead of wood this time. A 1920s renovation brought in bathrooms. The current owners purchased it in 1995.

Under new ownership Congress Hall has been restored to its nineteenth-century splendor. It occupies an entire beachfront and its L-shaped design, a tradition among Cape May hotels, gives most of the more than one hundred guest rooms a panoramic ocean view. The white-colonnaded, Tuscan-yellow hotel has tall ceilings and doors, gigantic Victorian mirrors, glossy black wicker, and potted palms. Carpets have vibrant stripes, beds are dressed in white linens, and baths are decadently huge. The hotel also offers lobby-level retail shops including a day spa, a full-service restaurant and lounge, and a nightclub.

The Tiffany-blue ballroom hosts receptions for 300 hundred seated. Sweeping verandas connect the ballroom to the grand lawn where Sousa's band marched, which is available for tented receptions. For smaller parties Congress Hall can accommodate all manner of themes and twists. The pool cabana or a subterranean candlelit nightclub called the Boiler Room is recommended for a different kind of wedding celebration.

Congress Hall
251 Beach Avenue
P.O. Box 150
Cape May, NJ 08204
(609) 884–8421
Reservations: (888) 944–1816
www.congresshall.com

Location: Cape May is a short ferry ride from Delaware, or down the coast off of New Jersey Highway 109 at exit 0.

Facility Rental, Amenities, and Policies: Site fees for weddings range from $500 to $1,500, depending on the day. Weddings can be reserved for either a daytime block, 11:00 A.M. to 4:00 P.M., or an evening block, 6:00 until 11:00 P.M. A Saturday wedding in June or September requires a minimum of 100 guests during the day and 200 during the evening. As a budget-conscious alternative to the Saturday wedding, Congress Hall recommends a Friday or Sunday date, or an off-season wedding. Not only do these dates offer flexibility with room restrictions and guest minimum requirements, but Congress Hall also offers

a discount on wedding packages on these days. (For instance, a Friday-evening wedding in March requires a minimum of only fifty guests.) This savings can also allow for an upgrade to the standard package, such as a twelve-piece orchestra.

Congress Hall can feasibly accommodate as few as fifty guests, though a wedding coordinator on staff mentioned that the hotel has hosted smaller, more intimate weddings during the week. Every ceremony must include a reception, however.

Catering: Congress Hall's reception "Wedding Package I," starting at $145 per person, includes a complimentary deluxe ocean-view room for the bride and groom, an on-site wedding coordinator, and coordination of overnight accommodations for the wedding guests. The package also includes champagne toast, five hours of open bar service, four passed hors d'oeuvres, two specialty presentations, plated dinner selections, and dessert presentations.

In-house chef Jeffery Klova offers a tailored menu with an extensive choice of meats, seafood, and fowl, as well as a vegetarian selection. A sample of the menu includes tenderloin of beef with shallot and green peppercorn sauce; stuffed grilled pork loin with pear and goat cheese and natural pan au jus; and roasted sirloin of lamb with garlic, rosemary, and a red wine demi-glace reduction. There is a chef attendant fee of $75 for the specialty presentations. Congress Hall's own pastry chef will custom-design a tiered wedding cake, included in the package. An additional fee may be applied if the wedding-cake choice requires extensive preparation.

Extras: Congress Hall offers a choice of chair rentals, starting at $7.00 to $11.00 each; chair covers may be added for $7.00 a chair. Italian banquet floor-length linens with white embroidered overlays are included in the package and upgrades are available. For that extra touch to a raw bar or specialty presentation, Congress Hall offers ice carvings starting at $400. Wedding coordinators can provide an extensive vendor list.

Accommodations: Congress Hall welcomes guests year-round, with rates during the week of $115 to $405 and weekends of $135 to $405 per night. There is a choice of 4 premium rooms: premium, deluxe,

luxurious suites, and connecting rooms, which are ideal for families. Many of the rooms have a spectacular view of the ocean, some a private balcony. Rooms can be blocked for wedding guests; rates and minimum night stays vary on the day or week and month of booking.

Keep in Mind: Recommended booking is a year and a half prior to the date, although the majority of weddings are booked even farther in advance. Three to four months is the shortest period that could be accommodated.

THE BISHOP'S LODGE RESORT & SPA

Santa Fe, New Mexico

Bishop's Lodge, huddled against the base of the Sangre de Cristo Mountains, was once the private retreat for Bishop Jean Baptiste Lamy. The subject of Willa Cather's 1927 novel *Death Comes for the Archbishop*, Lamy transferred from Ohio in 1851 to become the spiritual leader of Catholics in New Mexico, and purchased land north of Santa Fe for $80 to build a home and chapel. Tales circulating the property describe a man famous for hospitality, yet so stern he required parishioners to travel on foot to the chapel as an act of devotion. The devoted still come to revel in the resort that is the bishop's legacy and to marry in his chapel, now a Santa Fe landmark.

Built in the 1870s for prayer and private Mass, Lamy's Chapel still stands on the hill just above the Central Lodge. Although of adobe construction itself, the chapel is a bit incongruent amid the surrounding buildings with its blue double doors and whitewashed wooden porch and steeple, which are faintly reminiscent of midwestern chapels. Inside, the white walls are trimmed in pink; two

stained-glass windows with a harlequin design give off a charming glow. The bishop's celebratory cape, mitre (cap), and Bible are on display, and the wooden confessional booth awaits on the porch. This tiny chapel, which comfortably holds no more than twenty-two people standing, is popular for nondenominational weddings among locals and for elopements across the country.

Developed into a resort by the Thorpe family beginning in 1917, Bishop's Lodge has a number of beautiful locations for indoor and outdoor weddings. The East Garden lawn, adjacent to the chapel and surrounded by lilac bushes and cottonwoods, can be used for a ceremony or a cocktail reception for up to seventy-five guests. The Little Tesuque Gazebo, named for the creek that runs through the lodge's grounds, can shelter small ceremonies or become the backdrop for larger weddings with 150 guests, illuminated by a river rock fireplace in the evening. Poolside lawns surrounded by fruit trees are ideal for tented receptions for 100 to 400 guests. The Mesa Vista Overlook half a mile from the Central Lodge showcases views of blue mountains and red mesas for up to 350 people (shuttle transportation required).

French doors, original tin fixtures, *viga*-beamed ceilings, and a spectacular W. E. Rollins painting adorn the private Alcove and Fiesta Rooms in the Central Lodge, accommodating receptions for up seventy people. Directly through French doors the outdoor flagstone Chapel Terrace, just below Lamy's Chapel, is a pleasant place for an evening reception with its *horno* oven and *farolito*-lined wall.

Unchanged since it was built, the original El Charro Lounge and Thunderbird Ballroom downstairs in the Central Lodge features a colorfully hand-painted bar, copper-hooded fireplace, and tin chandeliers that reflect back to old Santa Fe. The lounge can be arranged living room style with Santa Fe artisan furniture, or seat one hundred for dinner receptions.

The Tesuque Pavilion Ballroom, seating 250 guests, is decorated in warm earth tones, with 20 foot ceilings, wooden chandeliers, and hand-carved doorways. Along the south wall, portal windows capture the sun during the day, and in the evening the grand flagstone fireplace lights up the ballroom. (The fireplace is lit in winter and can serve as a backdrop for a ceremony.) The lobby and pre-function portal, paved in flagstone, accommodates a cocktail reception. Through the south French doors, the *farolito*-lined Tesuque Terrace features a kiva fireplace and a delightful fountain and fishpond.

The Bishop's Lodge Resort & Spa
1297 Bishop's Lodge Road
P.O. Box 2367
Santa Fe, NM 87504

(800) 419–0492 or (505) 983–6377
www.bishopslodge.com

Location: 3 miles north of the Plaza in downtown Santa Fe. Santa Fe is 60 miles north of the Albuquerque International Airport via Interstate 25.

Facility Rental, Amenities, and Policies: Site fees for the various locations are $500 for a ceremony with catering on the property or $1,000 for a ceremony-only event. Lamy Chapel is $300 for one hour.

Catering: Bishop's Lodge offers an extraordinary selection in menus, from hot or cold hors d'oeuvres and themed buffet stations to elegant plated dinners, all for approximately $85 to $95 per person. Bishop's Lodge signature Southwest Mixed Grill includes salmon, beef, and lamb chop with herb wine sauce. Food and beverage minimums of up to $15,000 apply to ballroom receptions during the high season April 16 through October 31, and December; less during the off-season. The lodge does provide discounts for up to twenty-five guest rooms for Friday and Saturday nights for wedding guests of a ballroom reception. The Bishop's Lodge provides tables, linens with burgundy overlays, and tableware for all reception functions.

Extras: The setup fee for indoor bar services is $100; outdoor bar services are $150. Dance floors and a stage are each available for a $175 setup fee.

Accommodations: The lodge's 111 rooms are spread among 15 separate units built on a hillside beneath a canopy of evergreens and cottonwoods. Spacious lawns, delicate gardens, fountains, and southwestern statuary are everywhere. Although renovated, the rooms were kept in a style reminiscent of the old Santa Fe. Among the traditional and deluxe rooms and suites, some with fireplace, the lodge offers 18 new fireplace rooms with spectacular views. Rooms include welcome salsa made specially for Bishop's Lodge served with corn tortilla chips, newspaper, robes, and umbrellas. Nightly room rates are seasonal and range from $139 January through March to $309 mid-June through mid-October. The lodge offers horseback-riding tours, cookouts, tennis, an award-winning spa, and trap and skeet shooting.

Keep in Mind: Weddings at the lodge are beautiful in all seasons. At 7,300 feet above sea level, Bishop's Lodge enjoys sunny days and cool nights. The mountain air is dry and light, with a yearly average rainfall of 14 inches. The Santa Fe Ski Area often enjoys snowpack in excess of 100 inches.

CASA RONDEÑA WINERY
Los Ranchos de Albuquerque, New Mexico

Wine, that liquid romance in a bottle, is nearly a four-century-old tradition in New Mexico. Monks first produced sacramental wine here as early as 1629, and vineyards soon began sprouting along the Rio Grande—against orders from the king of Spain, who wanted no competition for his own wine. In fact, wine was the territory of New Mexico's leading export in the late nineteenth century—ahead of New York and Napa Valley—until nipped in the bud by Prohibition and other problems. Despite altitude challenges (at 5,000 feet) and late-spring frosts, however, some thirty boutique wineries have taken root in the state over the past few decades. One such producer is Casa Rondeña Winery in the village of Los Ranchos de Albuquerque.

Casa Rondeña is a newcomer to New Mexico's wine industry, yet its creator is native to Los Ranchos. Owner and vintner John Calvin went back to New Mexico's eclectic heritage to create an Andalusian villa and vineyard, drawing on his love of antiquities and his talents as architect, builder, and accomplished musician. The winery's name and form took inspiration from Ronda, an ancient town in southern Spain known for its Roman and Arabic country estates and its flamenco melodies (*rondeñas*). A departure from the brown flat-roofed or red-tiled haciendas that line Rio Grande Boulevard, the green-tiled, rose-colored winery incorporates artfully used stone, weathered timbers, tumbled marble, and unexpected Moorish, Asian, and East Indian architectural details. Calvin commissioned the hand-carved, sandstone grillwork from India that adorns the windows, for example. To celebrate Albuquerque's 300th birthday in 2006, he built an Andalusian and North African tower to house a bronze bell that was cast in Patzcuaro, Mexico.

With state-of-the-art equipment from Germany and Italy, Casa Rondeña ships out 5,000 cases a year. In 2002 *USA Today* claimed the winery to be one of New Mexico's best, and *Wine Spectator* awarded Casa Rondeña's 2000 Cabernet Franc its highest rating of any New Mexico red wine. "The culture of wine," Calvin writes, "is about people reaching for mystery, magic, and the highest refined aspects of culture in an effort to become conversant with their higher spiritual aspects." His winery indeed brings cultures—and the multidimensional facets of his persona—together.

Surrounded by aged cottonwoods, along with the formidable Sandia Mountains in the background that turn different shades of the grape at sunset, Casa Rondeña in Albuquerque's North Valley is a beautiful setting for weddings. The lush environment, classic architecture, fine handcrafted wines, meticulous attention to detail, and commitment to service are just part of what the winery has to offer. Rental of space at Casa Rondeña Winery includes use of the acoustically sound Old Fermentation Room, with its hand-hewn staircase leading to a balcony that frames views of the Roman arches. Two sets of large double doors open onto the portal and lawns alongside rose-bushes, bubbling fountains, pond, and the vineyard. The barrels, casks, and winemaking equipment of the fermentation room add to the charm. Guests can stroll among the rows of grapevines and savor their legacy.

Casa Rondeña Winery
733 Chavez Road
Los Ranchos de Albuquerque, NM 87107
(800) 706–1699 or (505) 344–5911
www.casarondena.com

Location: Casa Rondeña is fifteen minutes north of Interstate 40, 1 block off Rio Grande Boulevard.

Facility Rental, Amenities, and Policies: The price for a wedding involving up to fifty guests is $1,675, which includes one mixed case of wine; fifty-one to one hundred guests is $2,175, with two mixed cases of wine. Licensed servers are provided for pouring. Couples will need to rent chairs and other ceremony amenities.

Catering: Caterers of the couple's choosing are welcome and should be able to help with rental tables, chairs, wineglasses, linens, and other necessities for the day. Ask staff for recommendations.

Accommodations: None are available on the property but a fine choice would be Los Poblanos Inn, less than five minutes away. The property has twenty-five acres of agricultural fields and extensive historic gardens, which most recently acquired lavender. The 6 rooms, decorated in the valley's brand of Santa Fe style, are $175 to $250. Los Poblanos Inn and La Quinta Cultural Center are located at 4803 Rio Grande Boulevard, NW in Albuquerque. Call (866) 344–9297 or (505) 344–9297, or visit www.lospoblanos.com.

Keep in Mind: Casa Rondeña Winery can accommodate one hundred people before 6:00 P.M., and fifty thereafter, but the winery is most appropriate for a wedding with ten to twenty-five guests.

EL MONTE SAGRADO
LIVING RESORT AND SPA
Taos, New Mexico

The conscientious bride and groom will embrace El Monte Sagrado Living Resort and Spa, an environmentally sensitive sanctuary that takes feng shui to the next level. Offering luxurious accommodations and spa treatments in the rugged beauty of Taos in northern New Mexico, the resort is designed to coexist in harmony with the land. Guest rooms rim a grassy, shaded meditation space, called the Sacred Circle, bordered by waterfalls, stone water sculptures, a wooden footbridge, trout-stocked ponds, and drought-tolerant plants. The sights and sounds of running water, accompanied by sumptuous food and drink, lull guests into a deep state of pampered relaxation.

Behind its luxurious exterior, the resort incorporates most of the "green" construction techniques and water-recycling and purification technologies its owner and founder, Tom Worrell Jr., developed through his Dharma Corporation. For instance, an extensive network of trout ponds and streams fed by a rainwater-collection system runs through the heart of the resort; its wastewater is purified through a system known as a Living Machine. Worrell's holdings, innovations, humanitarianism, and preservationism are vast to say the least, but one recipient is Taos, where he purchased and restored many of the historical buildings in the downtown area.

Apparently environmentalism is not incompatible with indulgence. The spa offers all of the usual services along with those one might expect from Taos, such as private spiritual intuitive sessions, vibrational therapy, and Egyptian anointing, as well as treatments and programs inspired by local *curanderas* (healers).

Invoking the sense of a global village, the thirty-six suites and casitas that surround the Sacred Circle are each designed with art and artifacts of indigenous cultures from around the world. Eighteen junior suites draw from tribal influences throughout North America, while the remaining suites were inspired by the cultures of Tibet, Morocco, Mexico, the Caribbean, and other countries. A special Kama Sutra Suite is a favorite among honeymooners— with diagrams. Amenities include fireplaces, rooms with private views, and courtyard hot tubs.

Monte Sagrado can procure the services of a medicine man to perform a wedding ceremony in the Sacred Circle to Native

flute music, surrounded by mountain views, waterfalls, and historic towering cottonwoods. The Salon accommodates up to forty-five people for an intimate wedding reception and commands a view of the Sacred Circle and the Sangre de Cristo Mountains framed by a large geometric window. Receptions for up to one hundred can take place at Latir Ranch. The sprawling 6,500-acre ranch is home to the third largest and only certified organic yak farm in the United States.

De la Tierra Restaurant at El Monte Sagrado is one of only ten restaurants across the country to serve yak. Merging the flavors of the Southwest with creative American cuisine, De la Tierra, the resort's main restaurant, uses fresh, organic ingredients, and supports local farmers and growers as much as possible. Many of the restaurant's fruits and herbs have been grown in ecofriendly greenhouses, and meat is hormone-free. Also on site are the Gardens Restaurant, which serves breakfast and lunch with a tropical theme, and the Anaconda Bar serving a full menu of cocktails, wines, beers, and tapas.

El Monte Sagrado
317 Kit Carson Road
Taos, NM 87571
(800) 828–TAOS or (505) 758–3502
www.elmontesagrado.com

Location: El Monte Sagrado is south of Taos, New Mexico, on U.S. Highway 64 (Kit Carson Road), two and a half hours north of Albuquerque by car. Taos Municipal Airport is also available by small airplane or helicopter.

Facility Rental, Amenities, and Policies: Fees for the Sacred Circle are $850 to $1,000 for up to fifty guests, and include a backup location and theater-style setup. The Salon fee for Sunday through Thursday evenings, 6:00 P.M. to midnight, is $400, with a $2,200 food and beverage minimum; and $1,000 Friday and Saturday, with a $5,000 catering minimum. Daytime use of the Salon is $500, with a zero to $2,500 catering minimum depending on weekday or weekend wedding. The fees include white linens and on-site wedding coordinator. Fees for Latir Ranch were not listed.

Catering: On-site catering is provided by El Monte Sagrado, and starts at $75 per guest with a twelve-person minimum for all food functions, or a $125 labor fee is charged for groups of fewer than twelve. A sample reception plated dinner menu, priced at $85 per person, includes grilled bison tenderloin and bison sausage; rosemary skewered Gulf white shrimp; and spinach and herb cheese stuffed chicken breast.

Extras: El Monte Sagrado allows brides to bring in their own floral, music, and decor selections, depending on the scale of the event; however, an additional insurance liability policy may be required. El Monte Sagrado recommends all flowers be designed by the in-house floral artist in keeping with the decor. Dance floor rental and setup starts at $300.

Accommodations: El Monte Sagrado's junior suites start at $395 per night; the one-bedroom studio casitas from the Historic Artist Series, $345; the one-bedroom Exclusive Casitas, $595; and the two-bedroom Global Suites, $1,495. Additional discounts are available for three- and seven-night stays.

Keep in Mind: Only one wedding is booked per weekend, and therefore El Monte Sagrado books about nine months in advance. Most destination weddings are three-day events with Taos activities incorporated into that time period.

EL RANCHO
DE LAS GOLONDRINAS
Santa Fe, New Mexico

It's a warm day in May. Guests sit on wooden benches in the *capilla,* a tin-roofed, exposed-adobe chapel within a 400-year-old hacienda. The bride and groom face each other in front of the reredos (altar screen) decorated with brightly colored paintings of saints. Candle chandeliers hang from the *vigas.* The smell of freshly baking bread wafts through the wooden doors. Once the ceremony is over, the newlyweds and their guests burst into the *placita,* the small, fortified courtyard. A woman dressed in Spanish colonial skirts and apron pulls the bread from the *horno* (a large, beehive-shaped outdoor mud oven)

using a long paddle, and servers pass hot buttered bread chunks and champagne to the guests. Later a mariachi band will play "La Marcha" as experienced dancers lead the newlyweds followed by a single line of guests around the ranch. The parade ends in a circle, where men and women take turns dancing with the bride and groom for luck, and pay for the privilege by pinning money to their wedding clothes.

As weddings were centuries ago, so can they be today at El Rancho de Las Golondrinas, the ranch of the swallows. Las Golondrinas is a living museum of New Mexico's Spanish and Mexican heritage. The 200-acre ranch was once the last stopping place on the 1,200-mile El Camino Real from Mexico City to Santa Fe. Dating back to 1710, it is one of the most historic ranches in the Southwest.

El Rancho de Las Golondrinas grew from the vision of the Curtin-Paloheimo family, who acquired the property in the early 1930s. There are now thirty-three historic structures: Existing historic buildings were restored, authentic structures replicated on old foundations, and related buildings were brought in from other sites. An eighteenth-century house complete with defensive tower, a nineteenth-century home, outbuildings, a molasses mill, a threshing ground, several primitive water mills, a blacksmith shop, a wheelwright shop, and a winery and vineyards depict many of the essential elements of Spanish colonial culture. Shrines and places of prayer testify to the deep religious faith that sustained the early settlers.

Wedding parties can take advantage of the museum's unique combination of historic buildings and modern facilities. Brides can choose from several indoor and outdoor venues for their ceremony and dinner. In addition to the *capilla* described above, the kiva-shaped Education Center with a *viga* and *latilla* ceiling is a modern alternative for up to one hundred guests. The Plaza Salazar, a flagstone patio surrounded by a portal and romantic garden, is ideal for larger groups. The Lower Ranch has a large, shady Wedding Field for large ceremonies and receptions, and a grassy area near the Mill Pond is used for smaller ceremonies. Shuttles might be required for guests and the wedding party for both Lower Ranch areas—some brides choose to ride in on horseback! Receptions can be held in one of several more rustic plazas, or in the modern Placita Ortiz, which has a working caterer's kitchen and covered patio. The patio has a concrete floor for dinner and dancing, and side curtains that can be dropped in case of wind and rain.

The museum has hosted black-and-white formal weddings, as well as casual affairs with *rancheras* music and New Mexican food. One couple chose a Civil War theme with ladies in hoop skirts and men in uniforms. Another couple staged a fake shotgun wedding set in the 1850s, during which the groomsmen came dressed as mountain men, and dinner was served from a chuckwagon. Upon request staff will greet guests in period costume, and for an additional fee experts will demonstrate jewelry making, basket and rug weaving, storytelling, and straw doll making. There's even a shepherdess who will bring out nine socialized sheep for guests.

El Rancho de Las Golondrinas
334 Los Pinos Road
Santa Fe, New Mexico 87507
(505) 471–2261
www.golondrinas.org

Location: Las Golondrinas is near La Cienega 45 miles north of Albuquerque, and fifteen miles south of Santa Fe on Interstate 25.

Facility Rental, Amenities, and Policies: Pricing for use of the chapel only (sixty-five to eighty persons maximum) is $400 for two hours, and $100 for each additional hour. The chapel plus Golondrinas Placita together can be rented for $1,100; there is a one-hundred-person maximum in the Placita. The nonhistoric Upper Ranch is $1,500, for up to 150 people, with an additional $10 per person over that number. Use of the historic and nonhistoric areas combined (such as the chapel, and the modern kitchen and eating area) costs $2,000 for up to 150 guests, with a $10-per-person charge over the basic number. These prices will most likely increase in 2006.

In all site rentals three to four docents at $40 each must be hired if rooms in historic areas are open for guests. An extra charge will be levied if the Las Golondrinas staff must complete an involved setup and breakdown. All music must end by 10:00 P.M., and all events must end by 10:30 P.M.

Weddings can be scheduled in the afternoon or evening in April, May, and October. Weddings in June through August must be scheduled for early evening because the museum is open to the public until 4:00 P.M.

Catering: Las Golondrinas does not provide catering, but will work with the couple and their wedding planner or caterer to design a custom event.

Extras: Las Golondrinas offers demonstrations of authentic bread and *bizcochitos* baking on the premises, with a fee of $125 to $150. The baked goods could be served as part of the reception. Fees for demonstrating jewelry making, weaving, and the like vary.

Accommodations: Lodging can be found in nearby Santa Fe or the northern Albuquerque area.

HACIENDA DOÑA ANDREA DE SANTA FE

Cerrillos, New Mexico

Hacienda Doña Andrea de Santa Fe is one of the few venues that brings together all of the elements of a well-set and well-organized wedding. The hacienda sits on more than sixty acres in the foothills of the Ortiz Mountains, five minutes south of the old mining town of Cerrillos on the scenic Turquoise Trail. Travelers must endure a dusty, washboard road to get to the hacienda, but upon arrival all see the brief journey as a rite of passage and the reason for its reputation as an exclusive wedding venue.

It took native New Mexican Maximiliano Contreras five years to build this exquisite hacienda by hand with the help of a few local craftsmen. Simplicity is key; rooms are decorated with tiles, textiles, and antiques from Mexico, Guatemala, and historic New Mexico. Every angle is photogenic. Once settled, guests lose all sense of time, and weddings would start late were it not for Contreras's wife, Anne, and her staff, who expertly run the hacienda and weddings.

The variegated red roof tile and elevated patios give the appearance of a Spanish villa rather than a northern New Mexico hacienda. The 12,000-square-foot golden-brown building is terraced into the hill. Cars park at the top of the hill and enter the courtyard through an ornate, wrought-iron double-gate entrance. Many pre-ceremony and pre-dinner receptions are conducted among flowers and a fountain, with the mountain as a backdrop close by. Spanish guitarists play softly beneath the *portal,* and mission bells encased in corbelled arches above the roof are often rung by ropes upon the arrival of the bride and groom. In summer the owners open the huge main doors, salvaged from a sixteenth-century hacienda in Puebla, Mexico, to allow breezes and guests to flow freely into the *sala,* the colorful sitting and dining area.

Small elopements can take place in a reading area on the main level, with a wall-to-wall tiled mural of Our Lady of Guadalupe and picture windows of the view. In winter seated dinners and ceremonies are often set downstairs in an area flanked by a fountain, a fireplace decorated by ethnic masks, and another set of enormous doors. Summer ceremonies for up to 200 are set on the back plaza through those same doors. Surrounded by long portals on three sides, the 50-mile view of distant mountains on the fourth side becomes the altar for the ceremony. The big cobalt sky, whether patterned by clouds or not, is clear of haze and obstruction. Sunset dinners on this patio are the height of elegance, although midday July weddings can be warm—except for those sitting beneath one of the hacienda's large white muslin umbrellas.

A celebrated scenic route, the Turquoise Trail is home to the old mining towns of Golden and Madrid, today filled with galleries and curio shops. The nearby Cerrillos mine, first mined by the Ancestral Puebloans nearly 1,000 years ago, is the oldest of any kind in North America. The Tiffany Company in New York extracted $2 million worth of turquoise from the mine between 1892 and 1899. Area gold mines predate the California Gold Rush.

Hacienda Doña Andrea de Santa Fe
78 Vista Del Oro
Cerrillos, NM 87010
(505) 424–8995
www.hdasantafe.com

Location: Hacienda Doña Andrea is five minutes from Cerrillos on New Mexico Highway 14, an hour north from the Albuquerque International Airport and thirty-five minutes south of Santa Fe.

Facility Rental, Amenities, and Policies: The hacienda offers numerous packages, starting with two-hour intervals for elopements with six additional guests, five-hour

intimate weddings with up to one hundred guests, and two-day weddings for up to 200 guests with exclusive use of the hacienda.

The Destination Wedding package includes exclusive and private use of the entire hacienda, guest rooms, *salas,* courtyard, patios, and gardens, with overnight accommodations for guests in nine rooms with double occupancy. Destination weddings with a two-day option on the weekend are $6,750 to $7,500, depending on the season. One-day weekend options are only offered during the hospitality season for $5,350. Midweek destination packages, one-day option, Monday through Thursday, are less than $5,000, which is discounted during the hospitality season.

The hacienda also offers packages that include nonexclusive use of the hacienda and grounds, *salas,* courtyard and patio, and gardens, as well as the sound system, white wedding chairs, and grand piano. Elopement packages, for two-hour intervals with up to six guests, start at $475 to $675, depending on time, day, and availability. Intimate packages are available all year long, Monday through Thursday afternoon, for $895. Weekend weddings are only available in the hospitality season for $1,495 to $1,895. (The hospitality season is January through May 13, and October 16 through December 15.)

Prices differ between Web pages and printed materials to fit all occasions; it would be wise to contact the hacienda directly for current pricing.

Catering: The hacienda works exclusively with Walter Burke Catering, Inc., to assure its customers the finest service. Walter Burke Catering, Inc., offers a variety of buffet and plated menus ranging from $30 to $60 per person. The Southwest dinner, for example, presents citrus achiote grilled chicken breast with roasted red pepper sauce, three-squash calabacitis zucchini boat, traditional Mexican rice, gazpacho soup, or piñon Caesar salad with sage croutons. Visit www.walterburkecatering.com for more information.

Extras: Wedding cake, on-site salon services, flowers, photographer or videographer, and in-room massage and spa treatments are available for an additional price. The hacienda offers "full kit" buffet or plated dinner banquet rental packages for $19.50 per place setting. Banquet rental prices for a cocktail reception start at $8.00 a person, based on the menu.

Accommodations: The hacienda offers 9 double-occupancy rooms, some with sleeping lofts for small children, and can be rented out as a unit at a discounted rate of $2,300. A festive breakfast on the morning after the wedding is served to all overnight guests. If not participating in the buy-out package options, a 20 percent courtesy discount is offered to wedding guests for lodging, based on availability. Room rates for guests staying for additional nights are $155 to $355 a night, depending on season and room amenities.

Keep in Mind: The hacienda is often totally booked, but there might be room for last-minute plans.

HACIENDA MANZANAL BED AND BREAKFAST
Corrales, New Mexico

Pleasant and *simple* are the terms that best describe Hacienda Manzanal Bed and Breakfast in Corrales, New Mexico. Only minutes from Albuquerque International Balloon Fiesta Park (the first full week of October), the village offers unique shops, galleries, historical sites, and fine dining—we'll come to the fine dining in a minute. The Pueblo Revival bed-and-breakfast, with its clean lines and grounds, is newly built; it exemplifies southwestern architecture without asking guests to endure structural problems centuries in the making. Rather than retrofitting an old home into an inn, Hacienda Manzanal looks as if it was built with hospitality in mind with its paved parking area and low compound wall that leaves ample room for ceremonies on the sunny brick patio or shaded courtyard.

Hacienda manzanal is Spanish for "house of the apple orchards," reflecting Corrales's century-old endeavor and the neighborhood where the bed-and-breakfast sits. Edging Albuquerque's North Valley, Corrales is at once rural, trendy, and unpretentious. It was home to the Tiguex Indians for centuries before Spanish explorers first arrived about 1540. The area was part of the Alameda Land Grant, which the king of Spain had transferred to Spanish Captain Juan Gonzales in 1712 after the original recipient failed in his duties. Gonzales embellished upon a complex irrigation system of *acequias* (ditches) that the Natives had created to channel water from the river to their crops. Today most Corrales residents walk their dogs or ride horses along those ditch banks. It is said the village has more horses than people.

For intimate garden weddings Hacienda Manzanal can accommodate up to forty-five people in the courtyard and twenty people inside, if necessary. The carved front door leads into a comfortable great room with a massive stone fireplace. The great room opens to a covered portal.

As with many of New Mexico's bed-and-breakfasts, part of the attraction for the venue is the personable assistance of owners and innkeepers, Sue and Norm Gregory. Sue Gregory says she doesn't have a daughter and easily bonds with her brides, often doing much of the planning herself. Champagne toasts and cake after the ceremony are welcome, but usually the wedding party moves on to a local restaurant for celebration.

Casa Vieja Restaurant

The après-ceremony restaurant of choice is Casa Vieja, only four minutes away on Corrales Road. The restaurant is in a 300-year-old house that is a maze of fourteen rooms of varying heights, some containing the original *terrones* walls—30 inches thick in places—that support the original beamed *vigas*. Diners sit on mix-matched antique chairs and lace-covered tables that tilt a bit on the uneven brick floors. The rooms are heated by piñon-burning fireplaces in winter, and the wait staff must stop serving periodically to stoke the fires.

This old house was the ancestral home of the Martinez family, and is one of the oldest buildings in Corrales. Some sources claim that the house was built by Captain Juan Gonzales for his daughter, and Salvador Martinez purchased the land for 250 cows in 1718. Over the years Casa Vieja served as a military headquarters for the Spanish, a stagecoach stop, and an itinerant court and headquarters for an American cavalry unit. The calvary sword now hanging in the restaurant's Tijuana Bar was dug up in what was the area of the encampment. In the 1930s it housed a grocery store operated by the Moretto family. Casa Vieja became an exclusive restaurant in the 1970s. Most of the ghosts have been dismissed from the house by a professional, but one or two still linger for photographs.

Casa Vieja is open in the evenings only. With a food and beverage minimum, Casa Vieja can close for an evening reception and dinner for up to 120 people. Smaller groups of up to fifty people can be seated in private rooms during the evening hours without closing the restaurant. Casa Vieja has a full-service bar and serves traditional New Mexican and regional American cuisine taken to unexpected levels. Entrees start at $16.95. Casa Vieja is located at 4541 Corrales Road, Corrales, NM 87048 (505–898–7489).

**Hacienda Manzanal Bed and Breakfast
300 West Meadowlark Lane
Corrales, NM 87048
(877) 922–1662 or (505) 922–1662
www.haciendamanzanal.com**

Location: Hacienda Manzanal is on Meadowlark Lane 2 miles north of Alameda, off Corrales Road (New Mexico Highway 448).

Facility Fees, Amenities, and Policies: At Hacienda Manzanal wedding ceremonies are held May though September between 12:30 and 3:30 P.M. When all rooms are rented by the wedding party for the ceremony, the courtyard is available between 12:30 and 8:30 P.M. Fees for ceremonies in the great room are $250 for up to ten people and $325 for up to twenty, which is the maximum. Fees for use of the great room and outdoor patio run $450 for up to forty-five people. Chairs are provided.

Catering: No receptions are permitted on the premises. A possible choice is the Casa Vieja Restaurant.

Accommodations: Hacienda Manzanal has 4 bedrooms, each with its own private bath and fireplace. Rates for double occupancy are $85 to $135, and may be adjusted during holidays and special events. Rental of all 4 rooms is $420, discounted if rented for two nights.

Extras: Officiants and vendors abound in the Greater Albuquerque area for reasonable prices. Sue Gregory is a certified tea specialist and hosts tea parties for bridal showers and the like.

HACIENDA VARGAS BED AND BREAKFAST AND WEDDING CHAPEL
Algodones, New Mexico

Hacienda Vargas Bed and Breakfast is a casual wedding haven in the rural community of Algodones, New Mexico, which history and tourism have all but forgotten. Except for the occasional train running through, the setting is quiet and peaceful. That it is also close to Interstate 25 between Albuquerque and Santa Fe makes it convenient to shopping and sightseeing for elopements and destination weddings.

The Algodones (*al-go-tho-nez*) area is in the narrowest part of the Rio Grande Valley between the foothills of the Sandia Mountains and the volcanic-topped red mesas. Merchant wagon trains on the Santa Fe–Mexico Camino Real passed through here from as early as the seventeenth century, and the settlement of Algodones developed as a result of continuous Spanish efforts to control the pass in the eighteenth century. As Camino Real evolved into a stage route, railway, and the historic U.S. Route 66, Algodones continued to be a major thoroughfare until the parallel interstate was built. There has never been enough flat real estate to expand the town into anything more than it is. That's an advantage for visitors who want to rest their eyes on nothing but the native grasses and trees, dramatic mesas and bluffs.

Parts of the Hacienda Vargas date back to the 1840s. The site has been a stagecoach stop, Indian trading post, train stop, and U.S. Post Office. The Vargas family purchased it in 1991 and developed it into an inn. The territorial-style building is a classic square U-shaped hacienda, originally designed so that its inhabitants would not have to go outside to get from one end to the other. The *sala* (living room), with palazzo tile floors, exposed beams, and a plastered *banco* along one wall, leads to a series of sitting, reading, and eating nooks. The bedrooms were transformed into private guest rooms with their own entrances. The hacienda is oriented toward a covered veranda (*portal*) that lines the inside of the U on all three sides, forming a courtyard in the center.

At one end of the portal is a chapel, adorned by two purple-and-yellow stained glass windows, a kiva fireplace, and an altar covered in votive candles and flanked by stautes of saints. Current owners Cynthia and Richard Spence have purposely left the chapel's adobe brick wall, altar, and dirt floor unfinished. In the days when churches were few and far between, haciendas often contained their own chapels. An itinerant priest would have stopped by periodically to perform a Mass, christening, or small wedding. Today many nondenominational weddings take place in the chapel. Prior to all ceremonies, the innkeepers sweep the dirt floor and light the candelabra, votives, and wood in the fireplace. The glow in the late afternoon creates a dramatic tone for reciting vows. The Spences ring a church bell at the end of the ceremony.

Large weddings are held in the courtyard, the focal point of which is a 200-year-old elm. Celebrations for larger weddings usually take place in the sort of triangular side yard, enclosed by a compound wall and sheltered by trees. A host bar can be set up in a small pavilion, and the area is large enough for dining and catering tables, dance floor, and tent.

Hacienda Vargas is booked nearly every weekend in the summer months, and is host to some seventy weddings every year. The Spences work hard in the background to make sure all weddings run smoothly.

Hacienda Vargas Bed and Breakfast and Wedding Chapel
1431 Highway 313
P.O. Box 307
Algodones, NM 87001
(800) 261– 0006 or (505) 867– 9115
www.haciendavargas.com

Location: Hacienda Vargas is on New Mexico Highway 313, about half an hour north of the Albuquerque International Airport and south of Santa Fe. It is less than half a mile off Interstate 25 at exit 248.

Facility Rentals, Amenities, and Policies: An elopement or small wedding for up to twenty guests is $550, and includes a ceremony in the courtyard or candlelit chapel, chairs for a courtyard ceremony, wedding officiant and witnesses if needed, a honeymoon suite for the evening of the wedding, a full breakfast, and a bottle of champagne or sparking cider for the couple.

Packages for larger ceremonies with up to 180 guests in the courtyard and 250

guests on the reception lawn area are customized and priced anywhere up to $4,200. These packages usually include the facilities and coordination for the ceremony, reception, and rehearsal, whatever chairs and tables are needed (as well as their setup and takedown), free parking and attendant, all seven guest rooms and suites for one or two nights for up to twenty guests, and breakfast for all overnight guests.

Catering: Although there is no catering kitchen, the Spences can arrange catering through outside sources, or the couple may bring in their own licensed caterers. Caterers should do their own cleaning up after the reception.

Extras: The Hacienda does not have an alternative for rain and a tent should be put on reserve, starting at $900. A dance floor is required for receptions that include dancing. The hacienda offers cake-cutting and champagne-pouring services, plus coffee, sun-brewed iced tea, assorted sodas, ice, and extra linens for an additional cost.

Accommodations: The Hacienda offers 4 suites and 1 standard room, with 2 additional two-room suites in a historic house next door. Double occupancy rates are $89 to $189, plus $15 for each additional person, and include a full breakfast. All rooms have a bath (several have a Jacuzzi tub), and most have a kiva fireplace. Rooms are individually and sweetly decorated, and most are adorned with delicate stenciling.

Accommodations for other guests are available in small hotels in Bernalillo ten minutes south of Algodones. The historic Hacienda Grande in Bernalillo on the Camino Real can also handle overflow guests if not booked for its own weddings.

Keep in Mind: The historic hacienda sits right next to the railroad tracks, and children should be supervised.

HOTEL ALBUQUERQUE
AT OLD TOWN

Albuquerque, New Mexico

Northern New Mexico is known for its adobe chapels and missions. Beautiful for weddings, they are inconvenient for travel and prohibitive to couples who aren't Catholic or can't marry in the church. In a mountain-to-Muhammad gesture, Hotel Albuquerque at Old Town recently built such a nondenominational *Norteño*-style chapel on its property and has since attracted bookings from as far away as Germany.

Except for La Posada de Albuquerque (which is undergoing its own rise from the financial ashes), Hotel Albuquerque is the last of the territorial-style hotels in this city of nearly half a million. It separated from its Sheraton brand in 2005 to further distinguish itself as a landmark hotel, and along with recent renovations that added a number of exquisite wedding venues, including the chapel, it plans to install a city block of upscale villas and shops, with substantial upgrades to exiting guest rooms.

This 1975 eleven-story hotel is a microcosm of local culture. The Grand Sala lobby area features hand-carved wooden corbels in territorial-style windows, hand-forged iron chandeliers, historic photographs, and outdoor portals. The new nineteenth-century-appearing chapel, seating 156 people, has a dramatic vaulted beamed wooden ceiling, massive walls, deep-set windows, wooden chandeliers, and hand-plastered finishes. The focal point of both the wedding and the chapel's artistry is the intricately carved and plastered sanctuary space. A spiral staircase leads to the choir loft for musicians and photographers, and the bride and groom have their private dressing areas. Formal photography often takes place in the small, private courtyard paved with flagstone and thyme.

In addition to the chapel, the hotel now has an outdoor Victorian-era pavilion and rose arbor, Spanish garden lawn courts, a fountain plaza, and grand pool area, catering to parties between 10 and 2,000 guests. The Fireplace Room (opened seasonally), just off the pavilion area, offers direct access to spacious portals for indoor/outdoor receptions. Wood-planked floors, ceiling *vigas* and *latillas,* multipaned windows, a fireplace, Indian rugs, and pottery provide an elegant yet cozy atmosphere for groups of up to sixty people.

Apart from the standard conference rooms, Hotel Albuquerque has two newly renovated ballrooms named for the city's two extinct landmark hotels, the Alvarado and the Franciscan. The ballrooms blend the local Navajo, Pueblo, Mexican, and Spanish cultures in the form of handcrafted stamped tin chandeliers and carpeting patterned after Navajo rugs. The Alvarado accommodates 1,000 people, or 400 in half a ballroom; the Franciscan accommodates 225. The hotel books approximately 150 weddings per year, and May through August is the busiest time.

Hotel Albuquerque is just a five-minute walk from the Albuquerque Museum district as well as Old Town Plaza, the center of more than one hundred shops, galleries, and restaurants. Old Town has been the hub of diverse culture since Spanish settlers established Albuquerque in 1706, providing visitors a glimpse of Albuquerque's roots with Navajo and Pueblo merchants selling their wares under portals, quaint shops in quiet hidden patios, and summer fiestas on the plaza.

Cradled between the Sandia Mountains and the Rio Grande, and extending onto the West Mesa, Albuquerque's high-desert climate is conducive to year-round activities. The monsoon season cools down late-summer afternoons but also necessitates rain plans.

Hotel Albuquerque at Old Town
800 Rio Grande Boulevard, NW
Albuquerque, NM 87104
(877) 901–ROOM or (505) 843–6300
www.buynewmexico.com

Location: Just south of Interstate 40, Hotel Albuquerque is fifteen minutes from the Albuquerque International Sunport and five minutes from the Albuquerque Convention Center.

Facility Rental, Amenities, and Policies: The fee for a chapel ceremony is $1,500, which decreases with a reception on the premises. The two-hour rentals are scheduled for 11:00 A.M., 2:00 P.M., and 5:00 P.M. The fee includes ceremony rehearsal, sound system with technician, Carillon Chimes Bell System, candles for the candelabra, groom's dressing room with television, and bride's dressing room with vanities and a fruit and cheese tray with sparkling cider. The Pavilion ceremony rental fee is $1,200, which decreases with a reception on the premises. The two-hour rentals are scheduled for 10:00 A.M.,

1:00 P.M., and 4:00 P.M. Setup, ceremony, teardown of the room, and photography must take place during the two-hour period.

Catering: Food and beverage minimums are required, ranging from $22,000 for the Alvarado Ballroom (which can serve 1,000 people) to $3,350 for the seasonal Fireplace Room for sixty people. Wedding reception packages include suite for the bride and groom with wedding gift tray and breakfast for two, dance lesson for bride and groom, a one-hour hosted cocktail reception, champagne and sparkling cider toast for all guests, fountain with flowing citrus punch, wedding cake with full cake-cutting service, chocolate-dipped strawberries, complete table setup with china, silverware, and glassware, choice of several linen colors, centerpieces on mirror tiles with candles in crystal holders, sleeping room discount for guests, an area for entertainment and a dance floor, and ice carving. Menus run from $47.95 to $67.95 per person. The chef's elegant seven-course dinner is $125 per person. The New Mexico Heritage package, for example, features authentic Spanish appetizers and paellas.

Accommodations: The medium-size rooms have handcrafted southwestern furniture. The large rooms have desert-color appointments, hand-wrought furnishings, and tile bathrooms with southwestern accents. Request a south-side room, for a balcony overlooking Old Town and the pool. The hotel has 188 rooms plus 20 suites. Standard rooms are $99 to $219; deluxe rooms, $129 to $257; suites, $139 to $257.

HYATT REGENCY TAMAYA

Santa Ana Pueblo, New Mexico

Place yourself in the sixteenth century riding along with the first Spanish expedition into the Southwest in search of the Seven Cities of Gold. Imagine coming upon an enormous apartmentlike complex that rivals the largest castles in the Old World. That's what it's like to first see the new Hyatt Regency Tamaya north of Albuquerque, New Mexico. Sheltered by remote mesas on Pueblo lands, the first sight of Tamaya's sand-colored structure against a background of red buttes, the blue Sandia Mountains, and a thick stand of river cottonwoods is breathtaking. Perhaps Frank Lloyd Wright learned his architectural techniques from the Pueblos—even the Twin Warriors Golf Course blends in with the environment, routed in and around twenty ancient cultural sites.

This is not another Pueblo Revival facsimile; this is what happens when Pueblo people have the wherewithal to build something great. In partnership with Hyatt Regency, Santa Ana Pueblo built an exquisite first-class resort and spa named Tamaya. (Santa Ana owns the hotel, and Hyatt manages it.) The architecture tastefully reflects Santa Ana's abandoned ancestral village of Tamaya (tá-ma-ya) and their ancient agrarian culture.

Tamaya is laid out in three sections: The guest-room wings and grand courtyard are at one end, the ballrooms at the other, and the lobby, lounges, and restaurants in the center. The formal entrance is a three-sided courtyard flanked by a long veranda and shops with an above ground kiva at one end (housing the Tamaya museum).

The lobby great room is more typical of the Pueblo Revival architecture, with high beamed ceilings, indigenous fine art decorating the tables and walls, and comfortable couches and game tables near fireplaces. But just as most pueblo villages are divided into halves and named for Pueblo symbols of summer and winter, Tamaya's two mirroring guest-room wings are named Pumpkin and Turquoise. The grand courtyard has three swimming pools, water features, and gigantic seed-pot fountains. The large, round enclosed pool was modeled after the great kivas of Chaco Canyon in northern New Mexico; where niches would be aligned to the winter and summer solstices, lounge chairs are now oriented for sun-worshipping. On weekends local Pueblo women bake bread in the traditional beehive ovens for guests.

Sunrise Amphitheater, outside and to the east of the lobby, seats 150 theater-style for ceremonies with the Sandias as the altar. Ceremonies are also held at the Oxbow Pool at the north end of the property near the apple orchard against dramatic red and black buttes. The Puma and Wolf Ballrooms open onto the east terrace for indoor-outdoor receptions, seating 120 to 158 people each. Both rooms can be divided into thirds for a more intimate space that can accommodate forty to fifty-three people. The Tamaya Ballroom can accommodate more than 1,000 people, and 600 can enjoy a remote reception in a tented area under the cottonwoods.

Small wedding celebrations can take place in the Corn Maiden restaurant—Tuesday through Saturday evenings. Diners watch the chefs in the exhibition kitchen, or just gaze at the mountains as they feast.

Hyatt Regency Tamaya Resort and Spa
1300 Tuyuna Trail
Santa Ana Pueblo, NM 87004
(505) 867–1234
www.tamaya.hyatt.com

Location: Tamaya is on New Mexico Highway 550, 2.4 miles west of Bernalillo.

Facility Rental, Amenities, and Policies: Ceremony site fees range from $500 to $800, which includes setup of chairs and special table altars. Staff wedding coordinators can assist in selecting florals, entertainment, and photography.

Catering: Tamaya offers four wedding catering packages or "tiers" ranging from $85 to $149 per person. Each tier includes a one-hour cocktail reception with open bar, choice of four hors d'oeuvres, soup or salad, and entree (with a minimum of twenty people) or buffet (with a minimum of fifty), champagne toast, wedding cake, truffles, and chocolate-covered strawberries. Tiers increase in price with liquor and menu package upgrades, and the addition of action stations. Menus include a twist on traditional Puebloan fare: green chile asadero on fry bread or cured ham and manchego quesadillas, followed by Western chopped salad with jicama, roasted corn, and black beans over lettuce, and chicken breast Tamaya stuffed with black bean, wild boar, and jalapeno sausage with tequila sauce.

These catering packages include a complimentary deluxe bridal suite for the bride and groom, with champagne, strawberries, and turn-down service; reduced room rates for overnight guests; a professional banquet captain; white-glove service; bartender fees; selection of linens; centerpieces; and complimentary dance floor and staging.

Extras: Tamaya can arrange a bridal tea on the veranda, in the spa courtyard, or in the outdoor waterfall area, as well as a bachelor's golf tournament and cookout. Tamaya Mist Spa offers a variety of bridal preparation services and gifts for the wedding party. The day after the wedding, newlyweds might venture on a romantic trail ride through the *bosque* on Tamaya's own horses, ending in a sunrise breakfast on a blanket, a hot-air balloon ride with champagne and breakfast burritos, or an "Untie the Knot" breakfast-and-spa package. These range from $200 to $560. Horse-drawn carriages of various styles are available through the Tamaya stables for the wedding day.

Accommodations: All 350 guest rooms, suites, and public spaces are decorated with traditional Pueblo paintings, weavings, murals, and pottery, as well as contemporary artworks and historic photographs depicting early New Mexico life. With balconies or patios that overlook the mountains, grand courtyard, or golf course, there is no bad view. Rates May through October are $200 to $350; November through April are $135 to $250, depending on the type of room.

LA FONDA ON THE PLAZA

Santa Fe, New Mexico

No survey of Santa Fe wedding venues would be complete without La Fonda on the Plaza. A hotel, in one incarnation or another, has occupied this corner of the Plaza since Santa Fe was founded in 1607. Owners have seen to updating over the years, and yet it always retains a sense of Santa Fe's heritage and remains the vital heartbeat of a city that has many pulses. Nearly everyone who travels here passes through La Fonda at one time or another.

Literally the end of the Santa Fe Trail, the original inn saw trappers, traders, merchants, and presidents. The hotel played a role in opening the West to commerce when it welcomed the first expedition from Missouri in 1821. The current La Fonda was built in 1922, purchased by the Atchison, Topeka & Santa Fe Railroad, and leased as a Fred Harvey House until 1968. Since then La Fonda has been locally owned.

The hotel sits on a city block that corners the Plaza. Its architecture is Pueblo Revival, stacked adobe stories with wooden balconies and beam ends protruding over the tops of windows. Inside, the lobby indeed looks like an old Harvey House with people milling about as if they've got a train to catch or a long layover. There's much to see: beamed ceilings with intricately carved crossbeams and doorway arches, glossy brick floors, wrought-iron chandeliers, and expensive shops featuring pottery or rugs. The French Pastry Shop serves small sandwiches, crepes, and French onion soup (and, yes, the attitude that comes with it). La Fiesta Lounge draws many locals to its economical New Mexican food lunch buffet; La Plazuela offers southwestern cuisine in a skylit garden patio with painted glass tiles.

The Bell Tower Bar is the highest point in downtown Santa Fe and is a great place for a cocktail with a view.

Wedding venues in this old hotel are glorious. Winter ceremonies and receptions are often in the Santa Fe Room, which accommodates 50 to 125 guests, at a banquet table or theater style. This is no ordinary room—tin chandeliers hang from a high, intricately crafted *latilla*-and-*viga* ceiling. Although there is no altar, ceremonies are often oriented toward a blue door or flush fireplace. Other banquet and conference rooms can accommodate from 50 to 600 guests.

One of Santa Fe's more spectacular settings is La Terraza Room for 180 to 220 guests. Hand-carved wooden doors bridge the natural beauty of La Terraza's outdoor gardens with a panoramic banquet room. The French doors, which span three sides of the room, are removable for an indoor/outdoor reception or cocktail party with views of the adjacent St. Francis Cathedral and shops along the street. The room's tin chandeliers and sconces, a hand-sculpted kiva fireplace, and four enormous domed stained-glass skylights reflect the local craftsmanship. A kitchen across the hall is dedicated exclusively to La Terraza events. Banquets at La Fonda are led by one of the most gracious and attentive wait staffs in Santa Fe.

La Fonda on the Plaza
100 East San Francisco Street
Santa Fe, NM 87501
(800) 523–5002 or (505) 982–5511
Meetings and Banquets: (505) 995–2320
www.lafondasantafe.com

Location: La Fonda on the Plaza is at the end of Old Santa Fe Trail (merging with Old Pecos Trail) at Water Street. Old Pecos Trail is exit 285 off Interstate 25. Covered parking on San Francisco Street is subject to an hourly charge and availability.

Facility Rental, Amenities, and Policies: La Fonda offers 15,000 square feet of event space. The largest facility is the Lumpkins Ballroom, which offers 6,500 square feet and can accommodate up to 600 guests. This ballroom can also be divided to accommodate smaller events, such as receptions, buffets, and plated dinners. Rental fees were not disclosed.

Catering: Standard service is one and a half hours for a minimum of thirty people. La Fonda offers a variety of menus including several buffets beginning at $20 for lunch and $34 for dinner. The buffet entrees include grilled chicken over linguini pasta with roasted red pepper sauce; chicken or beef enchiladas with red or green chile; and char-grilled salmon served with papaya-avocado relish. There is a $50 culinary fee per chef per station, with one station per fifty guests. La Fonda also offers plated dinners for a minimum of thirty people, ranging from $28 per person for chicken La Fonda, breast of chicken stuffed with bacon, red onions, green chile and cheese; to $65 for a mixed grill of roasted beef tenderloin served with blackened tomato butter and stuffed jumbo shrimp.

Accommodations: La Fonda has 167 rooms and suites, some with traditional *vigas* and *latillas,* and others with fireplace and private balcony. Each guest room has hand-decorated wood furniture, wrought-iron light fixtures, and beamed ceiling. The 14 rooftop rooms are the most luxurious and include a continental breakfast, private concierge services, an exercise room, a garden, and an outdoor hot tub. Single and double room rates range from $219 to $319; suites, $219 to $319. La Fonda also offers 14 luxurious private rooms and suites on the third floor, with rates ranging from $399 to $519.

LA POSADA DE SANTA FE RESORT AND SPA

Santa Fe, New Mexico

La Posada de Santa Fe, only a couple of blocks from Santa Fe's Plaza, is like an adobe village full of artisans and landscape artists—and in fact that was one of its original uses. In the 1930s R. H. and Eulalia Nason constructed a series of Pueblo Revival–style adobe casitas around the existing Staab Mansion and carriage house, and called it La Posada, Spanish for "inn" or "resting place." La Posada became a summer arts school with many long-term guests who contributed to Santa Fe's flourishing arts community. With six acres of lush landscaping in full bloom May through November, statuary by local artisans, and fountains, this is one of the prettiest resorts in Santa Fe for weddings and portraiture.

The main building is a mix of southwestern and Victorian styles, typical of late-nineteenth-century architecture in New Mexico. The original part of the three-story brick mansion was built in 1882 by Abraham Staab, a German immigrant and prosperous merchant, for his bride, Julia. The

Staab family entertained Santa Fe society in their grand residence decorated with the finest European materials. In recent years Julia Staab's alleged spirit has been the subject of many ghost tours, an episode of *Unsolved Mysteries*, and *Weird Travels*.

Later the French Second Empire–style building was literally enclosed by an adobe structure to add a check-in area, lobby, and restaurant. The core Victorian mansion is still present in heavy black doors marking the original entrance, an Old West-style lounge, a wooden staircase leading to guest rooms, and a series of parlors. The stained-glass window in the Rose Room features a large, stylized rose burst in oranges, yellows, and greens.

After an extensive renovation in the late 1990s that included the construction of additional lodging, an Avanyu spa, and the Conference Center, La Posada opened as a member of RockResorts, and although it recently sold to two hotel investor companies in partnership, RockResorts will still manage La Posada until 2014. Fuego Restaurant specializes in excellent world-beat contemporary fare.

Here in the heart of Santa Fe, La Posada has enviable indoor and outdoor accommodations for weddings. Many couples choose to exchange vows on the landscaped lawn (seating 200 to 250 theater style) and then receive guests in the ballroom. The Montaña Ballroom, with grand fireplace, accommodates 150 to 300 for a reception, and can be partitioned into two rooms for a more intimate space. Smaller venues exist in the Conference Center, the Peyton Wright Suite, and the Staab House. The lawn and garden area surrounded by adobe architecture is beautiful and peaceful, but it is immediately adjacent to Fuego's patio and Avanyu spa. The wedding party will be so caught up in the proceedings they will not notice the quiet onlookers, but a few will end up in the background of the wedding photos.

La Posada de Santa Fe
330 East Palace Avenue
Santa Fe, NM 87501
(866) 331–ROCK or (505) 986–0000
http://laposada.rockresorts.com

Location: Two blocks east of the Santa Fe Plaza off Paseo de Peralta.

Facility Rental, Amenities, Policies: The hotel reserves the right to charge a service fee for setup of rooms with extraordinary requirements. An additional fee may apply if the event runs over the designated scheduling. The hotel will supply white linen for all functions; additional colors are available at an additional fee. Further site fees were not disclosed.

La Posada de Santa Fe Resort and Spa offers a complimentary five-day, four-night honeymoon to couples spending a minimum of $15,000 on their wedding event. The Honeymoon Reward may be enjoyed at any one of the RockResorts, regardless of where the ceremony takes place, for up to three months after the event.

Catering: A labor charge of $250 applies to all breakfast, lunch, reception, and dinner functions with attendance of fewer than fifteen people. The hotel has three buffet packages, with a minimum of twenty-five guests, ranging from $45.50 to $64.00 per person. La Posada also offers a three-course plated dinner, ranging from $37 to $49 per person, and a four-course for $42 to $54. A sampling of the menu includes blue corn crusted chicken breast with black bean sauce, cilantro rice, and pineapple salsa; Osso Buco Milanaise with saffron risotto and gremolata; and braised lamb shank with polenta and baby root vegetables.

Wedding-cake table setup, including the hotel cake knife, cutting, and service, is $3.00 per guest.

Extras: The lodge has a referral list of vendors, including photography, florists, music, and transportation. A dance floor is available starting at $350 for rental and setup. Valet parking is available at standard rates, and also quite necessary in the busy seasons. La Posada offers a variety of wedding gift baskets, ranging from $23 to $50.

Accommodations: The Lodge features 157 adobe-style rooms and suites interspersed throughout the property, many with patio and fireplace. All are decorated with ethnic throw rugs and local artwork; the newer suites are more modernly luxurious than the older casitas. The rates are seasonal: January 1 through June 15, rates begin at $189; June 16 through October 29, $239; October 30 through December 22, $169; and December 23 through December 31, $239.

LORETTO CHAPEL
Santa Fe, New Mexico

Loretto Chapel is interwoven into Santa Fe's history and lore, and is a popular site for local and destination weddings of all denominations. The delicate Gothic chapel was built in 1873 by the same French architects and Italian stonemasons who built the nearby St. Francis Cathedral. The chapel's legendary focal point is its spiral staircase, built without a single nail by a mysterious carpenter.

Bishop Jean Baptiste Lamy commissioned the chapel for the Sisters of Loretto, who two decades earlier had been the first to respond to Lamy's request for assistance in teaching and preaching "6,000 Catholics and 300 Americans" in New Mexico. The small group of sisters arrived in Santa Fe in 1852, opened the Academy of Our Lady of Light (Loretto), and for the next two decades struggled against smallpox, tuberculosis, leaky mud roofs, and even a brush with rowdy Confederate Texans during the Civil War.

Around 1870 Lamy brought in architect Antoine Mouly and his son, Projectus Mouly from Paris, France, to design and build St. Francis Cathedral, which turned out to be a ten-year project. During this time it became clear the sisters needed their own chapel, and Lamy encouraged them to take advantage of the French architects while they were in town. Mouly had been involved with the renovations of King Louis IX's 1243 Sainte-Chapelle in Paris, which was a favorite chapel of Lamy's childhood in France. It is no surprise, then, that Loretto Chapel was inspired by the famous medieval predecessor. Reportedly the sisters pooled their own inheritances to raise the $30,000 required to build it.

The sandstone used for the walls and the porous volcanic stone used for the ceiling were hauled to town by wagon. The ornate stained-glass windows were purchased from the DuBois Studio in Paris and freighted to New Orleans by sailing ship, to St. Louis by paddleboat, and then to Santa Fe by covered wagon over the Old Santa Fe Trail. The chapel was completed in 1878 and has since seen many additions and renovations such as the introduction of the Stations of the Cross, the Gothic altar, and the frescoes.

As the Loretto Chapel neared completion, it was realized there was no way to access the choir loft 22 feet above the floor. Carpenters concluded that a staircase would interfere with the interior of the small chapel, and that the choirboys would have to climb a ladder to get to the loft. The sisters made a novena to St. Joseph, the patron saint of carpenters, and according to legend, a man showed up on a donkey with a toolbox looking for work on the ninth and final day of prayer. Armed with only a saw, a hammer, and a T-square, he constructed this engineering marvel by soaking slats of wood (of a supposedly unknown variety) in tubs of water to curve them, and then assembled them into a spiral with wooden pegs. The staircase seems to rise from the floor like a vortex with no central support, taking two complete turns. When the carpenter finished, he disappeared without payment, and some concluded he was St. Joseph himself. Over the years the staircase has been the subject of many articles, TV specials including *Unsolved Mysteries,* and a movie called *The Staircase.*

The Loretto Academy was closed in 1968, and the property was put up for sale. At the time of sale in 1971, Our Lady of Light Chapel, now Loretto Chapel, was informally deconsecrated for Catholic Mass. Loretto Chapel is now a private museum operated and maintained, in part, for the preservation of the Miraculous Staircase and the chapel itself.

The Gothic chapel is a striking contrast to the adobe cathedral and churches already in New Mexico. Its intimate interior, with its vaulted ceilings, dominating stained-glass features, rich wooden pews and staircases, and sense of mystery, makes it a pretty place for weddings. At the end of the ceremony, it is customary for the couple to pose for photographs on the staircase. For fear that the staircase has seen too much wear and tear, couples are now permitted only to pose from the tenth step. Museum officials see to the meticulous running of every ceremony.

Loretto Chapel
207 Old Santa Fe Trail
Santa Fe, NM 87501
(505) 982–0092
www.lorettochapel.com

Location: Loretto Chapel is located in Santa Fe, fifty minutes north of Albuquerque, via Interstate 25.

Facility Rental, Amenities, and Policies:
The Loretto Chapel performs approximately 250 weddings a year, and has seating for 139 guests. Rates range from $550 to $1,850, depending on season, day of week, number of people, and special requests. The fees include the appropriate minister, candles, and the chapel for one hour. An organ player is additional. Ceremonies usually take place after hours, 5:00 P.M. mid-October to mid-May, and 6:00 P.M. the rest of the year. Contact Loretto Chapel for current pricing, which tends to be variable.

Catering: There are no reception facilities within the chapel, but the entire city of Santa Fe is at the couple's disposal.

Accommodations: The chapel is attached to the Inn and Spa at Loretto via the chapel museum's gift shop, although the two are not affiliated. Built to resemble Taos Pueblo, double-occupancy rates at this 135-unit hotel begin at $159 to $265 off-season, and $215 to $499 July through October. The Inn and Spa at Loretto is located at 211 Old Santa Fe Trail, Santa Fe, NM 87501 (800–727–5531 or 505–988–5531; www.hotel loretto.com).

Keep in Mind: The Loretto Chapel is currently booking about thirteen months out, but weddings can be booked with shorter notice depending on the couple's flexibility.

SANTA FE HISTORIC SITES AND MUSEUMS

Santa Fe, New Mexico

Enveloped by the foothills of the Rocky Mountains, Santa Fe—called the "City Different"—is America's oldest capital city. Founded as a capital city in 1607 by Spanish explorers, it has been claimed by the Pueblo peoples, the Spanish Crown, Mexico, and the Confederacy. The Mexican Federation ceded it to the United States in 1846, but New Mexico didn't become a state until 1912. Present-day Santa Fe is internationally renowned for its contemporary, cosmopolitan sophistication, particularly in the arts. With a museum older than the state itself, Santa Fe is also the center of archaeological and anthropological research. For the wedding different, check out these three historic locations: the Randall Davey Audubon Center, Museum Hill, and Pecos National Monument.

Randall Davey Audubon Center

The Randall Davey Home is 3 miles from the Plaza at the upper end of prestigious East Canyon Road, and owned and maintained as a museum by the National Audubon Society. The 135-acre property was originally a 1731 Spanish land grant, and the home was originally a stone mill built by the U.S. Army quartermaster in the 1850s. An artist ahead of his times, Randall Davey purchased the property in the 1920s and converted the sawmill into a home and studio, where he lived and worked for forty-four years. Today the 16-inch-thick stone walls are covered by plaster, but the massive, roughly hewn beamed ceilings of the mill are still visible. Two murals, *Burros Eating Pears* and the frog on the studio door, were both painted by Davey soon after he acquired the property. The lawn in front of

the house is available for rental. The center has hosted weddings as small as twelve people and as large as one hundred.

Museum Hill

The museum complex known as Museum Hill is just a few miles from the Plaza off the historic Old Santa Fe Trail, and includes the Museum of International Folk Art (MOIFA), the Museum of Indian Arts and Culture (MIAC), the Wheelwright Museum of the American Indian, and the Museum of Spanish Colonial Art. With ample free parking and spectacular views of the Sangre de Cristo and Jemez Mountains, the Indian Arts and Culture Museum and the Folk Art Museum separately offer unique spaces for weddings. Most of the spaces are off Milner Plaza, which connects the two museums to each other as well as to the museum cafe.

The **MIAC**'s changing exhibitions draw from an unparalleled collection of Native American art and material culture representing the Pueblo, Navajo, Apache, and prehistoric cultures of the Southwest. Weddings are held in MIAC's Sculpture Garden and Meem Auditorium. Small ceremonies of up to fifteen people can take place amid artworks in the tranquil, enclosed Doris and Arnold Roland Sculpture Garden. The historic Meem Auditorium is the perfect location for large events, receptions, or ceremonies with a uniquely southwestern flair. Built in 1929 in the Pueblo Revival style that John Gaw Meem himself conceptualized, the auditorium can accommodate 50 to 132 individuals depending on arrangement.

The **MOIFA** houses the largest collection of folk art in the world, with 130,000 pieces representing more than one hundred countries. The museum's Atrium is available for weddings or receptions for up to 225 seated, as well as several indoor and outdoor gardens and spaces, including the Milner Plaza Labyrinth. Some or all of the galleries will be open during the event for guests to enjoy.

Mission at Pecos National Historical Park

In the Sangre de Cristo Mountains 25 miles southeast of Santa Fe remain the ruins of a once powerful people called the Pecos. The weathered walls of a seventeenth-century Spanish mission rise above the pueblo ruins. Pecos was a major trading center for the Plains tribes to the east and the Pueblo villages of the Rio Grande Valley to the west from 1450 to 1600. Pecos National Historical Park preserves 12,000 years of history, including the ancient pueblos of Pecos, two Spanish colonial missions, Santa Fe Trail sites, the twentieth-century history of Forked Lightning Ranch (last owned by British actress Greer Garson), and the site of the Civil War Battle of Glorietta Pass. Under the auspices of the National Park Service, weddings are permitted in the roofless and ruined mission, reddish in color, serenely framed by archways and enveloped by mountain peaks and mesas.

Other Santa Fe Sites

Santa Fe is home to dozens of bed-and-breakfasts and haciendas, all of them blue-trimmed brown adobe (as required by city ordinance). Just about every inn will permit a small, understated ceremony in its *sala* or courtyard for no fee or a stipend, and innkeepers will even help organize the catering. Additionally, some of the local art galleries, such as Shidoni Foundry and Andrew Houser Gallery, will welcome a small wedding in their sculpture gardens. A couple of other well-known, high-end galleries extend an open invitation for small weddings as a courtesy to area officiants—and the privilege is so exclusive, it can't be publicized. Some ministers host weddings in private home chapels.

Randall Davey Audubon Center
1800 Upper Canyon Road
Santa Fe, NM 87501
(505) 983–4609
www.audubon.org

Location: Upper Canyon Road is off Paseo de Peralta. The last mile is a curvy dirt road that ends in a parking lot.

Facility Rental, Amenities, and Policies: The lawn, orchard, and gardens in front of the historic Randall Davey Home are available for events from 9:00 A.M. to 6:00 P.M. Rental also includes a private changing/gathering room and bathroom for bridal parties. The cost is $1,200. (A $200 tax deductible contribution to support Audubon New Mexico programs is given to those who rent the grounds for the full $1,200.)

Catering: Renters are responsible for all food and drink, serving pieces (dinnerware, flatware, et cetera), rental of an appropriate size tent, tables and chairs, cleanup, and trash removal.

Museum of Indian Arts and Culture
Laboratory of Anthropology
P.O. Box 2087
710–708 Camino Lejo, off Old Santa Fe Trail
Museum Hill
Santa Fe, NM 87504-2087
www.miaclab.org

Museum of International Folk Art
P.O. Box 2087
706 Camino Lejo, off Old Santa Fe Trail
Museum Hill
Santa Fe, NM 87504-2087
www.moifa.org

Location: From Old Santa Fe Trail, follow the signs to the museums.

Facility Rental, Amenities, and Policies: In the MIAC the Scultpure Garden rents for $250 per event, and the Meem Auditorium is $600 per event. Space is reserved Tuesday through Sunday after museum hours, from 5:30 P.M. to midnight. The museum is closed on Monday. Security must be provided at $25 per hour. Weather sometimes restricts use of the scultpure garden, but the auditorium can be rented year-round.

In the MOIFA the Atrium without gallery access rents for $750, or up to $1,500 with full gallery access, and includes the use of tables and chairs for guest use up to one hundred. The fee for the auditorium without galleries (seating 150) is $600 for evening events. Outdoor spaces are available May through October, including the Labyrinth for $250, and Overlook Garden for $100. Interior and exterior spaces together are available for $2,000 May through October. A minimum of two security guards are required at $25 per hour during the event. An insurance policy is also required.

Catering: In the MIAC the Museum Hill Café (operated by Walter Burke Catering; see Catering in Hacienda Doña Andrea chapter) can serve as a convenient lunch location for small groups, or the couple's contracted company may use the museum's kitchen facilities.

MOIFA requires that Walter Burke Catering be included in all bid processes. Menus that include nonstaining foods and beverages are encouraged, although red wines are permitted provided the renter accepts full responsibility. Deliveries must be arranged with the front desk, and security staff work closely with caterers to transform the event spaces into elegant reception areas.

Pecos National Historical Park
P.O. Box 418
Pecos, NM 87552-0418
Visitor Information Recorded Message:
(505) 757–6414, ext. 1
Special-Use Permits: (505) 757–6414,
ext. 236
www.nps.gov/peco

Location: Pecos National Historical Park is 25 miles east of Santa Fe off Interstate 25. Visitors traveling north on I–25 should take exit 299 at Glorietta to Pecos village and head south 2 miles on New Mexico Highway 63. Those traveling south should take exit 307 and continue 5 miles north to the park on NM 63. Pecos Mission is near a parking lot and is accessible by an easy walk.

Facility Rental, Amenities, and Policies: The flagstone-paved Pecos Mission can accommodate up to 200 people with a nonrefundable $100 special-use permit. In addition to the fee, each attendee must pay the $3.00 admission fee, and a ranger is required to monitor the event for $50.00. Call first to determine availability, and an application will be mailed. The park hosts about twenty-five weddings per year as an ad hoc service, often overseen by the security manager. Weddings are permitted seven days a week, except major holidays and during special events such as annual Civil War reenactments or the Pecos Feast Day on the second Sunday of August. Only one wedding is scheduled per weekend. Chairs and a wedding arch are permissible.

Catering: Pecos National Historical Park does not permit receptions of any kind on site, and most wedding celebrations move to Santa Fe because of the scant availability in the village of Pecos. An alternative is the Galisteo Inn (866–404–8200; www.galisteo inn.com) in the village of Galisteo, half an hour south. Its La Mancha Restaurant offers dining for parties up to sixty on the patio Wednesday through Saturday evening, as well as Sunday brunch by reservation only. A barbecue can be arranged for 125. Exclusive use of the facility, including guest rooms, is $1,850 to $5,000 depending on day of week and season.

Accommodations: Santa Fe has a wide variety of lodging, and part way between Santa Fe and Pecos National Historical Park is the breathtaking Inn at Mountaintop (505–310–7958; www.innatmttop.com). The inn's two cottages have wraparound porches with views of the surrounding mountains and valleys. A nearby outcropping of rock makes for an intimate mountaintop ceremony.

SUNRISE SPRINGS INN & RETREAT
Santa Fe, New Mexico

Sunrise Springs in the La Cienega Valley south of Santa Fe has been Megan Hill's canvas for thirty-five years, making it a tranquil and visually pleasing setting for weddings. The nourishing springs that seep through the valley had attracted various Native groups through the millennia until it was occupied by the Spanish in the seventeenth century, becoming a *paraje* or resting stop on the Camino Real. The current chapter in history begins when Hill and her former husband purchased the property in 1969 from a New Mexico governor. At that time the property now called Sunrise Springs was a solitary house with spring-fed ponds, an old barn, alfalfa fields, and a few stately cottonwoods and willow trees. "Something in the mystery of the waters and in the then beautiful open views of the valley, the deep croaking of the pond frogs, touched me deeply and permanently," Hill has written.

During a workshop in 1977, she had a vision of dragonflies and butterflies over the site that is now the Moonhouse, and thus began a process that resulted in the development of Sunrise as a healing retreat and conference center years later. By 2002 she had added twenty new casitas and a Meditative Arts Building to house a program that combines mindful arts, body work, and traditional movement practices. The new building also has a clay studio and a traditional teahouse for tea ceremonies.

Prior to focusing her attention on the healing arts, Hill was primarily a visual artist—and this talent shows in the layout of the grounds and buildings, which are particularly conducive to weddings. Spring, summer, and fall ceremonies for up to 300 guests are often set in Mulberry Meadow, a large grassy area near one of the spring-fed ponds that is surrounded by a spreading mulberry tree, fragrant Russian olive trees, cottonwoods, and rosebushes. The Ceremonial Circle area, bordered by a pink-stucco-covered half-moon *banco* overlooking the pond and gardens, can accommodate 150 to 175 for an outdoor ceremony.

The Moonhouse is a popular reception space, nearly 900 square feet with two smaller, circular rooms adjoining the main chamber. The flagstone floor, clerestory windows, and large fireplace all come together to create a rustic, intimate space.

The Moonhouse will seat fifty-six theater style, forty at round tables with buffet table. Glass doors open onto the wood deck overlooking the pond and can be tented for additional space, accommodating one hundred people in total. For larger weddings the Atrium is 2,500 square feet of plants, sunshine, wood, and saltillo tile floors. The room also has a wooden floor with a cushioned subfloor, specifically designed to absorb aerobic impact such as dancing. The front of the room features large windows overlooking the grounds and can seat up to 120 at tables or more than 200 theater style. Numerous other studios, galleries, and workshop spaces can accommodate smaller groups.

The Blue Heron Restaurant & Bar, the primary food and beverage operation at the resort, is named for the stately and elegant bird that occasionally seeks refuge in the spring-fed ponds. The restaurant seats seventy-five indoors, and another seventy-five on a deck under towering cottonwood and willow trees near the ponds. An upstairs room is perfect for small private parties. Chef de cuisine Prem Darlami specializes in natural and organic cooking that is light, satisfying, and healthy. His approach to food is to evoke the natural flavors, using the colorful, creative, and organic whenever possible. The restaurant presents global cuisines with a touch of Asian influence, focusing on locally grown produce, including that which is grown in the gardens of Sunrise Springs.

Sunrise Springs Inn & Retreat
242 Los Pinos Road
Santa Fe, NM 87507
(800) 955–0028 or (505) 471–3600
www.sunrisesprings.com

Location: Sunrise Springs is located in La Cienega, between Albuquerque and Santa Fe, off Interstate 25.

Facility Rental, Amenities, and Policies: All ceremonies on site must accompany a reception. Depending on the season, rates are $175 to $250 for the ceremonial space and $850 to $1,200 for the reception space.

Catering: Formal receptions require a minimum of thirty guests. Sunrise Springs offers nine menus prepared by the Blue Heron chef, for $65 per person. Sample entrees include grilled salmon with tarragon-cucumber salsa; chicken and cheese enchiladas with red or green chile; and roasted rosemary lamb loin chops and shallot demi-glace. Buffets are $65 per person for summer/fall weddings, which includes appetizers, and $40 to $60 per person for winter/spring weddings. A wedding brunch or lunch buffet following a Sunrise Wedding is $30 to $40 per person. Groups fewer than fifteen people are invited to dine at the Blue Heron Restaurant.

Extras: White wooden wedding chairs, currently priced at $2.50 each, plus a flat fee for delivery of $85.00, may be rented for the ceremony and celebration spaces. Some sites require tent rental for banquets. Check with Sunrise Springs staff for specific rental locations and pricing.

Accommodations: Sunrise Springs has a total of 60 rooms with ninety-three beds: 20 casitas with fireplace, kitchen, and private patio; 32 garden rooms with private balcony or patio; and 8 spa rooms and suites near the spa facility, each with its own balcony or patio. The nightly rates range from $90 to $275 depending on room size and season. Check the Web site for overnight packages, which include lodging, spa treatment, and breakfast.

CENTRAL PARK
CONSERVATORY GARDEN

New York City, New York

Dreaming of a Big Apple wedding, but have only a small budget? Look no farther than New York's own front yard. The Central Park Conservancy in New York City does weddings—and loves doing them so much, they request a photo of every ceremony performed there for a show album.

Central Park is one of the urban wonders of the world, an island in a sea of skyscrapers—rhapsody in green, it's been called. The *Greensward Plan* was how its designers and visionaries Frederick Law Olmsted and Calvert Vaux referred to it in 1858, even before the skyscrapers were built. With twenty-five million visitors each year, Central Park is the most frequently visited urban park in the United States. More than 56 miles of walking trails wrap in and around 843 acres, offering many romantic and idyllic locations for wedding ceremonies and photography.

The most popular wedding venue is the six-acre Conservatory Garden, Central Park's only formal garden, which takes its name from the huge glass conservatory that once stood there. Operated by the Central Park Conservancy, the Conservatory Garden is in fact three gardens representing different landscape styles: Italian, French, and English, each with its own particular charm. These Gardens of Europe present extensive displays of flowers, shrubs, and trees in bloom from early spring through late October.

Upon entering the garden from Fifth Avenue and 105th Street near Bergdorf Goodman, visitors pass through the Vanderbilt Gate, and an Italian-style garden opens immediately before them. A restful oasis of formal green lawn and clipped hedges bordered by crab apple trees, this stunning location is prime for many wedding photography sessions. On the west side of the Italian garden is a wrought-iron wisteria pergola sitting atop a series of tiered hedges, complemented by an elegant geyser fountain.

To the north is the classical French-style garden, centered by a fountain featuring the German sculpture, *Three Dancing Maidens* (circa 1910). An ornamental flower bed planted with purple germander is surrounded by sloped beds planted with 20,000 tulips in spring and 2,000 Korean chrysanthemums in fall.

To the south is the English-style garden, sheltering a reflecting pool where water lilies float in summer. At the pool's center is a 1936 bronze sculpture of the two children in Frances Hodgson Burnett's book *The*

CENTRAL PARK CARRIAGES

One of the most romantic ways to top off a wedding in Central Park is a horse-drawn carriage, even in winter—especially in winter! The carriages can be found lined up along Central Park South (59th Street) between Fifth and Sixth Avenues, at the southern end of Central Park across from the Plaza Hotel. Rides are $34 for the first twenty minutes, and $54 for a forty-five- to fifty-minute tour. Call for special wedding charters. Contact Central Park Carriages at (212) 736–0680 or visit www.centralparkcarriages.com.

Secret Garden; Dickon is playing a flute and Mary is listening. Surrounding the pool are seasonal beds planted with thousands of daffodils and other bulbs in spring, and more than one hundred varieties of annuals throughout the summer. Perennial plants, shrubs, trees, and grasses bloom in succession from early spring through fall in the outer ring of beds, and thousands more dot a woodland slope shade garden.

All wedding rental fees go directly toward garden maintenance and horticulture by the Central Park Conservancy, a nonprofit organization founded in 1980 that manages Central Park under a contract with the City of New York Department of Parks and Recreation. The Conservancy has raised more than $300 million to date, and has transformed Central Park into a model for urban parks nationwide.

Central Park Conservancy
Executive Assistant, Conservatory Garden
14 East 60th Street
New York, NY 10022
(212) 310–6600
www.centralparknyc.org

Location: The Conservatory Garden is on the east side of Central Park; enter at Fifth Avenue and 105th Street, or the 106th Street gate inside the park.

Facility Rental, Amenities, and Policies: Photography sessions and ceremonies in the Conservancy Garden require permits from the Central Park Conservancy. The fee for ceremonies is $400 for a maximum of one hundred people, plus $100 for photography (or just $100 for photography without the ceremony). The application is on the Web site, and requires submission of the fee as a money order payable to Central Park Conservancy, along with date and location of wedding or photography in the gar-

den. The date will be reserved and confirmed immediately. If a conflict exists, attempts will be made to reschedule. The permit will be mailed a month before the date. Bring the permit with you on the day of the event in case park or security personnel ask to see it.

Use of the lawn in the Conservancy Garden is prohibited, except for a thirty-minute photography session with the wedding party if previously reserved, which is limited to twenty-five people.

Catering: Receptions are prohibited in the garden. Some couples hold a champagne reception in a small lobby room or suite of a nearby hotel, such as the Kitano or the Mandarin Oriental.

Accommodations: Apart from the hotels listed in the catering section, a popular choice is A Greenwich Village Habitué (212–243–6495; www.gvhabitue.com). Two fully appointed private apartments are available in an owner-occupied 1830s Federal brownstone building in the historic West Village and Gansevoort Market Meatpacking District. The apartments overlook a formal English garden, although guests do not have access to it. Rates are $175 to $185 per night (single or double occupancy only). A minimum stay of four nights is required, and credit cards are not accepted.

Keep in Mind: Central Park has a number of ceremony sites besides the Conservatory Garden. Other popular places include the Pond, Cherry Hill, Bow Bridge, Shakespeare Garden, East Green, Cedar Hill, the Mall, Hernshead, the 100th Street Pool, and the Harlem Meer. For permits for these and other areas of Central Park, there is a fee of $25. For information call the Special Events & Permits Office of the New York City Department of Parks & Recreation at (212) 408–0226 or visit its Web site at www.nyc.gov/parks.

LAKE PLACID LODGE

Lake Placid, New York

Lake Placid Lodge is built into a hillside where white birches, sugar maples, and balsam firs come down to the shore and Whiteface Mountain looms. Lake Placid Lodge is the offspring of The Point Resort, a cloistered group of all-inclusive lodges on the peninsula stretching into Upper Saranac Lake. The Point was originally Camp Wonundra, the home of William Avery Rockefeller. Many such so-called Great Camp estates were built in the Lake Placid region in the 1880s by wealthy folks looking to escape the polluted, industrialized cities. The Point Resort became so popular by word-of-mouth that in 1993, owners David and Christie Garrett purchased the waterfront estate that became the Lake Placid Lodge and developed it into a resort to suit the same high standards.

Though not a great camp itself, part of Lake Placid Lodge's main building is originally from the nineteenth century, and a lot of the property has been rebuilt in the traditional Adirondack style. In addition to the mansion, owners David and Christie Garrett purchased smaller fishing cabins in the area and developed them into the Lake Placid Lodge's property. Such details as the cabins' beadboard walls and polished pine beams look convincingly old.

Rustic in the Adirondacks can mean antler chandeliers, but not here. In 1997 the Lake Placid Lodge was selected by Relais & Châteaux, and David Garrett is now president of Relais & Châteaux North America. Built with romance in mind, most of the thirty-four rooms and log cabins have deep tubs, double-headed showers, and peaceful lake views. Each is adorned with antiques, artwork, and one-of-a-kind rustic chairs, tables, and beds made by dozens of local artisans. Many of the pieces are for sale; should you fall in love with the bedstead sculpted like a tree root coming out of the floor, the lodge will put you in touch with its maker. All rooms have large stone hearths—in one lodge it takes up a whole wall.

At any time of year, Lake Placid Lodge provides a wide variety of natural settings and interior spaces for a distinctive wedding weekend. The rolling lawn can be tented or wedding parties can gather in the Wine Cellar for a small reception, or can be rowed out to a private island in Lake Placid for a rehearsal dinner picnic.

A dedicated staff member will help accommodate all wedding wishes, as well as plan activities and excursions. Lake Placid was the home of not one, but two Winter Olympics (1932 and 1980), and sporting activities are still a natural in this region. Public skating, nightly skating shows, and museums are available in the Olympic Village. There's also skiing and golfing, and guides can be arranged for hunting, fishing, and hiking.

A month or two before the event, the lodge's own executive chef, Ken Ohlinger, contacts the couple to arrange a uniquely tailored menu. Ohlinger combines innovative New American cuisine with classical French techniques, using local organic farmhouse products indigenous to the season.

The lodge promises to pamper guests with in-room massages and manicures, and to place their favorite homemade cookies on each pillow at turndown. Now, that's living!

Lake Placid Lodge
Whiteface Inn Road
P.O. Box 550
Lake Placid, NY 12946
(877) 523–2700 or (518) 523–2700
www.lakeplacidlodge.com

Location: Lake Placid Lodge is five hours from New York City and Boston, and two and a half hours from Montreal via Interstate 87. A small airport at Lake Placid accommodates private planes.

Facility Rental, Amenities, and Policies: The lodge is best suited for weddings up to 74 guests, although it can host up to 125 for a reception, with two additional tents. For large or formal weddings, a buy-out of the entire lodge is mandatory during the peak season of June through October at $22,000 per day with a two-day minimum. In addition, there is a food and beverage minimum of $24,000.

The lodge will accept smaller weddings with a maximum of twelve to twenty guests, as long as the party reserves lodging and a reception meal on the property. There is no fee for an informal outdoor wedding on the dock, for example, as long as no chairs, aisle, or wedding arch are required. The indoor ceremony fee is $1,500. Small ceremonies can take place in the den of the lodge, and a seated dinner for ten can be arranged in the adjacent Wine Cellar; a steep food and beverage minimum applies.

Catering: Sample menus forwarded to us ran $75 to $125 per person, the high end featuring zucchini "cannelloni" stuffed with goat cheese and morels; scallops cooked three different ways; filet topped with oyster and Maytag blue cheese; and chocolate molten cake. With a minimum of thirty-five people, the reception can order a gourmet Adirondack barbecue dinner for $95 per person.

Accommodations: Lake Placid Lodge has 17 guest rooms and 17 guest cabins available, sleeping up to seventy-four people. Lodge room rates are $400 for queens, and $475 for kings. Nightly rates for the cabins range from $695 to $1,300, depending on size.

Keep in Mind: During the peak season the lodge recommends booking one year in advance, although smaller weddings with flexibility may contact the lodge anytime. The lodge hosts some twenty weddings per year, with four or five renting out the entire location.

THE SAGAMORE
Bolton Landing, New York

Seventeenth-century French explorers considered Lake George sacred, and it would without a doubt be a breathtaking setting for a wedding. The Sagamore resort on the private seventy-acre Green Island on Lake George evokes a bygone era. Its expansive lawns and gardens feature spectacular views framed by the lush Adirondack Mountains.

A group of Philadelphia millionaires who summered on the lake opened the Sagamore's luxurious and spacious accommodations in 1883. Twice damaged by fire, the Sagamore was fully reconstructed in 1930. Throughout its history it has been a social center for the wealthy residents of Green Island and Millionaires Row, the stately mansions along the island's western shore. The hotel eventually fell into disrepair before closing its doors in 1981, but one hundred years after construction of the first Sagamore, builder and real estate developer Norman Wolgin of Philadelphia purchased the hotel and restored it to its former grandeur.

Listed on the National Register of Historic Buildings, the main hotel combines a central tower and veranda with rambling white clapboard wings. Guests register in a separate building as they enter the resort.

The Veranda Terrace, as a spectacular outdoor ceremony option, has a sweeping staircase leading from the historic hotel to the lakeside patio, with majestic views of Lake George as a backdrop. For receptions the Sagamore offers an elegant ballroom, a choice of dining rooms, and many other romantic locations. Guests can enjoy cocktails and a moonlit reception area for dinner and dancing beneath a tent on the lakeside lawn at the Shelving Rock Terrace, which takes advantage of panoramic lake views. Available May through November, this lakeside location can host up to 175 guests with a choice of brunch or classic dinner packages.

The turn-of-the-twentieth-century elegance of the main Sagamore Dining Room with its formal parlor area provides the perfect lake view backdrop for a formal affair. Available for evening celebrations September through June, it can accommodate up to 225 guests. The formal Trillion dining room, with its lake views from the outdoor terrace, offers an elegant setting for an afternoon brunch for up to 125 guests.

Enjoy the beauty of Lake George and the surrounding mountains aboard the 72-foot replica of a nineteenth-century touring vessel. During a four-hour reception cruise, guests can be served cocktails and hors d'oeuvres on the open-air topside deck, followed by a gourmet dinner on the enclosed lower deck. Cruise menus include a brunch package for up to fifty guests or classic dinner packages for up to eighty guests. A private cruise fee is assessed based on the number of guests attending. The Tudor-style Club Grill at the Sagamore Golf Course can host a reception on the covered porch, outdoor terrace parties of seventy-five guests, and a three-course dinner celebration in a clublike ambience.

Everything a bride and groom could need for the wedding is on the island, including a full-service salon. Guests will be able to take advantage of the resort's recreational offerings, including a full-service European spa, golf on the eighteen-hole Donald Ross course, boating and sailing from the resort's marina, and racquetball and tennis. Younger guests will enjoy the Teepee Club, surrey rides, and swimming in the lake or indoor pool.

The 32-mile-long lake, which is fed by mammoth underground springs, includes 109 miles of shoreline and about 300 islands; it covers an approximate area of 44 square miles. It figured prominently during the French and Indian and Revolutionary Wars.

The Sagamore
110 Sagamore Road
P.O. Box 450
Bolton Landing, NY 12814
(800) 358–3585 or (518) 644–9400
www.thesagamore.com

Location: The resort is located on Lake George Island, and is accessible year-round by air to Albany International Airport, by Amtrak from New York and Montreal, and by automobile via Interstate 87 (the Northway).

Facility Rental, Amenities, and Policies: A ceremony fee of $2,000 includes rehearsal arrangements, the ceremony setup, and coordination for the wedding day. The Morgan Wedding Cruise package incurs a cruise fee (in addition to the catering costs), which ranges from $2,000 to $3,000 for up to eighty people.

Catering: Reception packages and menus begin at $115 for Sunday brunch or cruise, $100 for the Winter Wonderland (November 13 through April 30), and $145 to $165 for the Classical Wedding dinner dance packages. Packages include site fees, wedding toast, open bar, hors d'oeuvres, displays, three- or four-course plated dinners, white-glove service, and wedding cake with many "opulent" options and upgrades. Ask about Friday and Sunday discounts.

Popular menu choices are the "duet entrees," such as pan-seared tenderloin of beef in red wine sauce and jumbo lump crabmeat cake with whole grain mustard sauce.

Accommodations: The Sagamore has 350 standard rooms, which range from $180 to $625 per night depending on the season, view, and size. In addition, 7 lodges

along the lakefront, including living rooms, kitchens, fireplaces, and balconies, are $149 to $745 per night. Wedding parties might consider renting one or more of the spacious condominiums, which have two bedrooms, two bathrooms, a living room, a dining room, and a fully equipped kitchen, and cost $485 to $815 per night. The historic Castle is a six-bedroom, four-bath home, and is ideal for larger family gatherings for $2,000 to $3,000 per night.

Keep in Mind: While destination weddings at the Sagamore average 125 guests, the facility will accommodate all weddings with a minimum of 20 guests depending on the couple's flexibility in dates.

The Sagamore requires that an indoor location be held in reserve when choosing an outdoor setting due to inconsistencies of weather. A 40 percent or greater probability of rain will necessitate the relocation for any outdoor function to the indoor reserve location, assessed by the staff four hours prior to the event.

TAVERN ON THE GREEN
New York City, New York

The legendary Tavern on the Green in Manhattan's Central Park is probably one of the best-known wedding venues in New York City—and most magical. This is Oz's restaurant, an explosion of color and light from its rococo-inspired ceilings to its custom French floral carpeting. Six distinctive dining rooms offer an array of crystal chandeliers, stained glass, hand-painted mural fantasies, and whimsical flower formations. Countless impatiens hang from London plane trees, lending a canopy of color

for outdoor parties. Thousands of daffodils and tulips in springtime make way for a sea of chrysanthemums and miniature evergreens in fall and winter. As the sun sets over Central Park and the evening's celebration beckons, the garden is set aglow by 1,000 chintz-covered lanterns and 750,000 tree lights. Nothing shy and retiring here.

The original structure was built in 1870 to hold 200 South Down sheep that grazed in the park's meadow. Parks Commissioner

Robert Moses decided to turn the building into a restaurant and banished the sheep forever from the park. Tavern's first incarnation was launched in 1934 with a coachman in full regalia at the door; the restaurant was quickly embraced as a gathering arena for New York's social strata. But by the 1970s it had declined and was eventually shuttered. Warner LeRoy then acquired the lease and—for $10 million—added the glass-enclosed Crystal and Terrace Rooms. Hand-hewn rafters and vaulted ceilings reemerged after decades of plastering. The Elm, Rafters, and Chestnut Rooms were paneled with a wormy chestnut. Rustic baroque gave way to the glitter of forty-five chandeliers from more than 15,000 pieces of crystal, sixteen stained-glass chandeliers, and fifty-two sandblasted, etched, and carved puntice mirrors.

When it reopened in 1976, Tavern enjoyed a fresh round of celebrity. Always a work in progress, updates are ongoing. The Menagerie of Topiaries from the film *Edward Scissorhands* took up residence in the gardens in 1993, for instance. Since LeRoy's death in 2001, his youngest daughter, Jennifer LeRoy, is leading another comprehensive renovation. Efforts have paid off; Tavern on the Green is now the highest-grossing independently owned restaurant in the United States.

Wedding parties from 20 to 900 can be accommodated through four dining rooms that open to each other. The Park Room, seating up to ninety people, is probably the best suited for a destination wedding. The Park Room is a salute to a bygone era, with antique Baccarat chandeliers, a private garden (seating forty) surrounding a period fountain, and a 52-foot mural depicting Central Park at the turn of the twentieth century.

The Tavern hosts 200 to 300 weddings per year. When we say "hosts," we actually mean "producers"; weddings at Tavern are indeed productions! (Just see what they can do with laser lights and a fog machine.) Experienced wedding specialists on staff can do everything from assisting with planning the flowers and menu, to selecting the calligraphy for invitations and hiring the hairstylists. Flowers and linens, in all colors and patterns, are provided at no extra charge.

Staff are amenable to e-mail contact, and people are encouraged to use the Web site. This is not just a platitude; we received a phone call less than an hour after filling out the Web site's online information request form. Many of Tavern's wedding clients are from overseas, particularly the United Kingdom and Japan.

Tavern on the Green
Central Park at West 67th Street
New York, NY 10023
(212) 873–3200
West View Parking: (212) 956–2280
www.tavernonthegreen.com

Location: Tavern on the Green is in Central Park. Parking is not included in event prices, and can be reserved for guests at West View Parking.

Facility Rental, Amenities, and Policies: Possible site fees were not disclosed, although prices might decrease for day events, Monday through Thursday. For functions of 150 guests or more, restroom attendants are required for additional gratuity or charge added to the account. A checkroom, if required, may also be added to the account.

Catering: Menus start at $125 to $150 per person. Tavern on the Green's menu options are as whimsical, varied, and rich as the place; the specialty is that there is no specialty. Executive chef John Milito can serve Lebanese, Vietnamese, Neapolitan, Old English, Old Czarist, Scandinavian, or pizza. The staff can even reproduce a classic banquet from past centuries. Milito grew up in his stepfather's Long Island restaurant and worked his way through New York City's kitchens, opening the Rainbow Room as the banquet chef in 1987. Having conducted his externship at Tavern after graduating from the Culinary Institute of America, Milito returned to the restaurant to become its executive chef. "Being at Tavern means hard work and long hours," he said. "But it also means a more hands-on approach in the kitchen, which will hone my creative edge."

Accommodations: Although there are many fine hotels in Manhattan, none are so critically acclaimed as the Sofitel (built in 2000). The hotel's 398 rooms meld modern, new-world amenities with European old-world elegance. The rooms are spacious, comfortable, and adorned with New York and Paris art. The lighting is soft and romantic, and the walls and windows are soundproofed (important in the city!). Rates range from $229 to $429 for double occupancy and from $359 for a suite. Less than ten minutes from Tavern on the Green, the hotel is located at 45 West 44th Street (between Fifth and Sixth Avenues, Times Square and Midtown West; 212–354–8844).

Keep in Mind: Tavern books wedding up to two years in advance, but six to ten months out is the average. There is no slow season, although February through April is often less fully booked—except Valentine's Day.

FEARRINGTON HOUSE COUNTRY INN & RESTAURANT
Fearrington Village, North Carolina

Fearrington Village, near Chapel Hill, North Carolina, is an Anglican country town with a southern style so sophisticated and well groomed, we've invented a new term for it: Farm Chic. Even the belted Galloway cattle grazing on the green lawn in front of the signature silo and barn look smart in their black tuxedos with white cummerbunds. In fact, this low-key, high-style combination is called the Fearrington Formula, and it is just the combination that will make your destination wedding a success.

Fearrington Village is an 1,100-acre synthesized community of homes, shops, and gardens, neatly organized around the Fearrington House Country Inn & Restaurant. The property began as an old dairy farm that had been handed down through the Cole family for 200 years, until R. B. Fitch of Fitch Creations, Inc., purchased it in 1974 from Jesse Fearrington, the most recent heir. Fitch slowly began to craft a town out of the rolling hills, beginning with several blocks of energy-efficient homes, soon transforming the 1927 farmhouse (the original homestead burned down) into Fearrington House Restaurant, and the granary into the Market Cafe. By 1986 Fitch opened the new Fearrington House Country Inn next door to the restaurant, joining the retail shops, residences, and gardens already thriving under the Fearrington Formula that fuses the historic with the innovative.

Weddings at Fearrington, however, are anything but factory made. Wedding specialist Gilda McDaniel sees to that, and emphasizes that it is her mission to make them stress-free. She is assisted by floral designer Bill Pressley, who completes the Farm Chic wedding with unique floral arrangements based on the seasonal beauty of the Fearrington gardens.

Fearrington House offers five settings for weddings. The **lawn** is framed by a perennial border and accented with an English dovecote and old pecan trees; it also features the intimate White Garden with roses, peonies, and hollyhocks. Daytime receptions are held on the **West Terrace** beneath a billowing white wedding tent with ceiling fans. The oak-tree-shaded, flower-lined brick terrace is attached to the **Fearrington House Restaurant,** which is still reminiscent of the historic family home. Private luncheons are welcome in the restaurant. A former granary, the **Market Cafe** served as a general store on the main road from Raleigh in the 1900s, and now houses a cafe, deli, bakery, and folk art shops. It offers a variety of private rooms for rehearsal dinners and small receptions. **The Barn,** where cows were once milked, is an enchanting venue that adapts to a range of decorating styles. Imagine a formal wedding reception with long white linens, candlelight, magical twig chandeliers hanging from the rafters, and stately decorative columns. Or go 180 degrees for a bluegrass barbecue hoedown, decorated with red-and-white gingham, hay bales, cornstalks, and pumpkins. As always the "Oreo" cows, those rare Scottish transplants, are nearby for guests to visit.

Fearrington House Country Inn & Restaurant
2000 Fearrington Village
Pittsboro, NC 27312
(919) 542–2121 or (919) 545–5734
www.fearringtonhouse.com

Location: Fearrington Village is 8 miles south of Chapel Hill, North Carolina, on U.S. Highway 15/501, just forty minutes from the Raleigh-Durham Airport, and is convenient to the Research Triangle Park.

Facility Rental, Amenities, and Policies: The ceremony fee of $3,000 includes pre-wedding photography privileges, use of the gardens, wedding rehearsal, white wooden chairs arranged on the lawn, and a superior suite for one evening for the bride and groom. Site fee for the barn is $2,500 for Saturday, and $1,500 for Friday or Sunday. Opening site fee for a private room at Market on weekends is $1,000, with a fifty-person minimum. Receptions must accompany all ceremonies on the property, but small weddings must weigh in the site fees.

Catering: Reception options vary with the number of guests, time of day, venue, and tastes. Fearrington has put together a reception menu, which is available on the West Terrace of the restaurant from 11:00 A.M. to 4:00 P.M., and at the Market Cafe from 5:30 P.M. to midnight. The menu includes hors d'oeuvres and specialty buffet tables for $3,000 for up to fifty guests, plus $45 for each additional guest. Large evening receptions are available in the Barn from 5:30 to midnight. The reception menu, including the site fee, for the Barn is $4,500 on Saturday, and $3,500 on all other days for up to fifty guests, plus $45 for each additional guest.

The Market's Southern dinner menu is $35 per person with a minimum of twenty people (plus site fee) for a generous selection of appetizers, entrees, and desserts. The Fearrington Market and Barn special events luncheon menu is $45 per person with a thirty-person minimum, and the dinner or buffet menu is $48 per person for two courses plus dessert. The Fearrington house special events dinner menu offers three courses plus chef's soup and dessert at $79 per person, or $81 to $90 per person for combined entrees. Finally, the Pig Pickin' rehearsal dinner menu, featuring southern barbecued chicken or pit-cooked pork, is $38 per person with a minimum of sixty people (plus the barn rental). Favorite dishes for weddings are the chocolate soufflé (although difficult for a large crowd) and the beef tenderloin, cooked to order on the day of the event.

Extras: Flowers and cake must be provided by Fearrington. Attendant and bridal bouquets start at $75 and $150, respectively. Decorations range from $50 for individual table arrangements to $500 for complete tent garlands. Prices for cakes range from $250 for up to twenty-five people to $750 for 200 to 250 people. The Belted Galloway groom's cake is charming.

Accommodations: The Fearrington House Country Inn offers 32 luxury rooms, each furnished with antiques and original art. 16 rooms open to an intimate courtyard, while the remaining rooms face Camden Park, a seventeen-acre garden open space. Rates are $220 to $450 per night for standard, deluxe, superior, or grand rooms, and include a gourmet breakfast at Fearrington House as well as afternoon tea. Fearrington House is a member of Relais & Chateaux.

OUTER BANKS
LIGHTHOUSES AND BEACHES
North Carolina

With more than 100 miles of pristine and often secluded beaches from Corolla to Ocracoke, North Carolina's Outer Banks have become increasingly popular for weddings. This thin necklace of islands curves out into the Atlantic Ocean and then back again into the sheltering embrace of North Carolina.

The main wedding season on the Outer Banks is April through October, though May and October are the most popular months thanks to mild weather, fewer visitors, and off-peak accommodations rates. Wedding service providers are available, but everyone recommends planning at least a year in advance. Remember, hurricane season is from July through early November, so make sure all contracts provide hurricane stipulations.

North Carolina law requires that a wedding ceremony be conducted by an ordained minister or a magistrate. The state has replaced its former justice-of-the-peace system with court-appointed magistrates. These officials perform wedding services for only $10. They are severely limited in the times and places they can accommodate, but are required to marry anyone who shows up with a marriage license and two witnesses. Most major Christian denominations are represented on the Outer Banks. Many do require a special counseling period, and some have specific requirements regarding remarrying divorced persons. There is no Jewish congregation on the Outer Banks; the nearest temple is in Norfolk, Virginia. Most Jewish couples bring a rabbi from their home temple.

A popular wedding option is to rent a large beachfront house (or several in a row) for a weekend event, holding the ceremony on the beach and the reception at one of the houses. Vacation rental companies are increasingly equipped to handle this, and some allow an unlimited number of guests for the reception.

Ocracoke and Cape Hatteras Lighthouses

Protected by the Cape Hatteras National Seashore under the National Park Service, the Ocracoke and Cape Hatteras Lighthouses and nearby beaches make beautiful backdrops for wedding ceremonies, which are permitted for a nominal fee.

The solid white 1823 Ocracoke Lighthouse at the south end of Ocracoke Island stands 75 feet tall and is crowned with an octagonal lantern. A primary consideration for the Ocracoke Lighthouse as a wedding site is Ocracoke Beach—named America's second best beach in 2005—4 miles north of the village of Ocracoke.

Cape Hatteras Lighthouse, with its two black and two white stripes, is the most famous of all North Carolina lighthouses and, therefore, the most crowded. It is the tallest in the country (depending on how it's measured) and historically a popular site for marriage proposals. (One tale runs that a man was so nervous, he dropped the ring all the way to the bottom, though he later found it.) The lighthouse was completed in 1870, but closed between 1935 and 1950 due to beach erosion. Now the Coast Guard owns and operates the navigational equipment, while the National Park Service maintains the tower as a historic structure. Visitors can climb the 248 iron spiral stairs.

Adjacent to the Cape Hatteras Lighthouse are a number of beach areas ideally suited for weddings. The large beach across from the visitor parking lot has plenty of parking and a new restroom facility. Smaller weddings may opt for the site

of the original lighthouse built in 1894, or the less populous beach on the park road leading to the point.

Currituck Beach Lighthouse

At the opposite end of the Outer Banks, and far less traveled, is the charming, well-kept Currituck Beach Lighthouse, where several dozen weddings take place annually and range in size from 5 to 150 guests. In 1875 the beacon of the redbrick Currituck Beach Lighthouse filled the remaining "dark spot" on the North Carolina coast. Two keepers and their families shared the duplex keepers' house, but were removed in 1939 after the lighthouse became automated. Now owned and operated by Outer Banks Conservationists, Inc., the grounds and walks of the compound have been restored.

Superintendent, National Park Service
1401 National Park Drive
Manteo, NC 27954
Special Park Uses Coordinator: (252)
473–2111, ext. 121
www.nps.gov/caha/fees.html

Location: Cape Hatteras Lighthouse at Buxton is approximately 40 miles south of Manteo and Nags Head, North Carolina. Ocracoke Island is immediately south of Cape Hatteras, and must be reached by ferry. Travel time by car and ferry averages about two hours from Nags Head, depending on the time of day. The ferry operates at different times during the day; for more information see www.ncferry.org.

Facility Rental, Amenities, and Policies: A written permit is required for all wedding ceremonies fixing the date, time, and place of the ceremony. To obtain one, simply write to the superintendent thirty days before the wedding, including a $100 check and all pertinent information. Allow two weeks to receive the permit. From Memorial Day until Labor Day, permits will only be issued for weddings occurring before 10:00 A.M. or after 4:00 P.M. daily. Parties will be charged for litter cleanup, any damage caused to the structures or environment, or any required participation or monitoring. The permit does not authorize exclusive use of any public lands. Weddings are not permitted in undisturbed dune areas, or within or upon any public park structure or its approach or steps. See the Web site for additional restrictions.

Since Ocracoke Lighthouse is immediately adjacent to wetlands and fragile grasses, it's best suited for ceremonies of three to twelve people. Parking is extremely limited; Ocracoke Lighthouse itself is closed to the public.

While the Cape Hatteras Lighthouse is open from time to time, weddings cannot be performed within the lighthouse itself or on its steps or paths. Continuous public access to the lighthouse is required at all times. Parking and restroom facilities are readily available, and this area is more suitable for larger weddings of up to twenty-five people. However, the area is less intimate given the great numbers of people visiting the lighthouse on a daily basis. Even larger weddings can more easily be accommodated at the beach area just beyond the lighthouse.

Catering: Receptions are not permitted at the NPS lighthouses, and restrictions at the beaches make receptions prohibitive. However, there are many restaurants and inns near these areas.

Accommodations: For complete accommodations listings go to www.ocracoke guide.com and www.corollaguide.com.

Currituck Beach Lighthouse
Outer Banks Conservationists, Inc.
P.O. Box 58
Corolla, NC 27927
(252) 453–8152
www.currituckbeachlight.com

Location: To drive to the Currituck Beach Light Station from North Carolina Highway 158 at Kitty Hawk, take North Carolina Highway 12 north, passing through the villages of Duck and Corolla.

Facility Rental, Amenities, and Policies: The site rental fee is $500, for weddings between 10:00 A.M. and 6:00 P.M. at the southwest corner of the site only. Parties must arrange their own chairs, tables, and setup on the day of the wedding. Amplified music is allowed. A staff member will be on duty and present on the site. However, there are no changing facilities or bathrooms. Portable toilets are available in season only (April through November). The site is open to the public daily from 10:00 A.M. to 6:00 P.M., from mid-March through Thanksgiving weekend, and there is a nominal fee for climbing the tower.

Catering: There are a number of restaurants and inns in the area.

Accommodations: Try the quiet and as-yet-undiscovered Inn at Corolla Light Resort. The inn has 43 new and individualized rooms and suites, many with gas fireplaces as well as separate sitting and entertainment areas, offering spectacular views of the Currituck Sound. Off-season rates are $109 to $249, and go up in summer. The inn is located at 1066 Ocean Trail, Corolla, NC 27927 (800–215–0772 or 252–453–3340; www.corolla-inn.com).

SMOKY MOUNTAIN MANSION

North Carolina

Why settle for a five-hour wedding when it can last all weekend? Smoky Mountain Mansion offers the perfect, cost-effective opportunity for a weekend wedding for families on both sides of the aisle to get to know one another in a beautiful setting. Smoky Mountain Mansion can accommodate most of the invited guests, as well as set up the wedding itself. With several national forests, rivers, and lakes in the area, there are plenty of diversions. Adventurous guests can hike to a waterfall or go white-water rafting, horseback riding, or trout fishing. The scenic Cherohala Skyway of the Appalachians or the extremely curvy Tail of the Dragon drives are close by.

The mansion was built in the mid-1990s as a private residence and, after many upgrades, opened in the spring of 2002 as a full-service rental facility attracting mostly destination weddings. This 10,000-square-foot luxury home is set in a forested area that lends to privacy and natural ambience and can potentially host weddings for 100 to 150 guests, although this venue is ideal for an affair half that size. The mansion has six deluxe bedrooms that can comfortably lodge sixteen to twenty members of the wedding party, and, more importantly, it has seven bathrooms. Overflow lodgings are available in nearby luxury cabins handled by the same company. Guests can relax in leather chairs in front of a fireplace or in a hot tub on the deck, or play pool or Ping-Pong. The mansion has a full catering kitchen downstairs and a guest kitchen and laundry room on the second floor. The large elliptical drive allows for plenty of parking.

The ceremony usually takes place on the lawn in front of the mansion's new gazebo. In case the weather doesn't cooperate, the wedding can move into the 1,200-square-foot indoor banquet room. The dining room itself can seat thirty people, but there is plenty of space in the new pavilion at the rear of the mansion for a casual buffet or formal dining for a hundred guests or more.

A relatively new facility, the mansion is gathering steam and receives twenty or more inquiries per day. We spoke with Peter Covert, a delightful, enthusiastic gentleman who admitted that the mansion is under-priced for what it offers. He suggested booking as soon as a wedding date is confirmed, with at least six to eight months' advance notice, although arrangements can be handled six to eight weeks in advance if there is an opening. May and October are their busiest months, followed by June and September. July and August tend to be slow.

All weddings at the mansion have live video coverage via mini cams placed around the property. Those who can't come to the wedding will be able to watch the ceremony, the receiving line, and reception through the mansion's Web site.

Smoky Mountain Mansion
P.O. Box 2059
Robbinsville, NC 28771
(866) 862–4220 or (828) 479–4220
Fax: (828) 479–2440
www.smokymountainmansion.com

Location: The mansion is near Robbinsville, North Carolina, ninety minutes on a twisty road from Knoxville, Tennessee, about two hours (more or less) from Asheville, North Carolina, and Chattanooga, Tennessee, and three hours from Atlanta, Georgia (if you avoid rush-hour traffic).

Facility Rental, Amenities, and Policies: When a couple rents the mansion for a weekend, the wedding with many accoutrements is included and it is set up for the bride and groom. The mansion's Weekend Wedding Plan for $6,995 includes use of the entire mansion, with two nights' accommodations for the wedding party (sixteen to twenty people); color-coordinated floral arrangements and decorations in the mansion, pavilion, and grounds; a casual outdoor catered cookout rehearsal dinner for up to thirty people, or a formal catered rehearsal dinner for up to sixteen; continental breakfast for the wedding party staying at the mansion Saturday and Sunday mornings; Saturday luncheon for the wedding party staying at the mansion preceding the wedding; use of limousine and driver for shuttle service; bartender for the reception; hairdresser(s) on Saturday prior to the wedding for up to four people; and live Web cam and personal Web site for information and photography.

Catering: The mansion's exclusive catering staff attends to all of the meals and events. Management has had the experience of owning and operating fine restaurants in past years, thus ensuring that meals are pleasing to both the eye and palate. The reception catering plan starts with a basic package for forty guests or more and builds from there. Simple hors d'oeuvres are $19 per person for assorted fruits, vegetables, and finger sandwiches. The expanded reception buffet is $29 per person and includes the hors d'oeuvres mentioned plus choice of one entree and two sides such as hot meatballs in BBQ sauce or a cold meat tray. The deluxe reception buffet is $39 per person and includes all items from the previous menus plus two entrees and two sides, such as chicken Mara Bella or eggplant Parmesan. Prices are based on a minimum of forty guests. The wedding cake begins at $165. All furniture, linens, glassware, and candelabra are included in the reception price. Outside caterers are not permitted.

Extras: Complete wedding services, such as officiant, flowers, photography, and entertainment, can be arranged by staff for additional costs. The mansion provides soft drinks, but alcohol is extra.

Accommodations: Although the mansion's Presidential Suite is beautifully decorated with French doors leading to a marble bath, the bride and groom may wish to stay in the secluded honeymoon cabin. The mansion offers 6 nearby fully equipped cabins, ranging from 1 to 3 bedrooms with pullout sleeper couches and hot tubs beginning at $95 per night. There is a 50-room Microtel 2 miles from the mansion for $65 to $135 per night.

Keep in Mind: The recently renovated Andrews-Murphy Airport is half an hour from Smoky Mountain Mansion, and has a jet-friendly runway with GPS approaches. Air-taxi service is available on request to commercial airports at each of these cities for up to five people. Contact the airport for more information. Rental cars might be available at the airport, or the mansion will dispatch its limousine to pick up wedding guests.

Smoky Mountain Aero at Andrews-Murphy Airport: (828) 321–5114.

CASTLE HILL INN & RESORT

Newport, Rhode Island

Ever since Jacqueline Bouvier and John F. Kennedy married in Newport, Rhode Island, in 1953, this yachting capital of the world has been synonymous with romance and bridal elegance. Whether family ties bring a couple back to Newport to wed, or they simply prefer a refined setting for a ceremony by the sea, Castle Hill Inn & Resort, on a forty-acre peninsula at the west end of Newport's world-renowned Ocean Drive, delivers a memorable wedding experience.

The island city of Newport was settled in 1639 by a small group of religious dissenters from Massachusetts, giving the city a reputation for tolerance. With an ideal location for trade at the mouth of Narragansett Bay, Newport became prosperous during the colonial era, specializing in furniture making, fishing, and candle making. By the beginning of the eighteenth century, Newport had become one of five major ports in North America and a center for shopping and trading, with more than 150 independent wharves and hundreds of shops along what is today known as Thames Street. A century later some of the wealthiest East Coast families built homes along the bay's rocky cliffs.

The city of Newport has preserved more than 200 pre-Revolutionary buildings and retained the small size that makes it so ideal for walking. Castle Hill was built as a summer home in 1874 for the Harvard University scientist and explorer Alexander Agassiz, who helped add a laboratory and lighthouse to the property. Recent extensive renovations restored the exterior of the Agassiz Mansion to its original look; a new gourmet kitchen was installed as well. Owner J. T. O'Connell is particularly excited about the suite added to the top of the

mansion's turret, which features 30-foot ceilings and a panoramic view of Narragansett Bay and the lighthouse. Aerial photographs reveal a dreamy setting of a Victorian estate on a sprawling oceanfront lawn—deep greens meet deep blues with striated cliffs separating the two as if to break the monotony. The granite Castle Hill Light, closed to the public, looks as though it emerges right out of the bedrock.

Summer weddings are held on the lawn overlooking Narrangansett Bay and Newport Bridge. The bridal platform is a terrace lined by an enveloping half wall of closely spaced stone columns, centered by a columned archway framing the blue sky and sea. The terrace setting can accommodate up to 250 guests. During the peak season the Chalet Terrace offers a semipermanent tent that is elegantly appointed with chandeliers and roll-down drapery on the sides. The inn itself has nine rooms and four dining rooms for the more intimate weddings.

Castle Hill can accommodate wedding parties of 2 to 250. During the peak season of April through November, Castle Hill hosts four weddings a week; thereafter, about two weddings a month are booked.

Castle Hill Inn & Resort
590 Ocean Drive
Newport, RI 02840
(888) 466–1355
www.castlehillinn.com

Location: Follow the signs for Ocean Drive to the coastal shore of Narragansett Bay and on to Castle Hill Inn.

Facility Rental, Amenities, and Policies: Site fees were not disclosed, although the

Web site frequently offers discounts such as the following: "Book your April, May & June, 2005 event, site fee will be reduced by 100%! Book your event for June–December, 2005, site fee will be reduced by 50%!"

Catering: The $145-per-person "summer menu" includes a three-course seated dinner with choice of appetizer and choice of two entrees. This packages includes a guest room for the bride and groom on their wedding night. The $195-per-person summer menu offers a "thrill of the grill" station, Castle Hill beverage service for one hour, a four-course seated dinner, and salad. This package also includes a two-bedroom suite for the bride and groom on their wedding night. Both menus offer a champagne toast and custom-designed wedding cake. Receptions include the use of fine china, stemware, flatware, round tables draped in elegant floor-length table linens, gold ballroom chairs, and valet service.

Extras: The schooner *Adirondack II* is also available for the wedding party to take a four-hour private charter through Narragansett Bay, passing right by Castle Hill.

Accommodations: The inn offers a total of 25 rooms and 2 suites in three locations: the main building, or Agassiz Mansion, the more modern Chalet rooms, and the Beach House rooms on the water. Room rates vary depending on the season, from $109 to $339 per night, January through March, to $395 to $850 per night during the high season of July 1 through September 4 for the deluxe rooms and suites. The exclusive bi-level turret suite is $300 to $450 per night, January through March, and $989 to $1,450 per night during the high season. All rooms receive a gourmet breakfast and afternoon high tea.

CHARLESTON PLACE

Charleston, South Carolina

Charleston Place Hotel is the focal point for Charleston's historic district "at the corner of heart and soul," as their slogan goes, in one of the most exciting and romantic cities in the world. It's the sort of high-end, high-gloss venue that appeals to royalty, celebrity, and the otherwise very wealthy, but all who stay here are treated as such. Weddings at Charleston Place are equally stately and fashionable. The question is: Do they do smaller destination weddings? Emphatically, yes, and in the same southern-comfort style that has made the hotel famous.

Now twenty years old, the hotel was the brainchild of a mayor who wanted to revitalize the downtown area of Charleston by building a world-class hotel and upscale shopping center. The hotel, now an Orient-Express property, "represents the New South at its most confident," one critic wrote. The eight-story landmark looks like a postmodern French chateau, colossal among the B&Bs and inns in the area. The fountain topped by four bronze horses at the hotel's Hassel Street entrance reminds one of the steed's significance in Charleston's history. (South Carolina was the first to secede from the Union, and the first to fire a shot in the Civil War.)

The Market Street entryway is used for grand entrances for special occasions. Guests enter on foot and the bride by horse carriage through a pair of brick columns supporting a black wrought-iron fence, and continue around the circular, brick roadway to the imposing facade. A sweeping view of the massive lobby includes a pair of plantation-style staircases that wrap around a 12-foot, one-and-a-half-ton Venetian glass chandelier as they rise from the white Italian marble floor. Picture all this in the wedding album!

Outdoor ceremonies usually take place in the Herb Garden (seating 300 theater style) and the Flagpole Terrace (seating 75). The responsive catering staff told us the smallest wedding the hotel can host would be for twelve people.

Charleston Place offers a wide range of reception options in eighteen function rooms. The spectacular Grand Ballroom can accommodate approximately 300 for a plated dinner, or 500 for "heavy hors d'oeuvres" with a dance floor, staging, bars, cake table, and gift table. The newly restored art deco Riviera featuring the rooftop terrace and Sottile Ballroom holds 220 to 350. Originally opened in 1939 on the site of the Academy of Music, the Riviera is listed on the National Register of Historic Places. It seamlessly combines the best of past and present with meticulously restored frescoes and hand-painted murals in lavish surroundings. The Palmetto Garden room and attached courtyard can hold about 100 people for a plated dinner, and 150 for heavy hors d'oeuvres for cocktail receptions before the dinner. Enshrouded by lush greenery, a bubbling fountain in the center of the bricked garden adds serenity. Smaller suites can host wedding dinners for parties of forty or fewer.

Charleston Place
205 Meeting Street
Charleston, SC 29401
(800) 455–2427 or (843) 722–4900
www.charlestonplace.com

Location: Charleston Place Hotel is at the corner of Hassel Street and Meeting Street, 1 mile from Interstate 26.

Facility Rental, Amenities, and Policies: There is a site fee of $500 for ceremonies.

Catering: Wedding packages are reception-driven: They primarily rely on food and beverage minimums for each function room based on the number of people, and these amounts were not disclosed. Reception packages include a complimentary "dinner sampling" to taste menu items of interest; customized menu cards; access to Charleston Place's preferred vendor list; discounted rates from the florist, Bloom, at Charleston Place; preferred room rates at Charleston Place for out-of-town guests; the Bridal Suite the night of the wedding, with champagne and strawberries; complimentary use of Charleston Place for portrait and wedding pictures (on the grand double staircase, perhaps?); and breakfast for two, either in the suite or in the Palmetto Cafe the morning after the event. As part of the "Honeymoon Never Ends" program, couples enjoy a complimentary stay on their one-year anniversary in an elegant room with a surprise awaiting them and room service breakfast the following morning.

Luncheons are $29 to $40 per plate, and dinners are $46 to $135 per person. Hors d'oeuvres are priced per hundred pieces, with an average of $5.00 per piece. Cooked-to-order action stations are around $17 to $24 per person per station with a minimum of four stations. For hors d'oeuvres consider venison and peppered brie tostada, spinach and cheese phyllo, and tandoori chicken on anan bread with cucumber crème fraîche. For dinner, perhaps enjoy the James Island cucumber soup with watercress and spiced sour cream, grilled local vegetables with goat cheese and pesto vinaigrette, sautéed crab cake and Angus beef fillet with tomato Creole sauce and truffled demi-glace, and mango orange mousse with kiwi coulis for $59 per person.

Accommodations: Charleston Place offers 320 deluxe rooms and 80 club-level rooms. Rates start at $239 for deluxe, $399 for club, and $599 for suites.

BROWN PELICAN INN
South Padre Island, Texas

Brown Pelican Inn, a bed-and-breakfast on the Laguna Madre side of South Padre Island, is an unassuming two-story beach house that attracts both birds and brides. For the part of the brides, and their grooms, the attraction could be the promise of rocking on wraparound porches, sleeping in decidedly Anglican and "spotless" guest rooms, and bird-watching, of course, or kite surfing at the other extreme. While we can't speak for the birds, a full 350 species are native to Padre Island. During their annual migrations thousands of bird species can be seen in Laguna Madre's lagoons and freshwater ponds. Common shorebirds along the Gulf beach year-round, to name a few, include black skimmers, great blue herons, sanderlings, long billed curlews, killdeers—and brown pelicans. The World Birding Center says that South Padre, particularly Laguna Madre around the jetties, is the second best place to spot brown pelicans. They make spectacular plunge-dives in the deeper waters of the open coast, and invariably they begin soaring just about the time guests at the Brown Pelican Inn begin their breakfast on the porch.

Extending 113 miles along the Texas Gulf Coast, Padre Island comprises stunning dunes of fine white sand, thriving grasslands, saltwater marshes, and myriad wildlife. With 70 miles of natural beaches, much of which are protected in a national seashore, Padre Island is one of the largest undeveloped barrier islands in the United States.

The inn maintains eight guest rooms appointed with American and English antiques, each with a private bath. Several rooms have bay views, and the covered porch is a favorite vantage point to experience "a Texas sunset like you have never seen." Texas's best beach is just a 2-block stroll from the front door, and fresh seafood is only minutes away. The Laguna Madre Bay with its warm and shallow water, its constant breeze, and its sheltered 7-mile width is one of the safest places in the United States to learn to windsurf or kite board. Lessons and equipment rentals are available.

Having purchased the inn in 1999, innkeepers Chris and Yves de Diesbach mix Old World values with casual hospitality. Guests have a sense of being treated like they're in a luxury hotel, while being at home at the same time. She's from Dorset, England, and he was born in Algeria and raised in France. American citizens now, they've pursued business ventures in other parts of the globe.

From our conversations with Chris de Diesbach, and judging by bridal testimonials, she attends to all details, preferring to speak with the bride directly on the phone to customize each wedding. The inn is quite small, and only twenty-five people can fit on the deck, although the inn can conceivably host a wedding for thirty-five. Chris has also facilitated weddings at a little chapel and a lighthouse on the island, as well as with the couple on horseback. The wedding party can have a small champagne reception with hors d'oeuvres at the inn, but will dine elsewhere on the island.

Brown Pelican Inn
207 West Aires
P.O. Box 2667
South Padre Island, TX 78597
(956) 761–2722
www.brownpelican.com

Location: The Brown Pelican Inn is on South Padre Island along the Laguna Madre Bay shoreline. From Brownsville–Port Isabel, Texas, take Texas Highway 100 to the island.

Facility Rental, Amenities, and Policies: A couple staying at the inn can marry on the inn's deck in an informal, small ceremony at no charge. The Brown Pelican Inn offers the ultimate wedding package for $2,300, which includes a minister or judge appropriate to the couple's religious convictions, three nights in a bayfront honeymoon suite, three dinners at the best restaurants on South Padre Island, a bridal bouquet, champagne, a photographer with one set of wedding prints, and a two-hour sunset dolphin-watch bay tour.

Catering: Chris de Diesbach will make arrangements with the couple's restaurant

of choice for celebratory dining. Many choose the Lantern Grill (956–761–4460). An upscale departure from South Padre's seafood shacks, the elegant restaurant is Mediterranean inspired, featuring light pink stucco outside, exposed brick and murals inside, and soft jazz on the weekends.

Extras: The inn has developed relationships with appropriate vendors such as officants, photographers, florists, and hairstylists. The de Diesbachs will also reserve bay and dolphin cruises, arrange bird-watching tours, or outfit guests for a day at the beach.

Accommodations: The inn has 8 rooms available, with maximum capacity of 2 guests per room. There are three applicable rates during the year: May 1 through Labor Day, rooms range from $135 to $150 per night; September 8 through February 28, $115 to $135; and weekends are $125 to $150. Weekends and holidays have minimum-stay requirements. Accommodations include a complimentary breakfast buffet served in the great room or on the porch. Morning buffets begin with coffee, a fresh fruit platter, and nut, date, or banana bread, followed by a hot entree such as Brown Pelican frittata. Additional lodgings may be found in the South Padre area if there are out-of-town guests exceeding the inn's 8-room capacity. There is a high-rise hotel next to the inn.

LUCKENBACH DANCEHALL
Luckenbach, Texas

You know the song, "Luckenbach Texas," made famous by Willie, Waylon, and the boys, but did you know you can rent the whole dang town for your wedding? Nothing there but a post office, general store, and beer joint all rolled into one, you say? Well, that *is* the town, and also the point.

Luckenbach, Texas, is an authentic ten-acre town set in the Texas Hill Country, surrounded by majestic old oaks and pecans. Established as a trading post in 1849, a post office/general store/saloon was first opened in 1886 by August Engel, an itinerant preacher from Germany, whose daughter, Minna, chose the name Luckenbach in honor of her fiancé, Albert Luckenbach. Go figure. The town is hardly more than a bend in the road, just a couple of old buildings beneath a grove of spreading oaks—population, three. The only other significant structure is a genuine, old-fashioned Texas dancehall where local bands play western music on most weekends.

It was Hondo Crouch, by strength of his eccentric personality, who put Luckenbach on the music map—with a bullet. He bought the town—lock, stock, and dancehall—in 1970 and became the town's "clown prince," appointing his friends as ambassadors and public officials. Hondo held such gatherings as "Hug-Ins," a Luckenbach World's Fair, Ladies State Chili Bust, and the Mud Dauber Festival. Thousands came to the town to hear Hondo tell stories and sing Mexican and cowboy songs on the porch. Jerry Jeff Walker, a Texas-style country-rocker, recorded the hit album *Viva Terlingua* in the old dancehall in 1973, using bales of hay as sound buffers. Four years later Bobby Emmons and Chips Moman wrote "Luckenbach Texas (Back to the Basics)," which became a massive hit for Waylon Jennings and Willie Nelson. That's when the tour buses really began to show up. Sadly, Hondo passed away in 1976, the year before "Luckenbach Texas" became a hit.

Luckenbach has since become a trademark, and the general store on the Web site sells such items as a personally engraved brick in the dancehall patio for $50. After spending some $75,000 in new wiring, septic system, and improvements, the old dancehall and general store have two-stepped Luckenbach into the twenty-first century. Nelson returns to Luckenbach annually for his 4th of July Picnic; Walker returned on the twentieth anniversary of recording *Viva Terlingua* to record *Viva Luckenbach*. The legendary dancehall still hosts monthly dances

by some of the best Texan musicians, many who were still in diapers when *Viva Terlingua* and "Luckenbach Texas" were recorded.

Somewhere in the neighborhood of fifty private parties (wedding receptions, birthday fetes, and corporate parties) are booked each year, keeping the dancehall alive almost every weekend. As many as 150 to 165 people can be seated on twenty-one picnic-style tables with pull-up backed benches, leaving a space large enough for dancing. Additional tables can be rented to accommodate larger crowds up to 300. The stage is equipped with convenient electrical outlets and lighting, a backstage loading area, and two backstage rooms. The main dancehall area has ceiling fans and twinkle lights throughout. Windows open on all sides of the dancehall for comfortable air circulation. A wheelchair ramp is available as well.

Luckenbach Dancehall
412 Luckenbach Town Loop
Fredricksburg, TX 78624
(888) 311–8990 or (830) 997–3224
www.luckenbachtexas.com

Location: Luckenbach, Texas, is approximately 10.6 miles outside Fredricksburg, off Texas Highway 290, 53 miles north of San Antonio, and 80 miles west of Austin. Stop and ask for directions; it isn't easy to find.

Facility Rental, Amenities, and Policies: Anytime the dancehall is in use, the general store, post office, and beer joint are also open. The dancehall rental ranges from $850 to $2,300. That includes the hall, up to twenty-one picnic-style tables and benches, one security guard, and a portion of the patio. The dancehall can be rented as a package for $1,350 to $2,800, which includes the above as well as a bar serviced with one bartender and one barback, plus grounds rental for the ceremony with up to 150 chairs. Rates depend on day of the week and time of the year.

Luckenbach "party perfessionals" will also work with the couple to customize the rental to fit any wedding. A licensed security guard is required for all private parties. Additional security may be required for parties larger than 150, or parties where guests arrive by the busload.

Open seven days a week from 9:00 A.M. to 10:00 P.M., Luckenbach's entire calendar is online for easy scheduling.

Catering: All catering is ordered through Luckenbach, which works with three vendors and two cake bakers. Menus range "from down-home, lip-smackin' BBQ to international cuisine," starting at $10 per person. Texas-style buffets are offered with a variety of menus, including southwestern—featuring entrees such as grilled sirloin steak with tobacco onions, and grilled chicken breast with corn relish; and the fajita buffet, featuring beef and chicken marinated in southwestern spices, tossed with bell peppers and onions. Elegant summer wedding buffets and plated dinners are also offered. How about smoked quail in tamarind barbecue sauce?

Luckenbach's license and insurance supports only beer, wine, and champagne; there is no BYOB option. You can choose to have the bar one of three ways: cash bar, modified prepaid tab bar, or open bar.

Extras: Entertainment must be booked through Luckenbach, and they say they can even get Willie Nelson to play for a wedding event. Realistically, choices include Luckenbach's DJ at $500 for four hours, or a live band starting at $1,200. Luckenbach books around 150 acts a year, so the selection is broad.

Accommodations: Plenty of good lodging is available in Fredericksburg, Texas. Receiving topflight reviews is the Hangar Hotel. Built new from the ground up, this 50-room boutique hotel was designed with the appearance and romance of a World War II hangar. A fly-in hotel, it's not just for pilots, according to the Web site. It is for anyone who wants more than just a bed and shower. Rates are $99 to $149. The Hangar Hotel is located at 155 Airport Road, Fredericksburg, TX 78624 (830–997–9990; www.hangarhotel.com).

MARION KOOGLER McNAY ART MUSEUM
San Antonio, Texas

Have Picasso and O'Keeffe as guests to your wedding. At the Marion Koogler McNay Art Museum in San Antonio, it's possible. Touted as the first modern art museum in Texas, "The McNay" is where brides from Houston, Dallas, and San Antonio know to set their weddings, receptions, and photography. The main attraction is the museum's setting in a 1929 Spanish Mediterranean-style mansion, with its lush gardens, koi ponds, fountains, modern art sculpture, and eternal views of the city. The artwork is a bonus!

The museum was originally the home of the founder for whom it was named, Marion McNay, "a discriminating collector, an earnest student of the fine arts, and a philanthropist of the first magnitude." Steadfast in her commitment to "the advancement and enjoyment of modern art," she bequeathed her important art collection, her twenty-four-room Spanish Colonial Revival–style mansion, the twenty-three acres upon which it sits, and most of her fortune to the development of the museum after she died in 1950. Because the home was not designed as a museum, the McNay underwent extensive renovations and reopened in 2001.

The house is in the section of San Antonio known as Alamo Heights located off Broadway. Developed in the 1930s, the neighborhood was revitalized and restored in the late 1970s when several new businesses recognized the area's potential. Today it's known for its restaurants, shopping, and art deco architecture. Alamo Heights is also home to San Antonio's Museum District. Another hidden jewel is the Witte, San Antonio's natural history museum, located near the intersection of Broadway and Hildebrand.

The McNay houses an impressive collection of impressionist art, focusing primarily on nineteenth- and twentieth-century European and American artists such as Cézanne, Picasso, Gauguin, Matisse, O'Keeffe, Cassatt, and Hopper. The museum also displays the largest collection of American graphic art in the Southwest. The Tobin Collection of Theatre Arts, including costumes, set designs, and rare books, is said to be outstanding. The McNay also hosts major traveling shows.

Wedding guests will enter a private world with first-class facilities, secure, free parking, and an opportunity to view some of the world's finest art. Combine the Rotunda, Courtyard, and Ballroom/Auditorium with a reception or dinner for a memorable, elegant event for discriminating guests.

Marion Koogler McNay Art Museum
6000 North New Braunfels
San Antonio, TX 78209
(210) 805–1761
www.mcnayart.org

Location: The McNay is located in San Antonio at the corner of North New Braunfels and the Austin Highway.

Facility Rental, Amenities, and Policies: For $4,500 the McNay permits rental of the entire Special Events area, which includes the Leeper Auditorium, Octagon Reception area, and Courtyard to outside grounds. The rental fee includes all three spaces, which cannot be rented separately. Maximum capacity in the Octagon is 100 guests; the Auditorium, 300 (seated or standing); and the Courtyard, 150. Rental includes free parking across from the Special Events Entrance. The grounds for the ceremony are not included and can be rented separately for $275. Ceremonies on the grounds will accommodate up to fifty standing guests and are limited to thirty minutes without chairs and props.

Catering: The caterers the McNay works with provide all manners of menus. Some will even e-mail a photograph of a particular dish. Hosted bars may also be set up in the rental areas.

Accommodations: Lodging is available in the Greater San Antonio area. It is recommended that rooms be booked at the same time as the venue during the peak season.

Keep in Mind: November and December are the busiest months for weddings and should be booked well in advance. May and June should be booked six months out, although if the museum has an opening sooner, staff will try to accommodate a wedding. July and August are the slowest time of the year due to the heat.

MARRIAGE ISLAND ON THE SAN ANTONIO RIVER WALK

San Antonio, Texas

The Alamo is the heart and soul of San Antonio, but when it comes to unique ceremony sites, forget the Alamo and remember the city's lifeline—River Walk. Since anyone can remember, couples have traditionally come to the river to exchange vows on what the locals have dubbed "Marriage Island." Near the red-and-white-flowered Garden of Hearts, this oak-shaded thumbnail of an island is the site of nearly a hundred ceremonies a year, a couple of dozen on Valentine's Day alone.

Sunk 20 feet below street level, the famed River Walk, or Paseo del Rio, is a diverted 2.5-mile water loop from the Gulf-bound river. Much like Italian life along Venice's canalways, the River Walk reflects San Antonio's boisterous and eclectic Tex-Mex culture. With multicolored outdoor umbrellas and old-growth trees framing the scene, the setting is enchanting. Instead of gondolas, the San Antonio River has slow-moving motored barges and water taxis. Pedestrians stroll along cobblestone and flagstone paths that line both sides of the river, and meander in and out of some of San Antonio's best hotels, restaurants, clubs, bars, and shops that crowd the waterfront, which stretches from the Municipal Auditorium and Conference Center to the multilevel Rivercenter Mall. Most people stop in intermittent gardens or on arched stone bridges for a moment to marvel at the masterpiece. At night the river is aglow with lights.

When the Spanish explorers and missionaries arrived here in 1691, they, too, marveled at the abundant water, the lush greenery, and towering trees. Camping along the river, which the Payaya Indians called Yanaguana, the Spaniards celebrated Mass in honor of St. Anthony's feast day on what is now Marriage Island, renaming the Yanaguana as Rio San Antonio. An unusual sculpture of swords, cross, and eucharistic hands now commemorates this first Mass.

The river became the centerpiece of a complex water system built to supply five local Spanish missions established between 1718 and 1731. In September 1921 the worst flood in its history killed more than fifty people and caused millions of dollars' damage to the city. Leaders wanted to pave the river over for an underground storage drain, but an architect named Robert H. H. Hugman proposed a plan for an urban park along the river, and a campaign swayed public opinion in favor of his vision. As part of a Works Progress Administration project, workers laid in much of the locks and stonework seen today. Primarily a park for many years, River Walk developed a dubious reputation as a crime area, but the 1968 HemisFair provided the impetus for turning it into the lively commercial waterfront it is today.

Up at street level hikers can see more of the city's historic and cultural highlights within a 7-mile radius. The King William District, just southwest of downtown, resembles New Orleans's Garden District, with lovingly preserved, stately homes (some open for tours, but most still residential). El Mercado is a Mexican-style marketplace with more than one hundred import stores, as well as open food stalls, restaurants, and street performers. La Villita, the little town, is an arts-and-crafts market with twenty-six shops and three restaurants in a square block of what was the original San Antonio settlement. Nearby are the Alamo, museums, art galleries, theaters, and the HemisFair.

Rio San Antonio Dinner Cruises

After the ceremony, have a small cocktail reception for thirty people or a dinner for twenty people aboard a flat-bottomed barge through Rio San Antonio Cruises. This cruise line can contract with more than seventy restaurants in the area, including local eateries such as Biga on the Banks and chain restaurants like Ruth's Chris Steakhouse. For all events, begin by contacting the catering establishment of choice (listed on the cruiser's Web site) to discuss needs, and then have the caterer book the cruiser. Cruisers are outfitted with two 8-foot tables for dinner or one for cocktails. The cruiser can be decorated as long as it is first approved by the company, as well as by Parks and Recreation. Be sure to book enough time for the caterer to set up and clean up. Events ending at or before 5:30 P.M. are $100 per hour for two hours, and $50 for each additional half hour overtime. Events ending after 5:30 P.M. run $125 for the first hour, $250 for the second hour, and $65 for each additional half hour.

Tickets for nonchartered river cruises, which are thirty-five to forty minutes long, are priced individually at $1.50 for children under five and $6.50 for adults. Water taxis are also available for $3.50 per person, one way, or $10.00 for an all-day pass.

San Antonio Parks and Recreation Department: (210) 207–7275

Paseo del Rio Association
110 Broadway, Suite 440
San Antonio, TX 78205
(210) 227–4262
http://thesanantonioriverwalk.com

Rio San Antonio Cruises
(800) 417–4139 or (210) 244–5700
www.riosanantonio.com

Location: The Marriage Island in San Antonio is across from the City Public Service Building and next to the Westin–Riverwalk Hotel, near Market and Navarro Streets. Stairs to street level are nearby.

Facility Rental, Amenities, and Policies: Call the San Antonio Parks and Recreation Department for a permit, and to reserve a date and time slot. The fee is $100 for thirty minutes. The space isn't roped off, but the permit can be shown to prove the reservation. However, the reservation assistant noted that the island is almost always available. The island is so small, there is only room for the officiant and the couple; the rest of the party must watch from the bank.

Catering: No receptions are permitted on Marriage Island. See Rio San Antonio Dinner Cruises.

Accommodations: Lodging is available along the River Walk and in the Greater San Antonio area.

Keep in Mind: Fall through spring are more pleasant than the scorching summers, but avoid the first or second week of January (when the 2- to 4-foot river is drained for cleaning). December is especially romantic, when the trees are decorated with more than 100,000 twinkling lights.

HARTNESS HOUSE
INN AND RESTAURANT
Springfield, Vermont

Hartness House Inn and Restaurant has a multifaceted personality. Set in a less traveled but accessible part of Vermont, it offers sweethearts log fires, cozy yet spacious rooms, a restaurant and a tavern with great inexpensive food, and helpful, friendly staff. Yet the scientific minded appreciate Hartness House's astronomy museum and antique observatory. Wide landscaped lawns, gardens, and parklike surroundings create an enchanting outdoor location for elegant yet affordable weddings, even by New England standards.

The Hartness House is set on a thirty-five-acre estate and is listed on the National Register of Historic Places. The two-and-a-half-story house is of a rare Shingle style that stands out in Vermont neighborhoods where the architecture is generally Federal and Greek Revival. The ground floor is a mass of stone that supports the upper floors with a combination of irregularly shaped roofs and windows that typify the Shingle style. The original house was basically rectangular, but has been extended in recent years by additions to accommodate its present function as a restaurant and inn.

The 1904 house was built for James Hartness at the height of his career. A New York–born machinist by trade, Hartness became president of a machine company before the age of forty and served as Vermont governor in 1921–1922. His home includes five underground rooms and an underground observatory containing a Russell Porter telescope.

Hartness House hosts about thirty weddings per year, from elopements to grand events involving 150 people (with a capacity of 200). Four locations on the property serve as wedding sites. Large and spacious, the Victorian ballroom, accommodating 45 to 150 people (depending on seating configurations), features two chandeliers, hardwood floors, a panoramic bay window and oversize windows, and an anteroom with fireplace. The Governor's Room (twenty-five to seventy) has oversize windows and a fieldstone wall and is next to the tavern, an outdoor deck, and swimming pool. The Library (twenty-five to seventy) is elegantly decorated with mahogany paneling and ceiling beams, and features an oversize fireplace. The Library's bay window overlooking the front lawns often serves as the backdrop for the ceremony itself, and the room is frequently used for dancing and buffets. The Wedding Gardens are a romantic outdoor location reminiscent of the Great Gatsby era. Starting from the Teahouse, sweeping lawns surrounded by gardens lead the wedding party and their guests to a private knoll approximately 100 feet wide by 250 feet deep. The wedding gardens include a pergola, a fountain, and a white house gazebo, along with lilacs, white lace, begonias, wisteria vines, roses, and hydrangeas. The location can serve large groups and is suitable for one or two banquet tents.

Hartness House offers thirty-five acres of meandering trails with flowing brooks and game playing (volleyball, horseshoes, croquet, and badminton). Area activities include golf, fly fishing, antiquing, canoeing, sailing, hiking, bike riding, tennis, craft exhibits and artisan demonstrations, house tours, and country drives. A state boat launch on the Connecticut River and the

Crown Point Golf Course are just 3 miles away. Though out of the way enough for quiet relaxation, it is convenient to other Vermont and New Hampshire towns.

Hartness House Inn and Restaurant
30 Orchard Street
Springfield, VT 05156
(800) 732–4789 or (802) 885–2115
www.hartnesshouse.com

Location: Just 3 miles off Interstate 91, Hartness House Inn and Restaurant sits atop a hill above the town of Springfield in the Connecticut River Valley.

Facility Rental, Amenities, and Policies: Hartness House offers a variety of packages geared toward destination weddings. The elopement package, at $695, includes an arrival welcome basket, two nights in the honeymoon suite, a ceremony in the Governor's Library, a romantic candlelit gourmet five-course reception dinner with champagne toast, and a honeymoon farewell champagne breakfast in bed.

Hartness House also offers three unique wedding packages with a minimum of twenty or thirty people, for $34 to $75 per person, depending upon day of the week and menu. Bookings are for five-hour periods (usually between 4:00 and 10:00 P.M.), with the sixth and final hour assessed at an additional $250. Each package includes bridal suite with fireplace and romantic champagne welcome for one evening, all facility fees for a ceremony in the Hartness Library, an hors d'oeuvres reception in the private Governor's Room or Library, a champagne toast, and a plated dinner or assorted dinner buffet that features country cooking such as Vermont roast turkey or London broil. The packages also include all necessary tables, linens, dinnerware, and glassware, and a hardwood dance floor.

Catering: For larger weddings, or outdoor events, plated or buffet dinners run $23 to $29. The couple may choose from a diverse menu, such as oven-roasted rack of lamb with cool mint yogurt sauce, herbed rice pilaf, and green beans amandine. A service fee applies for the setup and removal of furniture used during the ceremony.

Extras: Hartness House extends an invitation for a complimentary stay at the inn to assist in the decision-making process. Familiarization visits and tours are offered at a discounted rate of $129 per room, for up to two rooms for one evening, and include a tasting dinner and breakfast the next morning.

Accommodations: When the wedding date falls on either a Friday or Saturday, the client is responsible for the rental of a minimum of 11 rooms in the main house for two days. If the wedding date falls on any other day, the client is responsible for a one-day minimum rental of the Main House rooms. Hartness House offers three categories of rooms: the Main House, the Victorian Wing, and the Lena Hartness Wing. There are 43 rooms available, including 11 uniquely decorated rooms in the Main House, with overnight rates of $120 to $215, double occupancy. The Victorian Wing and the Lena Hartness Wing rates start at $99 to $120. All rooms include a full country breakfast.

For larger weddings there are other lodgings available within fifteen minutes of Hartness House Inn and Restaurant.

Keep in Mind: Weddings are performed all year long, although most are booked during the peak season of summer and early fall foliage. Ceremonies start after 3:00 P.M. Hartness House recommends booking the wedding one and a half years out, but tries to be flexible.

THE LILAC INN
Brandon, Vermont

Welcome to Brandon, Vermont, the "unhurried, unspoiled, unforgettable" village in a once productive corner of American industry. Chartered in 1761, Brandon's abundance of iron made it an important mill town for manufacturing railroad cars in the 1840s. Brandon has two village greens, with the Neshobe River flowing between them. During the boom years of the 1800s, many fine homes were built, and most of them are still in use today. Park Street, a broad, straight avenue with beautiful homes set back from the road, is a study in early American architecture. Brandon's historic downtown, with its entire core of 243 buildings, is on the National Register of Historic Places.

One such historic place is Lilac Inn, built as a summer residence for Brandon's favorite son, Albert G. Farr, which passed to his daughter, Shirley Farr, in 1942. Having made his fortune in Chicago, Farr could afford his generous philanthropy, which over the years gave Brandon an observatory on Mount Pleasant, its current sewer system, and the land to create Branbury State Park on Lake Dunmore.

The 1909 mansion that is Lilac Inn is a stately Renaissance-style building with magnificent gardens that reflect a casual yet enchanting elegance, and is today home to the "unhurried, unspoiled, unforgettable" wedding. The inn has hosted more than 500 weddings ranging in size from 2 to 250 guests. The historic Grand Ballroom is wrapped in oversize beveled French glass doors and windows to accommodate 135 guests. The Lilac Inn is built around a cobblestone courtyard that can accommodate a tented reception. A gazebo is the picturesque focal point for two acres of manicured landscaping. The cascading pond with frog fountain, Vermont stone walls, and slate benches provide the perfect setting for wedding photography. Ceremonies may also take place in the library, or near the grand staircase.

Decorated in a relaxed yet elegant style, the inn feels like a small luxury hotel with personal service to match. The dining room, overlooking the gardens, serves creative American fare. The Lilac Inn is proud to be an active member of the Vermont Fresh Network, which includes half a dozen farmers and food producers who serve only the freshest native ingredients whenever possible. Lilac Inn's menu changes regularly reflecting seasonal availability.

Innkeepers Shelly and Doug Sawyer purchased the inn in 2001, and loved the fact that it was an integral part of this charming Vermont town.

The Lilac Inn
53 Park Street
Brandon, VT 05733
(800) 221–0720
www.lilacinn.com

Location: In Brandon, Vermont, off Vermont Highway 73 east.

Facility Rental, Amenities, and Policies: The elopement package is an Internet special, and is available Sunday through Thursday for $899; Friday and Saturday, $1,299. Elopement packages include two consecutive nights' lodging, queen room with private bath, three-course breakfast for two served daily, and one evening dinner for two. The wedding itself includes a small wedding cake, a private indoor or outdoor ceremony with a local officiant, a bottle of champagne, fresh-cut flowers in the room, and a

Vermont gift basket. There is a $250 setup fee for ceremonies.

For larger weddings the facility and coordination fee is $3,200 and includes unlimited event consultation service, tables and chairs, white-on-ivory damask linens, all small wares (chinaware, flatware, and glassware), reception setup, kitchen staff, bartender, and wait staff. The packages are also subject to availability and exclude holiday periods and foliage seasons. The inn can accommodate up to 250 guests for tented receptions, and 135 guests in the Grand Ballroom. It is recommended that the inn be booked for at least a two-day event for the rehearsal dinner, reception, and a day-after wedding brunch.

Catering: The Inn offers three reception menus, priced $55, $70, and $90 per guest. All menus include a cold station, hot hors d'oeuvres, salad, vegetable, and coffee and tea service. The latter two packages include a champagne toast, dinner wine pour, and chocolate-dipped strawberries. The highest price also includes a soup choice and multiple choices of salad, entrees, and vegetables.

Extras: Lilac Inn's wedding cake is offered separately at $4.00 to $6.00 per guest, depending on the type of cake. The Lilac Inn has a list of wedding vendors available.

Accommodations: 9 guest rooms, each with a private tiled bath, feature amenities that are discreetly placed so as not to distract from the historic ambience of the inn. The bridal suite has a pewter canopy bed, whirlpool bath for two, and fireplace. The other individually decorated rooms are all furnished with claw-footed tubs, handheld European showerheads, and antiques and treasures from the innkeepers' thirty-year collection. Rooms start at $145 during off-season, and $175 during the peak foliage season. The Grand Suite is $250 to $295, depending on the season. The minimum stay is two nights on weekends, and three nights on holiday weekends. All rooms include a three-course gourmet breakfast. The town of Brandon has sixty rooms within walking distance of the inn, and another fifty within a few minutes' drive.

Keep in Mind: Many weddings are booked far in advance, up to two and one half years out. In 2004 every weekend was booked from May through October.

SHELBURNE MUSEUM
Shelburne, Vermont

Shelburne Museum, in Vermont's scenic Lake Champlain Valley just south of Burlington, contains one of the nation's largest collections of American decorative, folk, and fine art in thirty-seven buildings spread over forty-five acres. The more mundane exhibits include quilts, early tools, decoys, and weather vanes. But the museum also displays twenty-five whole buildings from around New England and New York. These include an 1890 railroad station, a lighthouse, a jail, a stagecoach inn, an Adirondack lodge, a covered bridge, and a round barn from Vermont. Even a 220-foot steamship is unexpectedly landlocked on the museum's grounds. A number of these sites are available for wedding ceremonies and receptions.

Electra Havemeyer Webb (1888–1960) established Shelburne Museum in 1947. The daughter of collectors of European and Asian art, she was a pioneering collector of American folk art in her own right. She sought to keep her collection "educational, varied, and alive" by exhibiting her pieces in a villagelike setting of historic New England architecture and landscape.

Webb's own Brick House, with sweeping views of the lake and mountains, is an incomparable location for ceremonies and receptions. The forty-room Colonial Revival house was actually a wedding gift to her and her husband in 1913. Used primarily as a foxhunting retreat, the house was in effect Webb's proto-museum for her collection, and many of its decorating and exhibition themes were transferred to Shelburne Museum.

Ever want to marry aboard a turn-of-the-twentieth-century steamship? The restored 220-foot *Ticonderoga* is a National Historic Landmark and the last walking beam side-wheel passenger steamer in existence—and it is available for weddings. Built in Shelburne in 1906, it operated as a day boat on Lake Champlain serving ports along the New York and Vermont shores until 1953. The *Ticonderoga* was then moved 2 miles overland from the lake to Shelburne Museum in a remarkable engineering effort that stands as one of the great feats of maritime preservation. Today the *Ticonderoga* portrays what it would have been like on board in 1923. The ship's carved and varnished woodwork, gilded ceilings, staterooms, grand staircase, and dining room bring to life the old-fashioned elegance of steamboat travel.

The 1840 Meeting House, which originally served a Methodist congregation in Charlotte, Vermont, demonstrates how churches were essential for gatherings, and is still used for performances, weddings,

and meetings of one hundred people. Notable interior features include trompe l'oeil wall paintings and an operating organ.

In addition, Shelburne Museum offers two garden settings for ceremonies. The elegant, circular Bostwick Garden, accommodating up to sixty for seated ceremonies, is planted with a medley of annuals and perennials designed to reflect a painter's color palette. The garden is surrounded by stone walls and trees, centered by a bronze *Turtle Baby* sculpture by Edith Parsons. Located next to the 1840 Schoolhouse and surrounded by perennials and historic houses, Alyssia's Garden accommodates up to 180 for ceremonies. Additionally, the graceful Pavilion Tent, encircled by apple trees and historic houses, accommodates 240 for a seated dinner with space for a stage, dance floor, and buffet.

Shelburne Farms, just two minutes from Shelburne Museum, is another famous attraction in the Shelburne-Burlington area and is an alternative location for a catered wedding. Created in 1886 by William Seward and Lila Vanderbilt Webb (related to Electra Havemeyer Webb yet totally separate from the museum) as a model agricultural estate on 400 acres, it serves today as an educational resource for practicing rural land use that is environmentally, economically, and culturally sustainable. Schoolchildren, adults, educators, and families come here to learn, while casual visitors may enjoy the walking trails, children's farmyard, inn, restaurant, property tours, and special events.

Nearby Burlington is Vermont's only real city (population 39,127), sited on a slope overlooking Lake Champlain and the Adirondack Mountains. Burlington is a lively place to visit anytime of year. Downtown shops, restaurants, theater, and clubs are priced for students at five local colleges.

Shelburne Museum
P.O. Box 10
Shelburne, VT 05482
(802) 985–3346
www.shelburnemuseum.org

Location: Off U.S. Highway 7, 7 miles south of Burlington, Vermont.

Facility Rental, Amenities, and Policies: Shelburne Museum schedules weddings beginning in May through the end of October. The museum will schedule a small ceremony without a reception, but if a reception is to follow a ceremony, a minimum of forty to fifty guests is required. The museum offers three ceremony-only sites for a fee of $500: the Meeting House, Bostwick Garden, and Alyssia's Garden.

For larger ceremonies and receptions, the Brick House accommodates 220 guests at a fee of $7,500. The Pavilion Tent hosts up to 240 reception guests, with room for a buffet, stage, and a dance floor, at a fee of $3,000. The *Ticonderoga* hosts up to 250 reception guests for $4,000, with a formal dinner for up to 100 guests for $5,000. The formal dinner is held in the State Room Hallway.

The larger facility rentals include the ceremony site, rehearsal, preparation room(s), security, visitor services, utilities, and parking. The Pavilion Tent fees also include restrooms, shuttle bus, dance floor, and caterer tent. The *Ticonderoga* includes the same additional amenities as the Pavilion Tent, with the exception of the caterer tent. (The Brick House does not include use of a restroom or catering tent.) Tables, chairs, linens, china, and the like need to be rented from local vendors.

Event fees include a complimentary one-year Shelburne Museum membership for the bride and groom.

Catering: Shelburne Museum provides a list of vendors with whom it has worked successfully in the past, although it is not mandatory to use one. The museum requests that couples contact the visitor services manager when not using a caterer on this list.

Accommodations: Overnight accommodations can be found in the nearby towns of Shelburne, South Burlington, New Haven, Burlington, Montpelier, Rochester, Moretown, Essex Junction, Weybridge, and South Hero.

WOODSTOCK INN & RESORT
Woodstock, Vermont

Woodstock is cradled between the serpentine Ottauquechee River and leafy green hills that turn a pristine white come winter. First settled in 1768, the village of Woodstock has thoughtfully preserved its architectural and natural heritage, with much of it included in a historic district. The colonial village would make a beautiful and fun backdrop for a destination wedding at any

time of year. Even a bronze bell on the property cast by Paul Revere can ring in the newlyweds.

Woodstock Inn & Resort, whose lineage has been in the hospitality service for more than two centuries, in many ways created the village's reputation as a resort town. The original tavern on this site, built in 1792, served as the transfer point and lodging for the region's stagecoach line, as well as the town's legal center. With the arrival of the railroad, Woodstock emerged as a summer retreat for rich city dwellers, and by 1876 the Woodstock Car was departing nightly from Grand Central Station. In 1892 the tavern hotel was replaced with the Woodstock Inn, which fostered winter tourism. Local skiers built the nation's first ski tow in a cow pasture, giving birth to the modern ski industry. Soon Suicide Six was a leading alpine resort and one of five ski tows operating outside of town.

The current Woodstock Inn, a formidable brick structure off the village green and across from a covered bridge, appears to be as old and historic as the village itself, but it wasn't constructed until 1969. That was when Laurance S. Rockefeller replaced the unsalvageable 1892 Woodstock Inn with the current structure. Under his genius direction, the new inn adopted the Colonial Revival look of the other shops and homes in the town. Inside, guests are greeted by a broad stone fireplace and sitting areas tucked throughout the lobby. Guest rooms are tastefully decorated in either country pine or a Shaker-inspired style. The best units, in the wing built in 1991, feature plush carpeting, fridges, and fireplaces. Recreational facilities include the Woodstock Ski Touring Center, which operates on the state's oldest golf course, and a state-of-the-art Health and Fitness Center. There are two restaurants and a tavern on the premises.

With several coordinators on staff, Woodstock Inn prides itself in adaptability when it comes to weddings. Weddings of all sizes are welcome at Woodstock Inn's storybook setting, whether outside on the spacious grounds surrounded by Vermont's Green Mountains, or at a number of indoor locations. Floor-to-ceiling windows overlooking the putting green illuminate the Garden Terrace, which is ideal for rehearsal dinners and standing receptions. Sophisticated afternoon receptions can take place in the Dining Room. The intimate Woodstock Country Club is also ideal for small, relaxed receptions and rehearsal dinners. Simple yet elegant, the Woodstock Ballroom hosts up to 225 guests and offers a clean canvas for expressing your own personal style. The ski lodge at Suicide Six can host large gatherings.

Woodstock Inn & Resort
Fourteen the Green
Woodstock, VT 05091-1298
(800) 448–7900 or (802) 457–1100
www.woodstockinn.com

Location: The Lebanon Municipal Airport is 19 miles to the east; Burlington International Airport is about 100 miles to the northwest; and Manchester Airport is 90 miles to the southwest.

Facility Rental, Amenities, and Policies: Woodstock Inn charges a $3,500 event site fee for weddings on the property for a five-hour maximum period. The Dining Room is available for afternoon receptions only and must be vacated by 4:00 P.M. The Woodstock Country Club and Suicide Six Ski Lodge are available at a rental fee of $1,750.

Catering: The inn offers buffet dining or a served dinner, starting at $75 to $100 per person. The menus are similar and include displayed and passed hors d'oeuvres, and a choice of salads and entrees. Woodstock's Signature wedding dinner, at $175 per person, with a minimum of one hundred guests, begins with the "Cocktail Hour," passed hors d'oeuvres; a choice of seafood presentation; and a seasonal harvest display of fresh vegetables, fruits, and Vermont cheeses. The next phase is the "Dinner Hour," which begins with a champagne toast, followed by a choice of salads and a choice of one entree, such as grilled petite filet mignon and crabmeat stuffed jumbo shrimp, seared salmon fillet, grilled tournedos of beef, or pan-seared natural chicken breast. All menus include the Woodstock Inn wedding cake, a traditional white wedding cake with white buttercream. Prices for special requests will be determined by the inn's chef.

Accommodations: Woodstock Inn has 142 rooms, and offers eight different room types, priced according to size, location, and amenities. Rates run from $215 for the Standard Room, to $629 for the Tavern Suite during the regular season. A $25-per-night fee is added to all rooms during peak periods and holidays.

Keep in Mind: Reception dates at the inn will be confirmed one year in advance. The Woodstock Country Club and Suicide Six Ski Lodge may be confirmed two years in advance. Those who wish to reserve a date farther out are placed on a priority wait list and confirmed one year from the requested date. Peak months for weddings are mid-June through mid-August, fall foliage (third week in September through Columbus Day weekend in October), Christmas week, and February vacation week.

BELL HARBOR ROOFTOP AND WORLD TRADE CENTER SEATTLE

Seattle, Washington

Mile markers for the New World Order begin in Seattle, Washington, with its software, dot-com, and espresso dynasties, yet its days as a rugged frontier aren't that far gone. Seattle's first settlers—fresh off the new Oregon Trail in the 1850s—were bachelors, and fifty-seven women were persuaded to travel west to marry them, thus setting a more civilized tone. Though the city is inventive and progressive, dress is outdoorsy casual, from flannel to, well, grunge—for good reason. Few cities are as immersed in, or poised for, the outdoor aesthetic. The sparkling waters of Elliott Bay, Lake Union, and Lake Washington envelop this city of shimmering skyscrapers, highlighted by the retro-twentieth-century Space Needle, which is dwarfed only by Mount Rainier in the background—when it's "out," of course. The Cascade Range lies less than 50 miles east of downtown Seattle, and the Olympic Mountains stand beyond Puget Sound. All of the views are best appreciated down near the waterfront, with a venti latte in hand by morning, or a microbrew by night.

A search for the definitive cityscape wedding can end here and now with the Bell Harbor International Conference Center on Alaskan Way. Ceremonies can take place on Bell Harbor's rooftop with sweeping views of downtown Seattle's skyline, Elliott Bay, and the Olympic Mountains. The Harbor Dining Room in Bell Harbor, with views and a connecting terrace, can accommodate up to 300 banquet style, and the Holland America Line Dining Room in the World Trade Center (WTCSE) across the street can accommodate up to 80 for more intimate gatherings. Elegant and architecturally stunning, the Holland America Line Dining Room also has a connecting outdoor terrace and floor-to-ceiling windows overlooking Elliott Bay and the Olympic Mountains.

Owned by the Port of Seattle and operated by Columbia Hospitality, Bell Harbor Conference Center offers 100,000 square feet of waterfront conference, meeting, and special-event space for groups from 10 to 5,000. The four-story World Trade Center Seattle, also owned by the Port of Seattle and operated by Columbia Hospitality, serves as a natural extension of the conference center. Columbia Hospitality manages a dozen other properties, many of which are worthy wedding venues.

Bell Street Pier 66 is a destination in and of itself with eleven acres of waterfront plazas and restaurants, plus a pleasure craft marina and the interactive Odyssey Maritime Discovery Center. The pier is within walking distance of the Pike Place Market (home of the Flying Fish), hotels, restaurants (including Anthony's Pier 66 restaurant), jogging paths, public parks, the Seattle Aquarium, and the Seattle Art Museum, among other entertainment and shopping facilities. Ferries to neighboring islands are also within walking distance.

Columbia Hospitality
2223 Alaskan Way, Suite 200
Seattle, WA 98121
(206) 239–1800
www.columbiahospitality.com

Bell Harbor International Conference Center
2211 Alaskan Way, Pier 66
Seattle, WA 98121
www.bellharbor.org

World Trade Center Seattle
2200 Alaskan Way, Suite 410
Seattle, WA 98121
(206) 441–5144
www.wtcseattle.com

Location: Columbia Hospitality (the managing company), Bell Harbor International Conference Center, and the World Trade Center in Seattle are across from each other on Pier 66, with ample parking in a covered garage and convenient pedestrian skybridge access.

Facility Rental, Amenities, and Policies: The Rooftop Plaza on the Bell Harbor Conference Center is the primary location for waterfront ceremonies at a fee of $1,500, which includes seating, speaker system, staging, two dressing rooms, and a backup room in case of rain. Bell Harbor has comparable-size rooms just below the rooftop, as well as fabulous decks and windows, and if it's raining, people can still enjoy the waterfront during the wedding. Rental periods are essentially from 10:00 A.M. to 3:00 P.M. for daytime events, and 5:00 P.M. to 1:00 A.M. for evening events.

Catering: The rental fee for the executive dining room in the World Trade Center Seattle is $800, with a food minimum of $2,500. The rental includes all tables, chairs, linens, china, dance floor, votive candles, bud vases, an on-site concierge, and an event planner. The room rental fee for the Harbor Dining Room in the Bell Harbor Conference Center is $1,500, with a food minimum of $9,000 for Saturday evening, and includes the same amenities.

Columbia Hospitality is a full-service food and beverage facility with its own chefs, menus, and serving staff; no outside food or beverage can be brought in. (The staff will work with a select few kosher caterers, however.) The plated three-course dinners at either location start at $37 per person, and the buffets at $43. There is a $50 fee per bartender per hour, as well as a cake-cutting fee of $1.50 per person. Entrees include sautéed fillet of salmon with lemon caper sauce and red pepper coulis; maple glazed roast turkey; and grilled filet mignon with Pacific wild mushroom sauté and cognac cream sauce.

Accommodations: The Conference Center is between the Edgewater Hotel and the Marriott Waterfront, with many more lodging options within walking distance or a short cab ride.

Keep in Mind: Alas, Seattle's popularity has turned the Emerald City into a traffic nightmare, but it is still a pedestrian's paradise. Metro Transit buses blanket the metropolitan area, and all bus rides are free in the immediate downtown area from 6:00 A.M. to

7:00 P.M. Seattle Trolley Tours, running every half hour, provide great downtown transport, and visitors may get on and off at leisure with all-day tickets. Stops include the Waterfront. Allow extra time to travel during rush hour from the Seattle's Sea-Tac Airport, which is 13 miles south of the city.

Seattle's other perpetual problem is rain. With just fifty-five days of annual sunshine, July and August offer the most likely sunny weather in Seattle, although October can be quite beautiful as well.

Bell Harbor is usually booked for weddings almost every weekend from late April through the first of October.

FRIDAY HARBOR HOUSE
Friday Harbor, San Juan Island, Washington

Of the 700 islands and reefs that comprise the San Juan Archipelago, the islands of Lopez, Orcas, Shaw, and San Juan have been luring explorers and visitors with their natural beauty since they were first discovered by Europeans in the eighteenth century. The islands offer views of rolling hills, distant farms, madrona trees, steep cliffs, and sandy beaches. Accessible by the Washington State Ferry Service, the islands make serene settings for Pacific Northwest weddings, whether held on the bluffs under Cattle Point Lighthouse, on the beautiful grounds of British Camp, or at nearby grand hotels and inns.

While each of these four islands has its own personality, San Juan Island may be most popular for its scenery and nightlife. Lined with shops and restaurants and exuding a decided seaport feel, the village of Friday Harbor is lively. Friday Harbor

House is rated at the top of the lodging options on San Juan and is poised for perfect views. Just minutes from the ferry landing, most of the inn's twenty guest rooms overlook the marina and San Juan Channel as well as the mountains on distant Orcas Island. The minimalist, yet distinctly Northwest architecture and furnishings bring contemporary sophistication to the island. Guests receive their first taste of understated elegance with the slate floors, a stylish water fountain, and whimsical driftwood furniture that accent the small lobby.

This understated style carries over into their weddings. The scenic bluff perched above the marina is ideal for a quiet ceremony in front of up to forty guests, followed by a reception in the sleek Harbor View Dining Room. Friday Harbor House is managed by Columbia Hospitality, known in the region for its crisp professionalism. Headquartered in Seattle, Washington, Columbia Hospitality manages fifteen conference centers, meeting venues, inns, and resorts in the Pacific Northwest.

Local activities include hiking, kayaking, sailing, powerboating, scuba diving, and playing golf and tennis, as well as renting mopeds and bicycles. It's an easy stroll to the docks, airport, parks, restaurants, shops, galleries, and lodging facilities. Whale watching is optimal here; more than eighty-five orcas comprise three pods (J, K, and L) that reside part of the year in the San Juan Islands and follow the salmon runs.

Friday Harbor House
130 West Street
P.O. Box 1385
Friday Harbor, WA 98250
(866) 722–7356 or (360) 378–8455
www.fridayharborhouse.com

Location: Friday Harbor House is a block and a half from Friday Harbor and the ferry terminal. Located 90 miles from Seattle, San Juan Island is accessible by ferry or by seaplane. Companies offering air transportation include Kenmore Air Seaplanes (866–435–9524), San Juan Airlines (800–690–0086), and Island Air (360–378–2376). If you are traveling by car, drive to Anacortes. The Washington State Ferry provides an eighty-minute scheduled service from Anacortes to the San Juan Islands.

Facility Rental, Amenities, and Policies: A one-hour site rental for small ceremonies

on the scenic bluff involving approximately forty people is $250. There is an additional $250 for the dining room for two-and-a-half hours, or $500 for four hours. Guest-service specialists are available to assist with reception menu selections, setup, and event coordination. The inn provides china and stemware. Other items, such as specialty linens, ceremony-site chairs, chair covers, tenting, wedding arches, candelabras, and floral arrangements and pedestals, may be arranged for an additional fee.

Catering: Receptions at Friday Harbor House require a food and beverage minimum of $1,500 for the two-and-a-half hour dining period, and $3,500 for the four-hour period. Entrees are $24 to $34 and include pork tenderloin, steak, halibut, and salmon from regional sources.

Accommodations: 20 guest rooms have floor-to-ceiling window views, European queen beds, fireplaces, and oversized whirlpool tubs. Standard-room rates range from $150 to $265 October through May and $240 to $310 May through October; a one-bedroom suite is $340. Rates include a Continental breakfast.

Keep in Mind: Weddings are welcome all year. The islands lie in a pocket between the mountains of the Olympic Peninsula and Vancouver Island, causing the weather to be dry and mild year-round. Spring commences with the nesting of some eighty eagle couples on San Juan, followed by the arrival of hordes of tourists.

ROSARIO RESORT & SPA

East Sound, Orcas Island, Washington

There is something hauntingly serene about the Pacific Northwest, triggered perhaps by the muted colors of the water and evergreen mountains under moody skies and that stimulating feeling of being far from home. Orcas Island is about as close as you can get to the proper British influences of Canada without leaving the friendly frontier individualism of Washington State. Moreover, it has a thriving cottage wedding industry. Getting to the remote island by water or by air is half the fun.

From a distance Rosario Resort & Spa, long the reigning royalty of resorts on the island, looks like an undulating cruise ship. Perhaps that's because the many-windowed, five-story mansion was built in 1909 by Robert Moran, the captain of Seattle's ship-building industry. Apparently the white mansion was originally burgundy from left-over ship-bottom paint. At the age of forty-six, his doctor ordered him to retire or die—so he retired here and lived another forty years. His health bespeaks the restorative quality of the island.

Harbored in an inlet where towering evergreen trees and sloping hills roll right into the cold water, the Rosario comprises nine buildings spread over eight acres. The resort's 127 guest rooms and suites offer fireplaces, sunken Jacuzzi tubs, and private balconies that overlook Cascade Bay, the marina, and distant ferry lines. Rosario boasts four separate restaurants and cafes on the premises, with a poolside bar and grill in summer. Everyone gets a window table in the Compass Room restaurant. The centerpiece of the resort is the mansion, lined with 6,000 feet of teak parquet floor and more than a hundred doors. The man-

sion's music room features a Tiffany chandelier and a working 1,972-pipe Aeolian organ that resounds through the mansion and the hearts of guests during a wedding ceremony. The music room is also a stately setting for a reception.

Rosario has seven venues for wedding ceremonies, four of which can accommodate up to 250 guests. Typically ceremonies take place on the Point Lawn, with its 360-degree views, but the music room will be held as an indoor alternative. Other venues include the Discovery Ballroom and Lawn, Figure Eight Pond Tent, Eagle Vista Lawn (cocktail reception), and Compass Room with Veranda.

Island wedding guests may wish to embark on a whale-watching tour from the marina, sail through the Rosario Straits on the *Morning Star,* hike to the top of Mount Constitution, relax in the spa, take a guided kayak tour, or scuba dive amid orca whales and octopi in waters that Jacques Cousteau claimed as one of his favorite dive spots in the world. At East Sound, the island's primary village, travelers can find traditional amenities, such as gas, groceries, and alternate lodging.

Rosario Resort & Spa
1400 Rosario Road
East Sound, WA 98245
(800) 562–8820 or (360) 376–2222
http://rosario.rockresorts.com

Location: Rosario Resort & Spa on Orcas Island is just 80 miles northwest of Seattle and is accessible by ferry, water taxi, private boat, or seaplane.

Facility Rental, Amenities, and Policies: Rosario's wedding package includes a one-hour ceremony, one-hour rehearsal, bridal water-view changing rooms in the Moran Mansion, and welcome gift for the bride and groom at check-in. Facility fees may vary depending on food and beverage expenditures, and are customized per event. Fees include white folding chairs, and setup and teardown. October through April is considered off-season, and facility rates are discounted for the seven wedding and reception venues—ranging, for example, from $200 to $500 for the Compass Room (for 50 to 65 people), to $1,500 for the Figure Eight Pond Tent (up to 220). During peak season facility fees are assessed depending on the day of the week and whether the wedding is held before or after 3:00 P.M. The Point Lawn during the off-season is $450 to $1,000 ($800 to $1,200 during peak season), depending on day and time.

Catering: Rosario Resort & Spa offers a complimentary five-day, four-night honeymoon to couples spending a minimum of $15,000 on their wedding event. The Honeymoon Reward may be enjoyed at any one of the RockResorts, regardless of where the ceremony takes place, for up to three months after the event.

Contact the resort for details on catering menus and prices.

Extras: Turndown service the night of the wedding, including scented candles, fresh chocolate-covered strawberries, and chilled champagne, is available to newlyweds for $75.

Accommodations: The resort features 116 rooms and suites. Nightly rates are seasonal and vary for weekday and weekend, ranging from $89 to $239. The rooms all include a patio or balcony, RockResort robes, and Avanyu spa amenities.

Keep in Mind: The Washington State ferry system runs multiple ferries each day out of Anacortes, Washington. Water-taxi and ferry services depart from the area in and surrounding Anacortes and Bellingham, Washington. The air- and seaplanes depart from various area airports, including Seattle. While the ferries provide views of the San Juan Islands, the most exciting mode of transport is a floatplane. Kenmore Airlines, operating from its Lake Union terminal in downtown Seattle, offers flights with forty-five minutes of unparalleled views. The resort's Web site lists all transportation contacts.

THE GREAT WEDDING TRAIN
Spooner, Wisconsin

The Wisconsin Great Northern Railroad in Spooner, Wisconsin, runs the only chapel railcar in the country. But it isn't a new idea. Between the 1890s and 1940s, thirteen chapel railcars (seven Baptist, three Catholic, and three Episcopalian) assisted in America's expansion from Chicago to the West Coast. As the railroads pushed farther into the frontier, chapel cars followed. Rather than invest scarce resources to build a church in a town that might never take root, a chapel car would be parked next to a depot to form a congregation. Eventually the locals would pool resources to build a church; the train would then move to another depot. Only three out of the original thirteen railcars are in existence today; one is in the possession of a private collector, and the other two are in museums.

The chapel car that's part of the Wisconsin Great Northern Railroad is a historic excursion and dinner train operating on approximately 20 miles of the former Chicago & North Western track between the northern Wisconsin towns of Spooner and Springbrook along the Namekagon River. Founded on April 1, 1997, by Greg Vreeland, with the help of family and friends, the railroad operates 1940s locomotives along with a fleet of mahogany interior passenger cars built between 1910 and 1930—twenty-eight in all. The cars have been rebuilt to give passengers the flavor of rail travel from this time period.

The idea for a chapel car came in 1996 when Vreeland helped a friend remove a 1915 Catholic chapel car, the St. Paul, from a Montana mountaintop. Impressed by the car's stained-glass windows and woodwork, he pledged to build a replica of the car where he planned to marry his own sweetheart. The project cost $50,000 (again from friends and family), and he named it Everlasting, Number 14. Eventually, Vreeland married his sweetheart, Mardell, on June 5, 2004, thus launching the Wedding Train.

Retrofitted in a Long Island commuter, the dark-blue-carpeted chapel car features rich oak trim accenting a light blue ceiling. The red oak church pews came from a small church in North Dakota; the altar, lectern, and communion railing were acquired through eBay from a church in Indiana. A stained-glass window custom made by family members adorns the altar. Extra-large windows, accented by sconces, line the sides so that guests may enjoy the scenery. The chapel car also features a clergy preparation room behind the altar, a passageway to adjoining cars, a state-of-the-art audio/video control room, and a pump organ.

The chapel car seats only about eighty-five, but additional guests can view the wedding from closed-circuit television in other cars. Couples can customize a wedding package by adding as many as three dining cars, a lounge, and a presentation car (upon completion), accommodating up to 200 guests for a reception—hence, the Wedding Train!

At a top speed of 15 miles an hour, the round-trip excursion takes about three hours, passing by a little bit of everything Wisconsin has to offer: farm fields, rivers, a lake, forest, even a trestle bridge. Spooner itself has a population of fewer than 3,000, but the region is a sporting destination for hiking, biking, hunting, and fishing.

The Great Wedding Train
On the Wisconsin Great Northern Railroad
426 North Front Street
Spooner, WI 54801
(715) 635–3200
www.spoonertrainride.com/wedding_train.htm

Location: The main ticket office is located in Spooner, Wisconsin, 100 miles northeast of St. Paul, Minnesota, at the crossroads of U.S. Highway 63 and Wisconsin Highway 70.

Facility Rental, Amenities, and Policies: The Great Wedding Train offers seven wedding packages, and in addition, the couple may customize a package for large weddings up to 185 people. The Stationary Wedding, the only package available year-round, costs $495 and includes one hour use of the chapel car while parked, silk flowers, unity candle, photos of the ceremony on disk, commemorative tickets, basic ceremony music disk, and a private wedding consultant. Additional time is available at $200 per hour.

The Wedding Dinner Train, representative of all the other packages, is available for $2,495, for up to forty guests on Saturday evening (Friday evening is $300 less). An additional 145 guests may be added at a cost of $34.95 each. In addition to the offerings of the Stationary Wedding Train, this package includes the private use of a changing room, silk flowers for the attendants, dinner in the lounge car, basic decorations, a champagne toast, keepsake crystal toasting glasses, a small wedding cake for the bride and groom, and a wedding sheet cake with keepsake silver cake servers.

Ordinarily, couples bring in their own ministers from out of the area, and the Vreelands are in the process of assembling a local list of ministers and officiants. The trains run May 6 through December 31, and scheduled weddings take place rain or shine.

Catering: For the customized a la carte package, four buffets are offered at $11.95 to $17.95 per person; the banquet is $12.95 per person. Menu options include chicken cordon bleu, roast beef, maple glazed baked ham, lemon breast of chicken, or honey glazed boneless pork chop. No outside food or beverages are allowed, except for the wedding cake.

Accommodations: The Private Car Flambeau is available in conjunction with the wedding train for a variety of purposes, such as to serve as a wedding party dressing room ($495) or wedding-night suite ($895). Spooner has five motels, and additional resorts can be found within a fifteen- or twenty-minute drive.

Keep in Mind: Due to its historic nature, the Great Wedding Train is not wheelchair accessible, but every effort will be made for passengers with special needs upon advance notice. All packages are available for online ordering and are subject to the "Wedding Guidelines," which are viewable via a link at the bottom of the ordering form.

SNAKE RIVER LODGE & SPA
Jackson Hole, Wyoming

A mention of Jackson Hole, Wyoming, might conjure up images of jagged mountain peaks against endless blue skies, audacious skiers riding white powder waves, and acres of cattle ranches stocked with cowboys who crowd the honky-tonks on Saturday nights. But weddings?

Things are changing in Jackson Hole. This wild glacial valley once predominantly attracted mountain men, hotdoggers, and year-round ski bums drawn to the epic ski terrain. With the appearance, however, of several new upscale hotels and condo developments in Teton Village, as well as an abundance of spas and restaurants right at the bottom of Jackson Hole Mountain Resort's main lifts, a wider variety of affluent skiers and snow lovers has been attracted to the area. It is time to update our imagery. Today three major ski areas have made Jackson Hole world famous. At the Jackson Hole Mountain Resort, Rendezvous Peak has the largest vertical rise served by one lift system in the country—at 4,139 feet above Teton Village.

The Snake River Lodge is one resort that recently evolved from rustic lodge to luxury hotel. It is now a RockResort. Reviewers call the decor rugged cowboy chic—a western-boots-and-champagne, hand-your-skis-to-the-valet-and-head-off-to-the-spa kind of chic. The lodge's exposed-beam ceilings, oxidized wrought-iron chandeliers, and deep leather lounge chairs near the fire put visitors in the lap of comfort year-round.

Snake River Lodge is the closest resort to Grand Teton National Park's south entrance. The lodge is a ski-in facility, and guests have access to the lifts via a heated walkway. The concierge can make arrangements for everything from mountain biking and horseback riding in summer to dogsledding and snowmobiling in winter. The indoor/outdoor pool area, where waterfalls cascade over large boulders and rocks, has a fire pit and views of the Jackson Hole ski area. The five-story Spa and Health Club has separate men's and women's floors with steam rooms and soaking tubs.

Weddings are something we can imagine at Snake River Lodge, which offers excellent packages for ceremonies both on the property and off site. Couples can exchange rings at the peak of Rendezvous Mountain (accessed by a tram ride), amid wildflowers on the banks of the winding Snake River, or next to the lodge's waterfall as it cascades over granite boulders. The Jackson Hole Golf & Tennis Club at the foot of the Teton Mountain Range is one of the country's most scenic and well-designed golf courses and makes an exquisite background to weddings. The new Sundance Center (accommodating 60 to 250 people) is poised for an evening of elegance, music, and dancing.

Whether a wedding is off site in Jackson's glorious alpine setting or held at the base of America's premier ski resort, the professional wedding coordinator will handle every detail. The lodge offers a variety of reception and dinner options; smaller weddings may wish to celebrate in the lodge's premiere GameFish Restaurant.

Snake River Lodge & Spa
7710 Granite Loop Road
P.O. Box 348
Teton Village, WY 83025
(866) 975–7625 or (307) 732–6000
http://snakeriverlodge.rockresorts.com/

Location: Snake River Lodge & Spa is 22 miles from Jackson Hole Airport, in Teton Village, Wyoming. The lodge is 1 mile from the Grand Teton National Park and an hour from Yellowstone National Park.

Facility Rental, Amenities, and Policies:
Wedding packages at Snake River Lodge are based by the catering, which offers a choice of three plated dinners, and one buffet, ranging from $99 to $119 per person with a one-hour hosted bar. All prices are based on 50 to 120 guests; higher-priced packages offer entree selections. Packages include a cocktail hour with butler-passed wines and champagne upon arrival, butler-passed hors d'oeuvres, a dinner service, entrees, side dish, champagne toast, and the traditional tiered wedding cake. Packages also include white floor-length linens, white chair covers, votive candles, a dance floor, all room fees, and all setup fees. However, a $200 fee is assessed for the wedding reception coordinator.

Snake River Lodge & Spa offers a complimentary five-day, four-night honeymoon to couples spending a minimum of $15,000 on their wedding event. The Honeymoon Reward may be enjoyed at any of the RockResorts, regardless of where the ceremony takes place, and the offer is good for up to three months after the event.

Catering: A sampling of the menu from just one of the packages includes beef Wellington with mushroom duxelle and bordelaise sauce, and herb crusted rack of lamb. The buffet package offers a western barbecue on its dinner menu, with barbecued chicken, smoked barbecued baby back ribs, and carved prime rib of buffalo.

Accommodations: The lodge features 130 rooms, suites, condominiums, and penthouses, with rates ranging from $150 to $3,000 per night. There are 88 rooms and suites, with goose-down comforters and plush robes. Junior suites add mini kitchenettes and fireplaces, while the two- and three-bedroom suites offer gourmet kitchens, workstations, and jetted tubs. Adjoining the lodge are 40 condominiums for an extra dose of privacy. Check with the lodge for additional discounts and special packages.

ABOUT THE AUTHOR

Travel writer and wedding photographer KATHRYN GABRIEL LOVING lives and works in the Santa Fe–Albuquerque area of New Mexico where she's been on the sidelines of many destination weddings. In this book she shares her expertise about the best of the best places to run away and get married throughout the United States.